THE STAMP YEARBOOK 1996

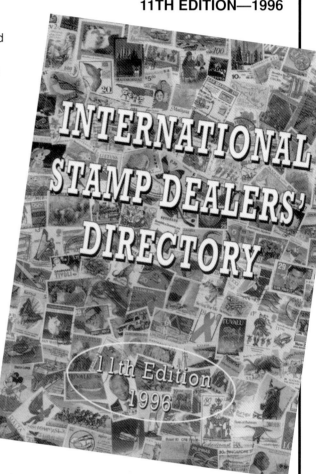

THE
STAMP
YEARBOOK
1996

A comprehensive compendium of philately and review of the past year

Edited by
James Mackay, MA, DLitt

ISBN 1 870192 09 5

Published by
TOKEN PUBLISHING LIMITED
PO Box 14, Honiton, Devon EX14 9YP

The Stamp Yearbook 1996
first published 1996

© Token Publishing Ltd.
PO Box 14
Honiton, Devon EX14 9YP

ISBN **1 870192 09 5**

Printed in Great Britain by Friary Press, Bridport Road, Dorchester, Dorset

CONTENTS

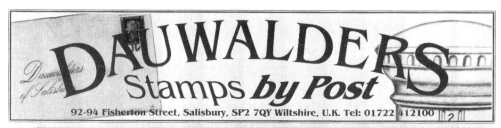

INTRODUCTION

JUST over ninety years ago—in 1904 to be precise—the first edition of *The Stamp Collectors' Annual* was published. Vicissitudes of war and peace meant that publication was suspended for eight editions at various times but, remarkably and despite paper shortages, it managed to keep going through the Second World War and survived the postwar austerity period. For many years it was edited by the late Tom Morgan who also edited *The Philatelic Magazine* and *The Philatelic Trader* for Harris Publications. Ironically, as philately was poised on the edge of a boom, thanks to the more enlightened policy of the British Post Office regarding stamp issues, *The Stamp Collectors' Annual* ceased publication in 1962.

For a few years thereafter (1969–74) Link House Publications filled the gap with an annual under the editorship of the late Arthur Blair. Unfortunately this annual was perceived, rightly or wrongly, by readers as just a bigger and glossier version of the monthly *Stamp Magazine*, with little of permanent reference value that one would expect to find in a year-book. For twenty years therefore there has been a vacuum just crying out to be filled. It has been a long-term ambition of mine to remedy this defect, but pressure of work has prevented me from realising it. When I embarked on this project I quickly realised that compiling the sort of data I would wish to find in an annual of this nature was a daunting task. Much depended on the co-operation of overseas postal administrations, some of whom responded readily while regrettably others ignored the questionnaire.

Whatever its shortcomings (and I take full responsibility for them), this *Year Book* is presented for your delectation, amusement and edification. I would welcome comments, suggestions, corrections and additional information from readers; by the time this edition is in print, work will already have begun on the edition for next year.

Philately has survived many ups and downs and weathered slumps and recessions. Today it is as buoyant as ever and in spite of so many other distractions and forms of recreation or entertainment, it has a worldwide following running into many millions. The prophets of doom and gloom have predicted that stamps will eventually disappear along with the letter-writing habit, yet more stamps are issued than ever before, the annual volume of different issues in 1994 having passed the 11,000 mark. Many have blamed postal administrations for issuing too many stamps at too high a price, and thereby frightening off the beginner and the juvenile collector; yet stamps remain one of the few genuine collectables which can be pursued at little or no cost, relying on the stamps on one's mail. The attraction of an exotic pictorial from a remote South Seas island or the pathetic primitives from war-torn Bosnia or Chechnya remains as strong as ever. Few hobbies are so redolent of human interest as stamps and postal history.

Attendance at philatelic exhibitions continues to grow, even though the figures for the United Kingdom seem minuscule compared with those in Germany or the Far East. Nothing reflects the universality of the hobby more than the increasing participation of postal administrations in the great shows of the world, while here in Britain the 1996 Spring Stampex had a distinct "Down Under" flavour.

In addition to the two great national exhibitions, held each spring and autumn, 1995 witnessed the first of what could be termed a mid-term international. Normally international exhibitions are held in London every ten years, on the decade, a custom which dates back to 1940 when Britain and the world celebrated the centenary of the Penny Black. Stamp '95 at Wembley in April was regarded as a powerful shot in the arm for the hobby and a wonderful showcase to take us through to the Millennium and the next full-blown London international. Such was its success that a repeat was scheduled for 1996. With luck this Wembley spectacular will now become a permanent fixture in the philatelic calendar.

James A. Mackay

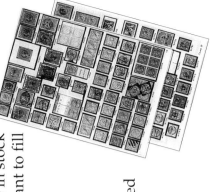

DO YOU COLLECT GREAT BRITAIN

- **OUR MONTHLY RETAIL PRICE LISTS . . .**

  Covers all issues from SG No. 1. Queen Victoria through to Queen Elizabeth II. At any one time, we expect to have in stock most of the stamps listed in this catalogue, so if you want to fill those blank spaces, we cordially invite you to . . . .

  SEND FOR A FREE COPY OF OUR LATEST LIST!!

- **PRIVATE TREATY CATALOGUES . . .**

  Aimed at the more serious collector, **these profusely illustrated listings** are extremely popular and are issued twice monthly, they contain a wide selection of **better Singles, Rarities, Proofs, Colour Trials, High Values, Multiples and much specialized material . . .** Seldom offered elsewhere!!

FREE MAY WE SEND YOU A COPY OF OUR LATEST CATALOGUE SO THAT YOU CAN SEE FOR YOURSELF WHAT YOU ARE MISSING. PLEASE WRITE, FAX OR PHONE US NOW!

THAT WAS THE YEAR THAT WAS!

1995 was seen by many to be a turning point in the hobby—a momentum that is becoming increasingly obvious as 1996 progresses, with Royal Mail issues enjoying unprecedented popularity and ever higher prices being achieved at auction, dealers stocks turning over faster than for many years and even societies experiencing increasing membership! Here we look back on the past year and present an at-a-glance résumé of the events that affected the hobby during the year . . .

February
Robson Lowe, Britain's longest-serving stamp dealer, celebrates his 90th birthday at a dinner in Bournemouth, and gives a display from his celebrated collection of Valentines.

March
Bruce Auckland, doyen of British postal historians, celebrates his 100th birthday with a lunch attended by philatelists from all over the UK. Still active, Bruce was pleased to add the distinctive Scottish version of the Royal telegram to his collection.

April
Thieves loot 100,000 of the R. J. Mitchell Spitfire stamp booklets from a security van shortly after it left the Walsall Security Printer. Quantities of other Walsall booklets were stolen at the same time.

Robson Lowe, Britain's longest-serving stamp dealer, who celebrated his 90th birthday in February 1995.

The Pobjoy Mint enters the philatelic market, forming Pobjoy Philatelic Agencies Ltd to market philanumismatic covers. The first, in conjunction with Benham, combines a Gibraltar crown with the British Peter Rabbit stamp.

Stamp '95, held at Wembley (April 27–30), attracts over 30,000 visitors from the UK and is voted a resounding success, with plans to become an annual event.

The International Association of Stamp Catalogue Editors and Philatelic Publishers (ASCAT) meet in Monte Carlo.

A market survey in the USA estimates that there are 6,425,000 stamp collectors in that country, spending $685 million a year on their hobby.

New telephone numbers, with an 01 prefix, are introduced throughout the UK, accompanied by a nationwide slogan postmark campaign.

May
Belgium and Ireland produce a joint issue of stamps to mark the 250th anniversary of the Battle of Fontenoy, the most decisive encounter in the War of the Austrian Succession. The stamps feature the Celtic cross that stands as a memorial on the battlefield to the Irishmen who fought and died on both sides.

Hawid mounts celebrate their half century. The concept of hingeless mounts was devised by Dr Hans

Widmaier (1911–66) as the Second World War was drawing to a close. He left his job with Siemens & Halske in Berlin and started the manufacture of the strips, setting up in his own home and using a secondhand Volkswagen engine to power the plant. By the time of his death Dr Widmaier had built up a thriving business with outlets in over 60 countries.

Guernsey issues Peace and Freedom stamps incorporating stereograms provided by 3-D images of London.

The *Philatelic Exporter* celebrates its 50th anniversary. Founded by Captain M. R. Musson at the end of the Second World War, it is now one of the world's leading trade papers. The inaugural number consisted of 12 small pages; the latest issue runs to 96 A4 pages with a full-colour cover.

June

Russia launches an RCM-50 ballistic missile from a Kalmar submarine in the Barents Sea carrying 1,270 items of mail (130 private letters and 1,140 serially numbered philatelic covers). The module flew over 5,000km before landing in the Kamchatka peninsula.

Leigh-Mardon, the Australian security printer, ceases stamp production on June 30.

July

Representatives of nine countries in southern Africa meet on July 5–6 and form the Philatelic Agency for a Greater Southern Africa. Participating countries are Angola, Botswana, Lesotho, Malawi, Mozambique, Namibia, South Africa, Swaziland, Tanzania, Zambia and Zimbabwe.

Rare Stamps of the World exhibition at Claridge's on July 6–8. 56 exhibitors assemble the largest and most valuable display of stamps ever mounted.

Her Majesty the Queen confers the KCVO on John Marriott, Keeper of the Royal Philatelic Collections,on the occasion of his retirement.

August

Dubbed "The Lady of the Century", Her Majesty Queen Elizabeth, the Queen Mother, celebrates her 95th birthday on August 4. Many countries (including a 16-country omnibus) mark the occasion with issues of stamps and souvenir sheets.

The latest Machin definitive stamp is a £1 denomination, the first to be printed in Iriodin ink

which acts as a transparent varnish with a reflective quality giving a three-dimensional effect to the Queen's portrait, as well as making it impossible to forge. At the same time, the Carrickfergus Castle motif, hitherto used on the £1 intaglio stamp, is transferred to a £3 purple stamp, prepaying the registration fee.

Canada Post issues a Birds sheet, but when it is discovered that the initial letter F is omitted from "Faune" on one of the stamps featuring a Belted Kingfisher, a reprint with the error rectified is ordered. This is the first spelling error to appear on Canadian stamps in their 144-year history.

September

Singapore '95 at the Suntec Exhibition Centre, runs for eleven days (September 1–11) and provokes a wide range of stamps, miniature sheets and souvenir covers from all over the world, many with the theme of orchids.

David Feldman holds his first auction in Singapore on September 7.

Royal Mail issues its last three stamp booklets with pictorial covers, a practice originated in 1968. Such pictorial covers are to be phased out at the end of the year and replaced by booklets in the standard glossy red livery.

Paul Fraser pays £1.17 million for Sir Ron Brierley's shares in Stanley Gibbons Holdings plc. Having acquired 77 per cent of the company's shares, Fraser offers to buy the remaining shares at 30p each.

The French catalogue publishing company of Yvert et Tellier celebrates its centenary with a two-day exhibition at the Hotel Drouot, a highlight being a demonstration of the new CD-Rom version of the catalogue.

Protesting against French nuclear testing in the South Pacific, New Zealand issues a $1 stamp with a strong anti-nuclear motif and the CND logo.

"Dick Barton's" is the name of the largest provincial stamp shop in the UK, opened by Paul Dauwalder in Salisbury, Wiltshire.

The 500th auction at Cavendish of Derby on September 15 marks the inauguration of Cavendish House, the new venue being formally opened by Francis Kiddle, President of the Royal Philatelic Society.

After a three year break, Stanley Gibbons re-introduces a Foreign Department.

Royal Mail issues Britain's first 60p commemorative stamp, part of the Communications series honouring Sir Rowland Hill and Guglielmo Marconi.

Netherlands Antilles issues stamps with a surcharge in aid of victims of Hurricane Luis. The 65c, 75c and 100c stamps of the 1984–85 definitive series are overprinted "Relief Stamps 1995".

Two of Britain's leading agencies, Harry Allen and James Davis, merge. As a result, stamps of some 50 countries are offered on agency terms.

Cameroons becomes the 52nd member of the British Commonwealth of Nations. Eritrea, Angola and Mozambique apply for membership.

Germany, Ireland, Italy, San Marino and the Vatican each issue a stamp of uniform design portraying Guglielmo Marconi and celebrating the centenary of the first radio transmission.

October
Israel launches its first duck protection stamp on October 1, depicting the Marbled Duck, an endangered species.

Zumstein, the leading Swiss catalogue publisher, celebrates its 90th birthday on October 5.

Autumn Stampex (October 10–15) is the last to be held at the Royal Horticultural Halls, ending a 25-year tradition. From January 1996 the twice-yearly show will take place at the Business Design Centre, Islington.

Total-Stampex philatelic exhibition at Johannesburg on October 19–21, marks the debut of the Philatelic Agency for a Greater Southern Africa with the UN 50 omnibus pack.

Stampa '95, the 24th Irish National Stamp Exhibition, opens in Dublin at the Riverside Exhibition Centre, attracting visitors from the UK, USA and Europe as well as Ireland, north and south (October 20–22).

Most member countries release stamps to mark the 50th anniversary of the United Nations. Many also celebrate the 50th anniversary of its first specialised agency, the Food and Agricultural Organisation.

"Designing Messages: European Stamp Design" is the theme of an exhibition at the Design Museum (October 26–February 11, 1996), sponsored by Harrison and Sons.

November
Corbitt's of Newcastle-upon-Tyne hold their largest sale ever, over 2,000 lots being devoted to specialised GB.

C. Angus Parker, one of Britain's foremost dealers in postal history, dies at the age of 68 on November 15.

December
Annual General Meeting of Stanley Gibbons. Paul Fraser announces profits to the end of June increased by 15 per cent to £7,326,000. The number of employees rises during the year from 103 to 120.

Israel releases a 5 sheqel stamp in mourning for Yitzhak Rabin, assassinated by a right-wing Jewish extremist on November 4.

At the Hard Rock Cafe, New York, on December 8, eight countries launch an omnibus issue honouring John Lennon and belatedly marking the 55th anniversary of his birth which actually took place on October 9.

Fifteen countries launch an omnibus to mark the centenary of the will of Alfred Nobel. Almost 500 stamps and 50 souvenir sheets portraying Nobel laureates make this the most ambitious omnibus issue ever.

Posta Limited takes over the operation of the Maltese postal administration, following privatisation.

The United States Postal Services announces that the 32c Marilyn Monroe stamp was the most popular single stamp of 1995, some 46.3 million being sold. The Civil War and Legends of the West stamps, each issued in sheets of 20, actually sold more—46.6 million and 46.5 million respectively.

THE YEAR AT AUCTION

The best barometer of the state of philately is the behaviour of the salerooms. The progress of an auction—or lack of it—and the outcome of the sale are more immediate indicators of the way the market is moving than the reaction of the trade in general, or the feed-back from one of the great national shows, where some dealers will do well and others fare badly.

The saleroom also provides us with an accurate notion of the worth of stamps and postal history material, often more precisely and certainly more up-to-the-minute than the vagaries of the stamp catalogue, with its six months lead time between compilation and publication. Moreover, so often it is the case that material comes up for sale which is either beyond the scope of the standard catalogues or difficult to quantify, that the price realised is the only guide to true value. And there is also material which is very seldom encountered in a dealer's stock, which may have been a sleeper in the stamp catalogue for years, and only establishes its true worth when two or more bidders fight over it in the saleroom.

ALTHOUGH the sales under review here belong in the main to 1995, we must stray beyond the confines of the year slightly, if only to include a comment about a very remarkable collection that came under the hammer at **Harmers** on December 14, 1994, devoted to stamps and covers of the world. **Sotheby's** sale two days later had a festive air about it, with a number of choice items which would have made the ideal Christmas present and ranging from the illustrated Victorian wrappers to the unusual Tibetan scarf covers sent by the Dalai Lama and other dignitaries to foreign diplomats in the 19th century. The sale also included the outstanding collection of Finland formed by Veijo Mannelin which fetched £60,000 in total. At the other end of the scale was a fine assemblage of French First World War Red Cross labels which went for £800. Among the individual rarities was a fine example of the NZ Christchurch Exhibition 1d claret instead of vermilion which sold for £11,000. The sale realised almost £500,000 in all.

As a rule, January is a quiet month due to the Christmas and New Year holidays. There is generally little activity in the London salerooms, but for the provincial auctioneers it's a case of business as usual. The new year got off to a fine start with a good general sale at Poole on January 20 when **Interstamps** had an excellent general sale, yielding good results. British unmounted mint Postage Dues, US Duck stamps and good ranges of Mauritius with B64 Seychelles

postmarks all sold well. The last had formed part of a collection which was previously unsold at auction, but when broken up into smaller lots all except one sold. This is further evidence of collectors moving away from the buying of whole collections at auction and the rising demand for better sets amd single items. Although this sale contained nothing spectacular it provided plenty of the bread-and-butter material which keeps the trade and private collectors happy.

Phillips held a general sale in London of stamps and covers of the world on January 26 which sold well. Although there was nothing particularly outstanding, there was much middle of the road material which generally sold on or above estimate. A mint example of the Thailand 2a on 24a with surcharge inverted made £170, while Turkey's suffragette series of 1935 in unmounted mint state made £210. In the same sale a USA 3c Wells Fargo envelope of 1858 with various express company markings and US PO charge mark sold for £360.

On January 28 Derby was the venue for an excellent sale. The old-established firm of **Cavendish** has gone ahead by leaps and bounds in recent years under the dynamic direction of James Grimwood-Taylor, and has attracted a great deal of material which traditionally would have gravitated to one or other of the major London auction houses. Although this was a general, whole world sale, it was strong in

British postal history material, attracting bids from around the world. Cavendish now have an excellent reputation as a saleroom where postal history is well to the fore and this sale was no exception. An unusual entire from the British ship *Monarch*, sent from the Dutch island of St Eustatius under British occupation in 1781, with Plymouth arrival mark, fetched £400, proving that collector interest in the Caribbean area is as strong as ever.

There was much useful material in the British and New Zealand sections. A stampless embossed free envelope for Ireland with the word FREE inked out and various handstruck charge marks, addressed to Hamburg, made £260, while an 1864 envelope from Canonbie to Langholm with crossed 1s as a cancellation made £150. A used example of the 1941 2d orange of NZ with double perforations at the top fetched £220, although this is one of only two recorded examples. By contrast, a 1910 halfpenny with green overprint reading upwards, with Hastings postmark made £650 despite a small crease. A St Helena postcard of 1902 to Germany, from a Boer prisoner in Deadwood Camp made £420.

Another indicator of the bullishness of the market is that when the hobby is on the up and up the major auction houses expand and diversify. At the beginning of 1994 **Stanley Gibbons** opened in New Zealand with a sale which netted half a million dollars —small by UK standards perhaps, but actually four times as much as any sale had ever achieved in that country previously. The Gibbons sale might not have been as big as some previous sales there, but the quality far exceeded quantity.

Harmer's auction on February 14 of 1557 lots realised a total of £391,470 with foreign countries selling well. A collection of China estimated at £1000 went for £5500, while a strong section of Ethiopia was practically sold out. The surprise of the afternoon session, however, was an 1870 Ballon Monte flimsy which had been carried from Paris to London and franked by a GB 3d stamp. This lot opened at £1800 and was finally sold for £13,200 to a telephone bidder.

A fine collection of Niger Coast sold extremely well, with a 10s on 5d surcharged pair, one stamp showing the surcharge vertically, selling for £11,000. A colour trial of the King Edward VII Northern Nigeria £25 stamp fetched £4125.

An extremely rare 1874 GB–Norway combination cover realised £1912 at the March 1 **Warwick & Warwick** sale. The cover, bearing a 7sk Posthorn of Norway, was addressed to Countess Dundonald in London, per SS *Argo*, and was franked and postmarked at Bergen. On arrival at Hull a ship-letter postmark was applied. At London the cover was re-addressed to Dorking and a GB 1d red plate 72 was applied alongside and cancelled by a London duplex handstamp.

Harmer's sale on March 2 was devoted to the stamps and postal history of Australasia, yielding a very wide range of material from this perennially popular field, with good sections devoted to the Pacific islands as well as Australia and New Zealand. Among the unusual items noted was a block of four of the Australia 2½d of 1947 from the upper right-hand corner of the sheet, showing misplaced perforations and imperforate vertically on the upper pair. This unusual piece fetched £319. An envelope of 1861 from Norfolk Island to London with the Paid

1870 Ballon Monte flimsy carried from Paris to London, franked by a GB 3d stamp sold for £13,200 against Harmer's pre-sale estimate of £1800.

Cover from the Thai occupation of Malaya, 1943, with Kota Bahru cancellations sold for £4620 at Phillips.

Auckland handstamp and red London paid handstamp on arrival fetched £1045. Several other Norfolk Island covers bore stamps of New South Wales and were keenly fought over. Among the stamps from this very popular island, a marginal copy of the 1947–59 1d imperforate vertically between stamp and sheet margin made £660 despite being unused without gum.

The **Gibbons** sale in Sydney, Australia on March 8 realised more than A$300,000, with 86 per cent of the lots sold. Collections sold above estimate and included a European accumulation which sold for $1450 against an estimate of $500, while a collection of Australia to 1984 went for $2850 (estimate $2000). A 1912 Kangaroo essay in pale brown (showing the "rabbit" flaw on the left) sold for $2600 despite minor blemishes. A first watermark 5s with CA monogram, believed to be only the second example to come to light, made $2400. The stamps of China also proved very popular, with just over 100 lots from classics to modern stamps totalling over $32,000.

On April 6 **Phillips** held a specialised Great Britain sale which yielded a total of £151,481, with a top price of £8800 paid for the unused or mint collection from 1840 to 1970. Runner-up was a fine example of the 1883–84 10s cobalt blue mint which made £8250. Other good prices included a 1799 entire with the rare ARMY BAG handstamp (£1320), a series of Telegraph essays from the De La Rue archives (£1078), an Inland Revenue £1 of 1901 (£1012) and matching 5s (£1155). The 1990 Stamp World miniature sheet in imperforate condition made £4180. The most keenly contested lots in the sale, however, were the 44 lots devoted to Railway parcel stamps formed by the late A. J. Lowe, all of which considerably exceeded their estimates.

The same auctioneer disposed of the specialised collection of Grenada formed by Dr R. P. Towers on April 20, making a highly gratifying £104,559. The beautiful mint marginal copy of the 1861–62 rough perf 14 to 16 made £4400 against an SG catalogue quotation of £3000. The 1861 die proofs sold extremely well and other good prices included £3960 for an 1876 envelope bearing the 1d, 1s and bisected 1d used to France, and £2750 for the 1883 envelope with mixed franking.

This was followed by a sale of British Commonwealth which was spread over one and a half days and totalled £352,904. This general sale, the best held by Phillips so far, was distinguished by the record number of postal bidders and the rich variety of the material on offer, but the undoubted attraction was the seven-volume collection of Australia which fetched £9000, about twice the pre-sale estimate. A specialised study of KGV heads made £2750, while a 1931 interpanneau pair of the £2 mint fetched £2860. A cover from the Thai occupation of Malaya, 1943 with Kota Bharu cancellation made £4620, while Tristan da Cunha covers from 1929 with the type IVa cachet fetched £2310 and £2035 respectively. There was keen competition for the stamps of the Bahamas, Bermuda, Canada, Cape of Good Hope, Cyprus, Dominica, Falkland Islands, Gibraltar, Hong Kong, Malaya, Malta, Mauritius, New Zealand, St Helena and Sierra Leone as well.

Christie's held two specialised sales in the same month. On April 11 the highly specialised collection of Bavarian stamps and postal history formed by Rudi Oppenheimer came under the hammer in Zurich. The star item was a registered cover of 1873 bearing the 12k reddish lilac, with 6k pale brown from Wurzburg to France, which was eventually knocked down for SFr 23,000. The runner-up was a registered cover of 1859 bearing four examples of the 12k red on the front and an horizontal pair on the reverse, from Munich to Naples via Marseilles, also bearing the 3k blue, 9k yellow-green and a pair of the 18k orange-yellow for good measure. This spectacular cover sold for SFr 19,550. Other fine pieces included two covers, each of which sold for SFr 18,400; a cover of October 1862 with the 6k Prussian blue combined with the 3k light blue from Augsburg to Austria and a cover of 1864 with the 12k yellow-green, 9k yellow-brown and 6k light blue from Straubing to Athens via Vienna.

Zurich was the venue, the following day, for the sale of the second part of Gary Ryan's incomparable collection of classic Hungary. The gem of this section was the 1867 3k red, error of colour, fine used, which made SFr 63,250. A cover of 1869 franked with the 50k from Pest to France sold for SFr 41,400. Among the more modern items the Madonna and Child 5000k of 1923 with inverted centre made SFr 12,650.

The **Phillips** general sale on April 27 realised a total of £144,120 with very few lots unsold. The mixed lots and collections were, as usual, incredibly popular, and yielded quite a few surprises, notably the £3250 paid for a Commonwealth collection which had been valued at £2000. A section devoted to French Antarctica produced some exceptional prices, especially for the earlier issues. There was also a good range of British stamps which generally sold well, and in many cases exceeded the estimates. A sign that the market is really beginning to recover after a prolonged period of stagnation is that a fine block of four PUC pound stamps made £1500, 50 per cent more than the estimate. Those with very long memories may recall that a fine single of this ever-popular stamp would have fetched four figures in 1970, having been hyped up and inflated by the investment mania of that period. When the crash came, a few months later, PUC pounds could be bought for a tenth of that sum, and the long haul back has been slow and painful. Significantly, there were many individual stamps in this sale which, because of their superlative condition, provoked keen bidding and went well above estimate.

A sale of British Commonwealth stamps and covers at **Phillips** on June 15 brought a total of £207,662 for 578 lots, most of which sold. Top price was £10,780 for a two-volume "New Imperial"

collection. Other good prices included £1115 for a mint Cyprus £5m, £1115 for the Falklands 1933 10s and £1 on covers, and £1155 for a Madagascar 1886 2s unused and without handstamp. The best of the other collections were Australia (£3190), Batum (£1012), Bermuda (£1760), British Levant (£1430), Cyprus (£1265), Falkland Islands (£1320), Morocco Agencies (£1430), New Zealand (£3960), Palestine (£2090) and Rhodesia (£2530).

Phillips held a specialised GB sale on June 22, yielding a total of £242,946. The Mulready 1d letter sheet which was re-addressed at least four times rose to a stupendous £3850. The 1840 1d black from plate V mint sold for £1760, while an example from the second state of the same plate, used on cover, made £2420.

Catalogued at £3500 this China 1897 4c on 3c revenue with "small" surcharge realised £6325 at Stanley Gibbons.

Some startling results were achieved at **Stanley Gibbons** on June 29–30. Notable among these was the China 1897 4c on 3c revenue "small" surcharge which went for £6325. This stamp is catalogued at £3500 and the current specialised China catalogue was only published a few months previously! Also going for well over full catalogue was one of the highlights of a very fine collection of the British consular mails of Madagascar. The 1886 3d handstruck in red (SG24a) made £4600 against a catalogue price of £3000, in spite of some defects. British Europem, Hong Kong, Far East and GB all did well, with total realisations achieving almost £310,000, one of SG's best results for the past few years. While most of the lots performed much in line with expectations, there were also some attractive lots of India and native states which excited considerable interest, showing yet again that nothing is too esoteric for collectors.

On the same date **Phillips** held a general sale which totalled £185,379. As usual with this saleroom, collections were well to the fore and generally sold extremely well. The best of these was an unusual collection of strike mail which made £2035. A thematic collection of Walt Disney material sold for £1650, while good general collections of Germany and GB fetched £1485 and £1980 respectively. Rather better collections of Italy and Hong Kong made £2860 and £2970 respectively. Some collections devoted to the Commonwealth as a whole, however, fetched excellent sums, going for £6050, £3520, £2750 and £2640. The best individual stamp was the French 1877–90 Peace and Commerce 1c black on Prussian blue in mint condition which fetched £1210.

Any lingering doubts that the market had made a good recovery after years in the doldrums were dispelled by the clutch of sales in June and July which brought the 1994/95 season to such a successful conclusion. **Harmers** held a sale of important stamps and covers of the world in July. This was the kind of sale which had much to offer which was difficult to evaluate—particularly covers the like of which had not been seen before and would probably never be seen again. The top price was £24,200 for a fine example of the Northern Nigeria £25 of King Edward VII. A mint De Pinedo airmail of Newfoundland fetched £16,500 while a fine early Victorian Albert and Victoria illustrated cover sold for £3575.

A new world record price for a Valentine was established at the sale of the Frank Staff collection on July 21 at **Cavendish**, £3080 being paid for a handpainted letter of 1805 from Brixham. This was not, however, the highest price in the sale: this went to an 1844 musical pictorial envelope at £3850, while a chromolitho envelope from Bavaria to Scotland

with six 3k rose made £3300. Twelve other lots went above the four-figure level, among them a Mons Thomson Mulready caricature which fetched £2420 and an 1841 Irish Heroes pictorial envelope which made the same sum.

Traditionally the major London salerooms are quiet during August, but there is no such thing as a closed season in philately so far as the provincial auctioneers are concerned. **Warwick & Warwick** had a good general sale on August 2, with nothing outstanding but a great deal of useful material, most of which found ready buyers. **Bristol Stamp Auctions** at Keynsham on August 5 had a sale which totalled £205,000, with quite a number of choice Commonwealth stamps and covers which passed the four-figure mark. Three days later **Acorn Philatelic Auctions** had a very satisfactory general sale in Manchester, attracting bids from collectors in many parts of the world beyond these shores. **PH Stamps** had an excellent whole world sale at Seaford on August 12, and while there were no howling rarities, there was something for everyone, and the lots were virtually sold out. Doubtless there were many other provincial sales throughout the year; they seldom hit the headlines and yet, among them, they must account for the bulk of the buying and selling for the bulk of the country's collectors.

The 1995/96 season got under way in fine style, with a splendid sale conducted by **David Feldman** in Singapore as part of the programme of the great Singapore '95 International Stamp Exhibition. This was a sale that concentrated on the rarities and

Francis Kiddle, President of the Royal Philatelic Society (centre) with James Grimwood-Taylor (left) and Geoffrey Manton, founder of the company, unveils a plaque marking the opening of the new Cavendish premises in Derby.

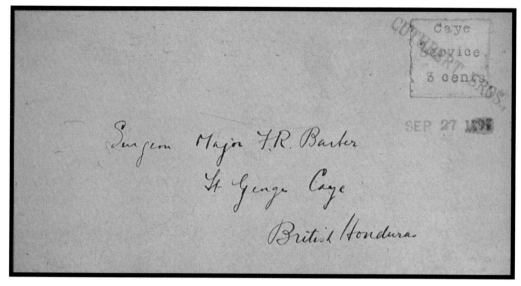

Cover bearing the typewritten local stamp from the Cayes of Belize, franked by CUTHBERT BROS. sold for £2970 at Phillips.

elusive gems pertaining to South-east Asia, and it drew spectacular bids from the countries around the Pacific Rim.

At home, the season was launched with a double celebration in Derby where **Cavendish** celebrated their 500th sale with the inauguration of their new, vastly more commodious premises at Cavendish House. The sale, on September 16, was preceded by a grand reception hosted by James Grimwood-Taylor and Geoffrey Manton (who founded the firm in 1952). The premises were formally opened by Francis Kiddle, President of the Royal Philatelic Society. The sale itself saw spectacular results with GB, Commonwealth and foreign stamps and postal history all reaching very good price levels.

Phillips held a specialised GB sale on September 5, yielding a total of £202,898. While there were no outstanding rarities, there was a great deal of material which is highly elusive, and consequently bidding was very keen. A Mulready with the distinctive Wotton-under-Edge Maltese cross cancellation fetched £2310, while a mint Penny Black from Plate 1b (ex-Seymour) sold for £1100 and a VR Penny Black formerly in the same collection fetched £1705. A good general sale on September 14 totalled £309,950 for 861 lots, well above expectations. A big surprise was in store for the vendor of the find of Japanese post offices in China which more than doubled estimates at £32,098. A Commonwealth sale on September 21 totalled £163,417. The Cuthbert Bros. cover from the Cayes of Belize, with typewritten local stamp, fetched £2970.

A Canada Twelvepence Black fetched £4400 despite defects.

Christie's held a sale on September 20 which concentrated on classic material from South Africa in the Salisbury collection. The top price was £82,900, paid for a splendid example of the Cape Woodblock 4d carmine error of colour, against an estimate of £50,000–£70,000 and, in fact, comfortably exceeding the Stanley Gibbons catalogue price of £80,000. Runner-up was a fine example of the Woodblock 4d deep blue which sold for £69,700, again well above estimate. There were several fine covers, the best of which made £42,200 (estimate £25,000–£30,000). The sale was nicely rounded off with several lots devoted to the siege stamps of Mafeking. One of the two recorded complete sheets of the 3d pale blue (the other is in the Royal collection) was knocked down in this sale for £45,500, slightly above the upper pre-sale estimate, and bringing the total for this sale to £826,000 for a mere 107 lots.

Christie's sold a superb example of the famous Cape of Good Hope "Woodblock" 4d carmine error of colour for the amazing sum of £82,900.

Harmers of London held a whole world sale on September 27 which yielded a total of £278,000. The opening lot was a valuable collection of George VI stamps which went for £7000 against an estimate of £5000. Among the foreign material there was considerable interest in the 15 lots of covers and postcards from the Aegean islands which attracted keen bidding and sold extremely well. In relative terms, however, the most spectacular result was the £1200 paid for the Danish Caravel Die I 15 ore scarlet of 1933–41 block of 16 overprinted MUSTER (Specimen). Despite damage to six of the stamps this block actually sold for twelve times the estimate of £100. British material sold extremely well, with fierce bidding for a fine selection of Mulready wrappers and caricatures. One of the more esoteric items which found a new home, was the reply half of a Bavarian 10pf postcard of September 1887, posted from Heligoland; not surprisingly, this sold for £2600 against an estimate of £1500.

Two days later, **Cavendish** disposed of the Swarbrick specialised collection of Jamaica. Top price was £11,550 paid for a fine example of the Queen Victoria statue 1s stamp of 1919–21 with inverted centre, formerly in the collection of King Carol of Roumania. One of the covers in the sale, from the Dummer packet service of 1702, has the distinction of being reproduced on a postage stamp, issued by Jamaica in 1971 to celebrate the tercentenary of the postal service. This was fiercely contested and eventually sold for £4620, more than three times the pre-sale estimate.

The Jamaica inverted centre 1s of 1919–21, previously in the collection of King Carol of Roumania, realised £11,550 at Cavendish when they disposed of the Swarbrick Collection on September 29.

The auction season really got into its stride on October 5. **Christie's** staged what is undoubtedly the sale of the year, when they dispersed the incomparable TES Collection of Great Britain for

The Heath "Blank Head" essay with "POSTAGE" and "ONE PENNY" labels added (left) sold for £65,300—top price at Christie's GB sale in October.

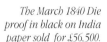

The March 1840 Die proof in black on India paper sold for £56,500.

£1,088,226. This spectacular collection of classic GB was formed over the past 20 years and illustrated the origins and development of adhesive stamps, from the Treasury Competition of 1839 onwards. It was undoubtedly the finest collection of its kind ever formed, surpassed only by the collections in the National Postal Museum and Buckingham Palace. Top price was £65,300 (estimate £25,000–£30,000) for the Heath "Blank Head" essay for the Penny Black; the only other examples are in the two great institutional collections already mentioned. The runner up was the master die proof for the Penny Black, with blank corners, which was knocked down for £56,500 (estimate £20,000–£25,000), one of two copies believed to exist in private hands. The completed master die proof with stars in the upper corners fetched the third best price of the day, £40,000 (estimate £15,000–£18,000). Conversely, the item which had been expected to take the highest price failed to reach its lower estimate of £40,000. This was the unique vertical corner pair of imprimaturs from the first registration sheet of the VR Penny Black. This superlative item found a lucky buyer at the rather disappointing price of £34,500. No matter, the overall result surpassed expectation and proved that the market was now in an extremely buoyant mood again, after several years of stagnation.

On October 27 **Cavendish** disposed of the specialised collection of stamps and postal history of Madeira formed by John Sussex. The best price was £16,760 (estimate £4500) paid by a European collector for the cover of September 1842 bearing the very rare crowned paid mark of the British post office. This is the earliest and by far the clearest strike of this postmark. An entire of 1816 with the two-line

Top price in the John Sussex collection of Madeira, sold by Cavendish on October 27, was £16,760 paid for this September 1842 cover with the crowned PAID AT MADEIRA mark.

PORT/BRITISH accountancy mark sold for £2010, just over double the pre-sale estimate.

Harmers had a good general sale on October 31, attracting considerable attention on account of the strong sections of Bechuanaland and Cyprus as well as the Australian occupation of German New Guinea in 1914. A fine example of the GRI overprint on the 5 mark realised £6705, more than twice estimate.

Christie's held three sales late in October and the beginning of November, in London, Melbourne and Hong Kong, reinforcing their global predominance. While the results underlined the buoyancy of the international market in general, it is significant that the most spectacular results were achieved in Hong Kong in respect of material from the Far East. This is an aspect of philately which has been surging ahead of late, reflecting the upswing of interest in the newly affluent countries of the area, most notably Taiwan and Korea; but there is now clear indication that the sleeping giant of mainland China is waking up to the potential of philately.

On October 24, a worldwide sale of postal history material provided a very wide range of covers and postcards to suit every level of collecting, and while there were no outstanding rarities there were numerous pieces which sold for £1000 or more. Even at the more modest level, in the price range from £100 to £500, many items sold for well above estimate and were keenly contested. Two days later, in Melbourne, the stamps and postal history of Australasia included the specialised collection of Gilbert and Ellice Islands formed by Thomas Belknap, and the study of New South Wales stamps used in Queensland formed by Robert Horley Taylor. The star item in this sale, however, was the unique cover of 1854 from Norfolk Island to Tasmania with a 4d orange of 1853–55 and a fine framed Norfolk Island paid handstamp. This superlative item sold for

Highlights of the Christie's sale in Hong Kong on November 1 were the 1941 Sun Yat-Sen $2 black and blue with inverted centre which realised the top price of HK$207,000; the unused 1922 2c on 3c with inverted surcharge which sold for HK$172,500 and the used 3c on 4c inverted surcharge which made the same price.

A\$20,700, in line with the pre-sale estimate.

On November 1 the sale in Hong Kong yielded some really spectacular results, especially for material from the collection of Hong Kong formed by Robert Horley Taylor. Mint multiples of Victorian stamps produced the fiercest bidding, and a horizontal pair of the 96c of 1863–71 went for HK\$16,000, twice the estimate. A mint block of four of the 20c on 30c of 1885, however, sold for HK\$22,000 against an estimate of HK\$2500–\$3000. Best price in this section was HK\$126,500 for the set of proofs pertaining to the 1954 series of Queen Elizabeth. However, it was in the section devoted to the stamps of China itself that the best prices were produced. A fine example of the 2c on 3c of 1922 with inverted surcharge went for HK\$172,500, while a slightly defective copy of the 3c on 4c inverted surcharge in used condition made the same price, despite small defects. Top price of the day was HK\$207,000 paid for the fine unused example of the Sun Yat-Sen \$2 of 1941 with inverted centre.

Phillips held a sale of Commonwealth material on November 9, totalling £300,110. This sale was dominated by specialised sections of Australia and New Zealand formed by the late J. G. Evans. Top price was £9680 for an accumulation of Australian material which was snapped up by a dealer from Down Under. Another, mainly mint, accumulation rose to £5500 against an estimate of £1000, while an accumulation of George VI material estimated at £800 went eventually for £5060. Best of the individual items was the se-tenant strip of five of the 37c Wildlife stamps of 1987 with the buff colour omitted, which sold for £1012 against an estimate of £500. A whole world sale on November 16 brought in £276,625. The highlight was the Mendelsohn collection of French Indochina, which included an 1897 registered cover from Mongtse to Shanghai (believed to be the earliest known), which made £3080. The large section of

Germany included many good prices, especially for the booklets and specialised items. Italian states were in demand, with the two best Naples Trinacria selling for £2240 each and a Tuscany 3 lire of 1860 in used condition reaching £3300.

Sotheby's hold stamp sales infrequently, but when they do the results are guaranteed to be spectacular. The year was well rounded off on December 15 by a whole world sale which realised a total of £540,765. One of the lots which attracted considerable attention was the set of three Olympic stamps prepared by East Germany but not issued on account of the decision by many Communist countries to boycott the Los Angeles Games. Four years later stamps in identical designs but with the date altered to 1988 were actually issued. The set on offer was one of several which had been sold over a Leipzig post office counter by accident. Attempts by the German authorities to suppress sale of previous sets from the same source had been quashed by a court ruling in 1992. In the end, this set was sold for £7475 to a US collector, against an estimate of £6000. The penultimate lot in this sale was an old-time accumulation of British stamps, still in the original envelopes as purchased from dealers before the war. This lot was estimated at £5000 to £7000, but was hotly contested until knocked down at £47,700.

Five days later, **Harmers** produced gratifying results in their whole world sale. The morning session was dominated by lots from specialised collections of Ethiopia and Tibet, two of the more out of the way countries which can always be guaranteed to attract keen bidding. There were some interesting and unusual covers from 1864 onwards, all of which found buyers at well over £1000 a time; but the best price in the Ethiopian section was £2458, paid for a 1g stationery postcard from an Italian, taken prisoner during the Abyssinian campaign of 1896–97. The Tibetan material produced even better results, with

East Germany's decision to boycott the 1984 Olympics and the consequent cancellation of the stamp programme attracted a bidder to pay £7,475 for these unissued designs when they were offered at Sotheby's on December 15.

a cover of 1933 from Gartok to Belgium selling for £7822.

The afternoon session moved to more familiar ground. The GB material sold strongly in line with pre-sale expectation, a strip of three Queen Victoria £5 stamps going for £3911, pretty well in line with the estimate. The best price, however, was paid for the Victorian £1 overprinted I.R. OFFICIAL in fine used condition; despite defects it fetched a satisfactory £8381 in line with the estimate which proved pretty accurate in view of the fact that this stamp is not priced in used condition in the Gibbons catalogue.

The highest price paid for a single stamp at auction during the past year was $660,000 paid by Greg Manning of Australia for the unique unused example of the Hawaiian Missionaries 2 cents of 1851 which was sold on November 7 in the **Robert Siegel** *auction. This famous rarity had formerly been in the Ferrary and Burrus collections and also featured in the Cary Grant and Audrey Hepburn thriller* Charade. *Manning, incidentally, had been prepared to go to a million dollars for it, and considered the result very satisfactory from his viewpoint.*

DIX AND WEBB

AUCTIONEERS AND VALUERS

1996 Sale Diary

Wednesday 3rd July
British and World Stamps and Postal History

Wednesday 18th September
British and World Stamps and Postal History

Wednesday 11th December
British and World Stamps and Postal History

All auctions are held at the Westbury Hotel, Bond Street

Lots for inclusion in any of the above sales can be accepted up to 5 weeks before the sale date.
Specialised sales may be held throughout the year in addition to those shown above.
For further information, please contact James Grist, Director of Philatelic Auctions.

DIX AND WEBB LIMITED

AUCTIONEERS AND VALUERS
1 OLD BOND ST • LONDON W1X 3TD
TEL:0171 499 5022 • FAX:0171 499 5023

THE GOOD, THE BAD AND THE UGLY

One of the most popular—certainly the most provocative—features of the old *Stamp Collectors' Annual* which ceased publication in 1962 was L. E. Scott's survey of the ten best stamp designs of the previous twelve months. In view of the vast increase in the volume of new issues—about 12,000 in 1995—it would be impossible to examine them all and select a Top Ten these days; but some of the problems of 1961 are still with us thirty-five years later, while many others have emerged in the interim.

LOOKING over the new issues of 1961 Scott lamented the abysmal state of industrial design in Britain generally, and of stamp design in particular. "Shoddy and out-of-date" was his description; harsh words indeed. Things have come a long way in the past three decades. Despite Scott's dismissive attitude, British stamps were the subject of a great deal of deliberation in the higher echelons of the Post Office. There was arguably more time spent, and more expertise tapped, than in a stamp from anywhere else in the world. Perhaps that was the problem.

British stamps are still the result of considerable planning, and in commissioning artists to execute the designs Royal Mail clings to the tradition of seeking the best and most varied talent available. Whether the end product of all this effort lives up to the promise is a matter for debate and often controversy. But looking back on the stamps issued in 1995 we may be relieved that they were no worse, if no better, than any of their predecessors.

The year got off to a splendid start with the set of five cat stamps designed by Elizabeth Blackadder, one of Britain's best-known painters of nature subjects. It emerged that the cats depicted were real animals—Sophie, Puskas, Tigger, Chloe, Kikko, Rosie and Fred—all living in the Edinburgh area in fact; so here we have an interesting breach of Royal Mail rules against the depiction of living persons other than royalty. Thus, a cat can not only look at the Queen, but do it on our stamps.

The Springtime series, however, proved a let-down, with Royal Mail getting all arty on us again. The stamps featured plant sculptures by Andy Goldsworthy, created by the artistic arrangement of such material as garlic leaves and dandelions. The results are then photographed before they curl up or are scattered by the four winds. The result, I'm afraid, defied description.

Greetings in Art was the theme of the greetings booklet released in March and featuring, for the most part, couples in clinches, dancing, kissing, eyeball to eyeball and ranging from "The Kiss" by Rodin to a charming Edwardian photograph of Alice Keppel with

The Centenary of the National Trust was marked by a set of five stamps depicting the wide range of subjects covered by the Trust, from protecting the land to repairing historic buildings.

her daughter Alice Hughes. Everything from Persian miniatures to Eric Gill was thrown into this pot-pourri of passion, but there's no doubt about it: they do brighten up our social mail (as Royal Mail quaintly describes anything these days that isn't a bill or a circular).

Hard on the heels of the greetings booklet came another disappointment—the National Trust Centenary set which did not compare too well with the set of 1981 covering much the same ground (though ostensibly marking the jubilee of the National Trust for Scotland). Close-up details of a fireplace decoration or the Tudor timberwork at Little Moreton Hall did not do justice to the subject, while the oak seedling on the 25p looked like a refugee from Goldsworthy's nature sculptures.

The year really hit rock bottom, however, with the Europa issue in May. It never ceases to baffle me why Royal Mail do not make a straight-out, honest-to-goodness Europa issue like all the other countries participating in this hardy annual. Instead, we have the confusion of only two stamps in the set actually bearing the CEPT logo. Confusion was compounded this year by producing two stamps by one designer and three by another. The trio came in for a great deal of criticism, being the work of the controversial Belgian artist Jean-Michel Folon, creator of the 1991 Europa pairs which totally defied description. The latest offering was in the same genre, combining wishy-washy pastel colours with obscure symbolism

(elongated human hands), but actually intended to mark the 125th anniversary of the British Red Cross and the 50th anniversary of the United Nations. The set was redeemed by the pair designed by John Gorham. Based on actual photographs, they showed British troops and French civilians celebrating the liberation and St Paul's Cathedral with searchlights making a giant V in the night sky. No-nonsense, and providing a clear message; the essence of good stamp design in other words.

Siobhan Keaney designed the four stamps marking the centenary of the publication of *The Time Machine* by H. G. Wells. The man himself was not portrayed, much to the disgust of Wells fans, and the psychedelic treatment of the motifs intended to symbolise four of his best-known works left much to be desired. The designs were cluttered with words and slogans which had no actual relevance to the titles or their subjects.

After two disappointments in a row, came the Shakespeare strip of five se-tenant stamps in August, celebrating the reconstruction of the Globe Theatre but providing a glorious opportunity for a panorama of the South Bank in the early Jacobean period, with the principal theatres of Shakespeare's heyday prominently depicted. The Bard himself was depicted on one of them, if you looked closely at the fine detail with a good magnifying glass.

Best of the year's stamps, however, were the set of four released in September to mark the

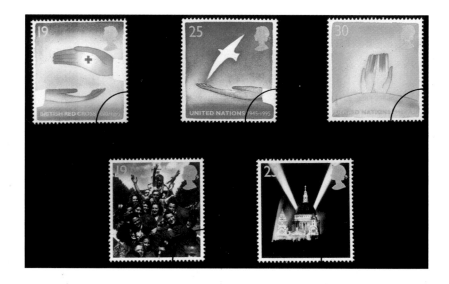

The confusing and controversial Europa issue which celebrated the 125th anniversary of the Red Cross and the 50th anniversary of the United Nations.

In August a panorama of the South Bank in Shakespeare's time celebrated the reconstruction of the Globe Theatre.

bicentenary of the birth of Rowland Hill and the centenary of Marconi's early experiments with radio. All four married a lithographed background with finely engraved portraiture by The Master himself, Czeslaw Slania who must, by now, be approaching his thousandth engraving since his debut in Poland in the early 1950s. Call me old-fashioned, but there is nothing to touch intaglio for the finest quality of stamp printing, and the mere fact that the motif has to be engraved by a skilled craftsman actually does force the designer to give rather more thought to such matters as layout, balance and good lettering. The Rugby League and Christmas robins which rounded off the year were pretty well par for the course.

Comparisons are invidious, but one cannot help noting how they do things in the Channel Islands and the Isle of Man. Guernsey's greetings set of February featuring the welcoming face of Guernsey was a masterpiece of whimsy and pawky humour— not too much of that around in stamp design (outside Tunisia, that is, where Hatem Elmekki is still producing gems of surrealism). All three postal administrations devoted considerable coverage to the Europa theme, made all the more poignant in the case of the Channel Islands which celebrated the 50th anniversary of their liberation after years of Nazi oppression. Separate issues for the latter subject were released simultaneously.

Guernsey's Europa stamps were of considerable interest technically for using stereograms to create a three-dimensional image. This was claimed as a first, but unfortunately French Polynesia got there first, having adopted the same technique for the 1994 Christmas stamps. The Liberation set consisted of a strip of five and matching miniature sheet reproducing contemporary photographs. Even little Alderney got in on the act, producing a £1.05 miniature sheet in November to mark the 50th

Sir Rowland Hill was the subject on two of the Communications set issued in September. Engraved by Czeslaw Slania the set of four stamps proved to be the best of the year's designs.

Rugby and Christmas robins rounded off the year

Jersey's contribution to the celebration of the 50th anniversary of their Liberation included a £1 miniature sheet.

anniversary of the return of the islanders. Jersey's contribution was a booklet of six different designs capturing the historic moments of liberation, accompanied by a miniature sheet whose £1 stamp showed Churchill with the Royal Family on the balcony at Buckingham Palace acknowledging the cheering crowds on VE-Day.

The Isle of Man produced a splendid set of eight which showed scenes of celebration and included the campaign stars and medals for good measure.

Peace and Freedom were the twin themes of the Europa stamps in 1995 and were interpreted in diverse ways by the member countries. Denmark and Norway opted for press photographs of 1945; others chose a symbolic path, with a rash of peace doves and broken strands of barbed wire. Interestingly, Germany produced a stark reminder that it, too, had been a victim of Nazi oppression with a miniature sheet symbolising the destruction due to enemy air raids. This was coupled with a very austere sheet, showing the striped clothing worn by inmates of the concentration camps. The sheet margins bore the

names of some of the more notorious death camps. Incidentally, these were the first stamps (since the shortlived Amgots of 1945–46) to bear the country name Deutschland, reflecting the privatised nature of what used to be the Bundespost.

The Holocaust was to be a recurring theme throughout the year, ranging from the miniature sheet produced by Israel itself to the 45c released by Canada in November. Striped clothing and yellow stars predominated, often using actual photographs, though from the artistic viewpoint the best of the designs was that produced by Slovakia, using line engraving.

Both the Crown Agents and the Inter-Governmental Philatelic Corporation launched omnibus issues to mark the 50th anniversary of the end of the war. The former was the more coherent of the two, each territory producing four stamps illustrating its contribution to the war effort, together with a miniature sheet in a uniform design, showing the war medal against a field of poppies. By contrast, the countries in the IGPC ensemble were allowed

The Isle of Man set of eight stamps commemorating VE Day includes the campaign medals of the war.

considerable leeway, both in the number of stamps and the treatment adopted, though it cannot be denied that the results were colourful and interesting.

Both of the major agencies also produced omnibus issues for the 50th anniversary of the United Nations in October. Here again, the Crown Agents omnibus had a clearly defined structure, with the interesting contemporary topic of UN peacekeeping activities in the world's trouble spots. Elsewhere, most member countries of the United Nations marked the jubilee with a stamp or stamps featuring the approved 50th anniversary logo, but relying heavily on rather vapid symbolism rather than actual

content to maintain the status quo, these countries polarise between the ones which rely on indigenous printers and those which have gone to the world's leading firms. Slovenia and Croatia, Estonia and Latvia produce their own stamps and have come a long way in a very short time. It seems like only yesterday that Lithuania was using rather crudely lithographed imperforate stamps from East Germany; today its stamps are as sophisticated as any to be found anywhere, but they are printed in Hungary which has also produced quite a few issues for the Ukraine. By contrast, the stamps of Armenia and Azerbaijan are now printed by Questa in Britain. This

Germany issued a stark reminder of Nazi oppression with this austere miniature sheet.

pictorial examples of what UN membership had meant.

On the one hand there continues to be a vast outpouring of provisional local issues in Russia and the Ukraine, as their respective currencies spiral into orbit. A big question mark hangs over this material, much of which may well be quite bogus, despite the existence of commercially used covers which reflect the total chaos in the postal services in much of these countries. On the other hand one also notes the improvement in the design and printing of the stamps in many of the new republics of central and eastern Europe. Apart from Slovakia, which is

company, incidentally, must surely print half the world's total output, judging from information on new issues, and certainly outperforms all other stamp printers.

Questa have become the past-masters of the composite sheet. Many of the stamps they print are released in sheets of 12, 16, 18, 20 or 24 in which each stamp is self-contained but forms part of a larger picture covering the entire sheet. This, I suspect, is done largely for marketing reasons and it certainly makes for greater convenience all round, from the designer who can think on a grand scale, to the collector who can mount a sheet with a few transparent mounting corners, in a fraction of the time required to cut and trim Hawid strips for the same number of individual stamps. But somewhere in between I feel that something is being lost. Does one ever come across postally used examples of the individual stamps? And if so, how does one reconstruct the sheet tidily when different cancellations are bound to obtrude and spoil the symmetry? Personally I would like to see far fewer of these composite sheets and a return to traditional sheets.

This also raises the problem of sheetlets with decorative margins. These have been around for many years, but in 1994 assumed alarming proportions when the German Bundespost announced its intention to release commemoratives in this format, thereby pressurising collectors into buying complete sheets where a single stamp, pair or block of four would have previously sufficed. Since then the Netherlands has followed suit. There is immense danger, both for the quality of design, and for philately in general, when postal administrations resort to such dubious practices in pursuit of profit.

The concept of joint issues has come a long way in recent years and is by no means as unusual as it once was. Late in 1994, in fact, the concept was taken to its logical conclusion by Italy and San Marino which produced a joint issue of 750 lire stamps celebrating the 900th anniversary of the dedication of St Mark's Basilica in Venice. Stamps were issued in tete-beche pairs, in sheets of 20 or miniature sheets, inscribed for use in Italy or San Marino, depending on which way up the vertical pair was. An inscription on the back limited the validity of the pair to the appropriate country. 1995 witnessed quite a number of twinned issues, including Nobel (Germany and Sweden), Tycho Brahe (Denmark and Sweden), St Olav (Norway and Faroes), and air service (Iceland and Luxembourg). Formerly such issues involved two countries but increasingly three countries are taking part. A prime example of this came in April when Estonia, Latvia and Lithuania each issued a stamp and miniature sheet to celebrate the Via Baltica motorway project. The sheet reproduced the stamps of all three countries, but were inscribed for use in the country issuing the sheet, an interesting and novel permutation on the theme. Later in the year there was even a five-country issue portraying Guglielmo Marconi, using a common design of German origin for Germany, Ireland, Italy, San Marino and the Vatican, though some of these also contributed a second stamp of their own design.

Of course, this was the year in which the twin

Joint issue from Italy and San Marino.

media of the silver screen and the postage stamp collided in a very big way. The centenary of the cinema was the occasion for numerous stamps and miniature sheets from every part of the world. Indeed, celebrations are on-going, with a set from the United Kingdom issued in April 1996. Amid the welter of stills, pictures of camera equipment and portraits of film stars I must single out the Brazilian miniature sheet which provided the best coverage of the development of cinematography, and the sheetlet from Sweden whose six se-tenant stamps were beautifully engraved multicolour images derived from stills—a combination of two quite different media at its best.

1995 was a remarkable year for centenaries, with the death of Pasteur and the discovery of X-rays by Roentgen exciting a certain amount of global interest. The centenary of the strip cartoon should have been a natural for philatelic reproduction, and indeed, it yielded a sheet of 20 from the USA and a booklet of ten from Canada, but disappointingly little else—though this seems too good a theme for other countries not to pick up on ere long. By contrast, the strangest centenary to attract attention was the making of Alfred Nobel's will. No matter that the poor man lingered on a further twelve months before

Marconi was the theme for a number of different issues.

actually expiring, so we should not be celebrating his death centenary till 1996, and the fact that a further five years elapsed before the first of the celebrated Nobel prizes were awarded. Germany and Sweden had a joint issue, and Hungary also marked the occasion, with a portrait of Nobel and reproductions of the medals. But this was the opportunity for a fifteen-country omnibus from IGPC that promised to outdo all previous omnibus issues. Each country released one or more (and in some cases as many as six) sheetlets of nine or twelve stamps, together with appropriate souvenir sheets, making a grand total in excess of 500 stamps and sheets that provided a veritable portrait gallery of Nobel prizewinners past and present.

Other celebrities who have attained international status also did well, with stamps from the USA in honour of Elvis Presley and Marilyn Monroe, multiplied several times over by issues from a number of other countries. Belatedly, the 55th anniversary of John Lennon's birth was the subject of an eight-country omnibus in December.

One other trend which developed in very recent times was well established in 1995: the se-tenant sheetlet. This is something with which the United States has dabbled in previous years, but led to the controversial Legends of the West issue and, latterly, the sheet of 20 portraying the heroes of the Civil War. As neither of these issues was tied to a particular anniversary, a dangerous precedent has been established, and no doubt we can look forward to many more of these sheets in the years to come. At least the individual stamps are quite distinctive, which is more than can be said for the Dutch and German sheets of ten previously mentioned.

Not quite a centenary, perhaps, the Queen Mother's birthday in August excited a number of issues from both Crown Agents and IGPC countries. I imagine that the world's presses are already getting geared up for her 100th birthday in the year 2000, but doubtless the Millennium itself will be the great topic in that momentous year.

ISLE OF MAN POST OFFICE

Philatelic Bureau
P.O.Box 10.M
Douglas,
Isle of Man
IM99 1PB
01624 686130

Depicted here are just a few of the recent themes covered by the Isle of Man Post Office :- Lighthouses, Fungi, Cats, Heraldry in the Douglas self Adhesive stamp and motorbikes in the forthcoming TT issue. Others to look forward to later in the year are Dogs, The British Legion, UNICEF & Christmas

THEMATICS!

Manx Cat First Day Cover

If you need further information on any of these issues write the address above or phone 01624 686130

Maxi Cards

Stamp Cards

LIGHTHOUSES

Trust the Isle of Man Post Office to cater for the thematic collector!

THEME OF THE YEAR— CATS ON STAMPS

It is strange to think that the domestic cat (Felis domesticus), probably the commonest and most familiar of animals throughout the world, was one of the least represented on postage stamps until quite recently. Up to the 1960s, in fact, you would have been hard put to find more than a dozen examples, and in every case you would have had to look closely to find the cat tucked away in a corner of the design.

THE first cat stamp was an airmail issued by Spain in 1930 to commemorate the solo Atlantic flight of Charles Lindbergh in 1927. The stamp portrayed Lindbergh and showed his monoplane, *Spirit of St Louis*, beside the Statue of Liberty. In the bottom right-hand corner of the stamp, however, is Patsy, a tiny black kitten, which should have been Lindbergh's companion and mascot on his epic flight; but at the very last moment the tender-hearted aviator decided that, while he was quite prepared to risk his own life, he could not take chances with the nine lives of the cat, so Patsy was left behind.

Cuba celebrated the golden jubilee of the Young Helpers' League by issuing a stamp in 1957 which depicted a boy fondling a cat. A boy holding a kitten was featured on one of the stamps in the Dutch Welfare set of 1952. Luxembourg showed a cat on one of its Animal Protection stamps of 1961.

Cats in folklore fared little better. In 1959 Hungary issued a series of stamps depicting various fairy tales. The 30f stamp showed the Sleeping Beauty—and, peeping round the foot of the bed, was a black cat. The following year Hungary issued a second set and this time Puss-in-Boots himself appeared on the 60f stamp. Germany issued a set of Child Welfare stamps in 1961 depicting scenes from Hansel and Gretel; two of them showed the wicked witch with her black cat.

One or two "strays" could be found on stamps depicting works of art. East Germany issued a set of stamps in 1959 showing famous paintings in the Dresden Art Gallery. The 10pf stamp featured Gabriel Metsu's "Portrait of a Needlewoman" and her cat appears beside her in the picture. Belgium's 1960 anti-TB set featured various arts and crafts, and the top value, devoted to ceramics, showed a porcelain cat. The previous year, Belgium issued a set devoted to various local festivals; the 3fr depicted the town jester of Ypres in fancy-dress and holding a cat. A Roman terracotta figure of a cat appeared on one of the stamps in the Dutch Cultural Welfare series of 1962. In 1972 Monaco belatedly celebrated the 150th anniversary of Baudelaire with a stamp showing two of the cats that featured in his bizarre poetry. The following year the birth centenary of Colette was marked by France which issued a 50+10c stamp showing the novelist with a stylised cat in the background—an allusion to her lifelong devotion to cats. In 1991 Finland celebrated the centenary of the confectionery industry by issuing a 2.10mk stamp showing kittens playing with a giant "Kiss-Kiss" sweet.

Cats only came into their own in the mid-'sixties. In 1964 Poland brought out a magnificent set of ten large stamps featuring various types of European, Siamese and Persian cats. This was the sequel to a very popular series on dogs. This encouraged Roumania and the Yemen to produce colourful cat sets in 1965. The Roumanian series consisted of eight multicoloured pictorials showing a wide range of animals, ranging from a tabby (5b) and a ginger tom (10b) to the more exotic White Persian (40b) and the haughty Siamese (1.35L). Kittens at play, with an old shoe (55b) and a ball of wool (60b) proved that cats were cats, no matter which side of the Iron Curtain they lived on.

The Yemeni series depicted three different kinds of Persian cat—the Black, the Cream and the Silver Tabby, as well as the Tortoiseshell, the Red Tabby and the Sealpoint Siamese. This was followed in 1967 by a set of seven from Fujeira (now part of the United Arab Emirates), featuring a Sealpoint Siamese, a Red

New Zealand's Health issue, 1993.

Tabby, a Tortoiseshell, a Longhaired Black, a Silver Tabby, a Chinchilla and a Maine Coon. In 1966 Albania had a set devoted to farmyard animals, but depicted a cat on the 50q value. Later Albania jumped on the bandwagon with a set of seven showing different breeds.

Since then cats have appeared in abundance, with long sets from Nicaragua, North Vietnam, Mongolia and Paraguay among others. In 1988 the USA issued a block of four featuring two breeds on each stamp: Siamese and Exotic Shorthair, Abyssinian and Himalayan, Maine Coon and Persian. In 1993 Belgium, Venda and Italy each had sets of four, while Sweden had a booklet containing four different cat stamps in 1994. New Zealand produced a booklet of greetings stamps with the caption "Thinking of You". The five different stamps depicted a cute marmalade cat in different poses. New Zealand also had a stamp in the annual Health series, showing a little girl cuddling a kitten. Tonga's Family Planning series included a pair showing girls playing with kittens, and in 1994 the miniature sheet captioned "Kindness to All God's Creatures" included an 80s stamp showing a girl stroking a ginger cat. This sheet was subsequently overprinted for Christmas.

During 1994 the Falkland Islands produced a set of stamps featuring islanders' pets. The 34p showed a puppy licking a ginger kitten, while the 39p showed another kitten rearing up on its hindlegs. The stamps were re-issued in February with an overprint in honour of the Hong Kong International Philatelic Exhibition. St Helena released a set of four stamps for the same occasion and showed pet animals, including a gorgeous tabby on the 25p. Later in the year Sweden issued a greetings booklet of four designs, including one showing a black cat with the slogan Puss och Kram (love and kisses—Puss actually being the Swedish word for a kiss).

These paled into insignificance compared with some of the countries whose stamps are handled by the Inter-Governmental Philatelic Corporation. Guyana produced a sheet containing eight different stamps featuring cats of the world. One cannot quarrel with seven of the breeds selected—Russian Blue, Havana Brown, Himalayan, Manx, Cornish Red, Black Persian and Siamese—but I can't help feeling that the Guyanese postal authorities were ill-advised to include a Scottish Fold, a breed which is not recognised in Britain on account of the deliberate deformity of the ears which it encourages. A sheet of twelve from Sierra Leone showed different cats of the world—including that dreadful Scottish Fold again! The Gambia issued a sheet of twelve depicting Oriental cats, while Nevis produced a similar sheet showing different breeds of Persian cat, against a background of a Persian carpet. Subsequently the Gambia had stamps reproducing paintings showing cats, and ranging from some of the famous paintings by Steinlen, a famous cat-lover, to a nineteenth century poster for Jayne's Tonic Vermifuge and artwork for a Christmas card by Raphael Tuck. Jersey celebrated the 21st anniversary of the local cat club by releasing a set of five stamps showing both fancy breeds and ordinary moggies. The Isle of Man has had several issues featuring the famous tailless cat and in 1994 produced a prestige booklet telling the story of Postman Pat and his cat Jess on a visit to the island.

Jess was by no means the only literary cat to appear on stamps in 1994. Earlier in the year the Faroe Islands had a stamp showing the giant Brosakjull's black cat, from a saga which has some similarities to our tale of Jack the Giant-killer. Brazil issued a block of four stamps to celebrate the centenary of the publication of the first children's book in that

Postman Pat and his black-and-white cat visit the Isle of Man.

Jersey portayed their cats in classical style.

country. The stamps featured fairy tales and two of them included cats—*Puss in Boots* and *Joao and Maria*. Britain's greetings booklet devoted to children's literary characters included Orlando the Marmalade Cat. Previous greetings booklets had featured the Cheshire Cat from *Alice in Wonderland*. which also appeared on a British stamp of 1979 marking International Year of the Child.

Although the impression is given that the British Post Office has been rather niggardly towards cat-loving philatelists, the truth is quite different. Apart from the three stamps featuring Lewis Carroll's grinning feline, there have been quite a few cat stamps, including a pantomime cat on a Christmas stamp, two stamps (and a miniature sheet) depicting an alphabet cat and *The Owl and the Pussycat* by Edward Lear, a Scottish wildcat in the Nature Preservation series of 1986, a cat nuzzling up to a chimney pot on another Christmas stamp, and a wistful kitten on one of the 20p stamps of 1990 celebrating the 150th anniversary of the RSPCA. In addition, the Good Luck greetings booklet of 1991 had no fewer than four stamps showing a lucky black cat, although on three of them you will need a magnifying glass to find them!

The first set from Royal Mail entirely devoted to cats was issued on January 17, 1995. Not tied to a specific event or anniversary, it is purely thematic. The stamps were designed by Elizabeth Blackadder, Scotland's foremost lady painter and a devoted cat-lover. Interestingly the cats featured on these stamps are real animals. "A cat can look at a Queen" runs the old proverb, and this is certainly true in this case, for it seems that real cats can look at the Queen on stamps, even though this privilege is denied to ordinary human beings (unless they are dead).

For the record, the black cat on the 19p is Sophie, whom Elizabeth Blackadder named after Sophia Loren because she was so elegant. On the 25p are a Siamese called Puskas (named after the famous Hungarian footballer) and a tabby named Tigger. On the 30p appears a ginger cat named Chloe, while the 35p shows Kikko the tortoiseshell and Rosie the Abyssinian. The 41p depicts Fred, named after Fred Astaire, because of his black and white markings resembling the film star in white tie and tails. The cats belong to Elizabeth Blackadder or her neighbours in the Edinburgh area.

These British cat stamps were closely followed by several in different parts of the world, belonging to the Felix, Sylvester or Corky category, being caricatures or cartoons rather than the real thing. From Taiwan came a miniature sheet of four $5 stamps for Children's Day. The stamps show children playing and on the first of the strip can be seen a little boy sailing a paper boat, with a red-ribboned black cat looking on approvingly. The black cat also appears in a paper boat, in the top right-hand corner of the sheet itself.

For St Valentine's Day Slovenia issued a 20 tolar greetings stamp. Apart from the visual pun, highlighting the word LOVE in the country name, the stamp shows two cats gone a-courting, with a flurry of red hearts above them. This love stamp was the result of co-operation between readers of a teenage paper *Pisani List* and the postal administration, the magazine inviting entries from its readers to a competition for a stamp design. The winner was twelve year-old Jure Kos whose design, entitled "Kittens in love" was finally selected. June 1 was Children's Day in the Czech Republic, which marked the occasion in 1995 by issuing a 3.60 crowns

Publicity sheet from the Isle of Man pays homage to the famous Manx tailless cats.

stamp, designed by Josef Palecek and engraved by Vaclav Fajt, showing a multicoloured puss.

On April 25, 1995, St Vincent issued a sheet of nine different $1 stamps depicting cats of the world. Dennis Burckhardt designed the sheet in such a way that it forms a composite picture of a West Indian verandah, with a view of sea and mountains in the background, and a coterie of cats engaged in a variety of activities. In the picture one can see (from top left to bottom right) Snowshoe, Abyssinian, Ocicat,

Tiffany, Russian Blue, Siamese, Bicolour, Malayan and Manx, while the accompanying $6 souvenir sheet shows a Birman, characterised by "white gloves" on all four paws.

Guyana had already produced several sets of cat stamps but in May produced a sheet of twelve $35 stamps in connection with the Singapore '95 World Stamp Show. Thomas Wood designed this sheet which shows a Norwegian Forest Cat, the Scottish fold (yet again!), the Red Burmese, the British Blue-hair, the Abyssinian, the Siamese, the Exotic Shorthair, the Turkish Van, the Black Persian, the Singapura and the Calico Shorthair. The accompanying souvenir sheet depicts a Maine Coon, with another cat studying a butterfly in the sheet margin.

From Equatorial Guinea comes a strip of three stamps with the theme of domestic animals. The stamps, designed by Pedro Sanches and printed by the Spanish Mint, show an Iberian hog, a Pekingese dog and a Persian cat. On July 5 the Marshall Islands released a block of four different stamps entitled "Captivating Cats" and featuring four pairs of fascinating felines. Created by the noted artist, Don Blake, each stamp displays a colourful portrait of two different breeds of cat: Siamese and Exotic Shorthair, American Shorthair and Persian, Maine Coon and Burmese, and Abyssinian and Himalayan.

France marked the tercentenary of the death of the writer Jean de La Fontaine on June 24 by issuing a strip of six 2.80 franc stamps featuring scenes from his best-known Fables. One of these was *Le Chat, la Belette et le petit Lapin* which tells the story of the weasel and the rabbit. One day, when the rabbit was out and about, the weasel took possession of his burrow, saying, in effect, that possession was nine points of the law. The rabbit argued that the burrow was his by custom and usage, and had been passed down from generation to generation in his family. In the end the weasel agreed to put the matter to the arbitration of Raminagrobis, a wise old cat who lived like a devout hermit, "a saintly man of a cat, well-furred, big and fat" (a sly dig at the clerics of 17th century France).

The cat said, "Approach, my children, come close, for I am deaf, advancing years are the cause of my affliction". The weasel and the rabbit came close, suspecting nothing. The cat suggested that they get on to the scales so that he could weigh his judgment, and when he had them there, arguing with each other, with one swift blow he struck out with his claws and put the litigants in accord. La Fontaine concludes: "This strongly resembles the squabbles which petty rulers sometimes have among themselves, before they are swallowed up by mighty kings".

The stamp, which shows the cat holding the balance between the weasel and the rabbit, was designed by husband and wife Roland and Claudine Sabatier. This strip was issued in booklets and sheets and also impressed on stamped envelopes and postcards. A special edition of the six fables was also published, illustrated by enlarged prints of each stamp and containing a mint strip of the stamps.

St Vincent's sheet shows nine different cats of the world in a composite picture.

On August 28, 1995 Antigua and Barbuda issued a sheet of twelve different 45c stamps forming a composite picture of cats doing what cats do best. The ingenuity of stamp designers never ceases to amaze me, in continually coming up with motifs that are fresh and full of interest. But I read the other day that there are about forty different breeds of cat, and if one were to include all the colours and patterns within each breed you could develop a range of more than two hundred different cats.

Chinese-American artist Yuan Lee has chosen a patio as the setting for his charming picture, with a bit of wall, paving, a household chair and an ornate wrought-iron garden seat, with shrubs and trees in the background and a couple of butterflies that have merited an inspection by some of the more inquisitive cats.

On top of the garden seat is a proud Somali and, keeping his distance on the arm-rest, a Persian. Below them, a haughty Himalayan stalks along the bench, while an Angora perches precariously on the branch of a tree. At the nearer end of the bench a moggy (captioned here as "Nonpedigree") leans over to talk to a black and white American Curl. Under the bench an American Wirehair takes a well-earned rest. A Devon Rex stares at the butterflies from the back of the chair on which reclines a Maine Coon. On the patio floor there is a British Shorthair, while a non-pedigree black cat and a Birman stalk another butterfly at the foot of the picture.

This sheet, printed by Questa of London in

Twelve cats make up Antigua and Barbados' sheet designed by artist Yuan Lee and printed in England by Questa.

multicolour, is accompanied by a $6 souvenir sheet depicting a Siberian cat on the stamp, with a Norwegian Forest cat in the decorative margin. Though inscribed for use in Antigua and Barbuda it should be noted that Barbuda also issues its own stamps, usually stamps of Antigua overprinted BARBUDA MAIL, so I would not be surprised to find this cat set appearing shortly with the distinctive overprint.

The Netherlands Antilles, another group of islands in the Caribbean, produced a more modest issue of five stamps on September 29. The stamps were designed by John Baselmans and lithographed in Holland by Johan Enschede.

The 25 cent stamp shows a Siamese Sealpoint. The

The Netherlands Antilles set of five include the Siamese Sealpoint (left) and the Maine Coon which is now regarded as the national cat of the United States.

National Thai Library in Bangkok contains the world's earliest book on cats, a handwritten and illustrated manual from the ancient Siamese capital of Ayudha in the 15th century. This book describes a light cat with dark feet, tail and ears, showing that the breed was well known centuries ago. Siamese cats were first brought to Europe from Bangkok in 1848.

The Maine Coon (60 cents) is now regarded as the national cat of the United States, and derives its name from the fact that its thick bushy tail resembles that of a racoon. It is also allegedly the largest and heaviest of all known domestic breeds but from its close resemblance to the Norwegian Forest cat it is believed that the breed is derived from cats brought by the Vikings to America about 1000 AD.

The Egyptian Mau (65 cents) is the direct descendant of the cats which were regarded as sacred in the time of the Pharaohs. Mau is, in fact, the Egyptian word for "cat" and probably comes from "miaow". This breed is a relatively new one, having developed since the 1950s when a pair of cats with an exceptionally spotted fur were brought from Egypt, via the Lebanese embassy in Rome, to the USA. Since then distinct varieties, such as the Mau Silver,

Mau Brown Smoke and Mau Cinnamon, have been bred. Characteristic of the Mau is its fine silky coat which has a luminous sheen.

The Angora (90c) first appeared in French and Italian manuals on cats in the 18th century, but interest in the breed spread rapidly at the turn of the century when Ardebil, the capital of Azerbaijan, began holding a twice-yearly cat fair which attracted buyers and cat-fanciers from all over Asia and Europe. Today, there is a special breeding programme at Istanbul Zoo to ensure the purity of the Angora cat, with the characteristics of two centuries ago.

The Persian Blue Smoke (150c) is a breed which has developed over the past century and a quarter. Traditionally Persian cats were white or black but in 1870 breeders in England began evolving a blue longhaired cat. As long ago as 1876 Gordon Stables, author of one of the first cat books in English, raised the question, "Why in heaven's name do they call this cat blue? It is neither ultramarine nor sky-blue nor navy-blue." In fact this cat presents an over-all grey effect, its silver undercoat having a bluish tipping, but the tip of the nose and the toes are blue-grey.

On October 9 Finland issued a booklet containing six different 2.80 mark stamps. The cats depicted on the four smaller stamps on the left are Somali, Siamese, Persian and Norwegian Forest breeds but quite rightly, in my opinion, prominence is given to the domestic moggy on the two large stamps on the right. The upper stamp shows a mother cat watching anxiously while her three kittens (lower stamp) stare in wonderment at a frog. The stamps were designed by Asser Jaaro who was also responsible for an international prestamped envelope which features a feline illustration.

The only breed specific to Scandinavia is the Norwegian Forest cat, the newest of the domesticated breed and still found wild in its homeland. The ubiquitous domestic shorthair is now officially called the European. It is not regarded as a pedigree breed, but it is the most widespread breed in the world. Apparently there are 25 different breeds of cat in Finland, the number of registered pedigree cats now exceeding 10,000.

Two of Jersey's recent Christmas stamps feature cats. The subject of the four stamps, designed by Victor Ambrus and printed by Cartor of Normandy, is Christmas pantomimes. In Jersey pantomine is still largely a homespun entertainment produced by church groups and amateur dramatic societies in village halls around the island. The 19p shows Puss in Boots at his swaggering best, while the 23p stamp shows Cinderella examining the glass slipper the morning after the Prince's ball, with her black and white moggy looking on.

After such a prodigious year for cat stamps, 1996 looks like maintaining the momentum. On March 14 the Isle of Man returned to the theme of its distinctive tailless cats with a set of five designed by Nancy Corkish to show how the breed has now spread all around the world. The 20p shows a white cat in its island habitat, with the Manx arms, but the other four stamps show different cats with the Stars and Stripes and the Statue of Liberty (24p), playing with a Union Jack ball and red, white and blue streamers (36p), against a beflagged map of Australia (42p) and lying on the German flag with the Brandenburg Gate in the background (48p). The cats, incidentally represent the four main types: the Rumpy, Stumpy, Rumpy Riser and Longtail (which, in this context, means a fairly short tail by comparison with other breeds).

The Channel island of Alderney will release a set of six stamps on July 19, 1996 showing cute and cuddly household cats in various settings.

Cats, cats and yet more cats . . .

DESIDERATA

World-Wide Colour Advertising of Philately on the Internet

It is now cost-effective for Philatelic businesses to advertise their products or services world-wide on the Internet. DESIDERATA is the only UK-based site on the World-Wide Web specialising in Fine Art, Antiques and Collectibles, including Coins and Stamps.

We are the Web site of choice for:

>The Philatelic Traders' Society (PTS)
>
>The British Numismatic Trade Association (BNTA)
>
>The British Antique Dealers' Association (BADA)
>
>and many others.

Advertisers in DESIDERATA do <u>not</u> require their own Internet connection or computer equipment.

For a brochure, or for a free demonstration at your premises, please contact:

Interweb® Systems Limited

Tel:	0171-221 7102 (Int'l: +44 171 221 7102)
Fax:	0171-221 7109 (Int'l: +44 171 221 7109)
E-mail:	info@desiderata.com
URL:	http://www.desiderata.com

HAIL
AND FAREWELL

Four stamp-issuing countries disappeared in 1994, and only one new country emerged. Parodoxically all five involved were affected by the peace process whereby two of the world's most intractable political problems were seemingly solved. The four which ceased to exist at mid-year did so with the minimum of fuss or fanfare, and apparently gave the lie to the fiction of their truly independent sovereign status. The fifth which came into existence about the same time is not yet a country in the true sense, but an autonomous region with its own defence force, tax system and postal service.

THE four countries which are no more were so-called black homelands, established in South Africa as a logical outcome of the Apartheid system. Briefly, they were set up to create the notion of independent black "bantustans" whose citizens migrated to neighbouring South Africa in search of work. As citizens of foreign countries, therefore, these black migrant workers could be denied political rights in South Africa proper, and could be deported back to their respective homelands whenever necessary. Although these countries did offer some hope of separate development, they were quickly perceived by the world at large as a cunning ruse to deny blacks in South Africa their civil rights, and for that reason they never received de jure recognition. Interestingly a fifth homeland, Kwa-Zulu, never exercised its rights to issue its own stamps but throughout its notional existence was quite content to make do with South African stamps.

The concept of the bantustan or black homeland had been developing during the early years of Apartheid but came to fruition in 1965 when the Transkei was established with local autonomy under Chief Minister Kaiser Matanzima. At the same time, the South African government established Bantu homelands development corporations through which it was hoped that European investment would be chanelled to assist in African tribal areas. Over the ensuing years Transkei assumed more and more powers, and even created an Apartheid situation in reverse by declaring certain towns to be all-black. But, in reality, Transkei's administration was closely monitored and controlled from Pretoria.

The second homeland was proposed in 1966 for the territory occupied by the Tswana-speaking Bakwena of Mokgopa, a tribe of some 80,000 people led by Chief Nerothodi Mamogale who bluntly told the South African government to wait thirty years, after which the Bakwena would say whether they wanted a bantustan or not. Additional concessions to the Transkei, including the formation of a defence force, were made in 1967. Meanwhile plans to create other bantustans on the Transkei model went ahead. In 1968 black officials began replacing white in Transkei and in November proposals to create a second bantustan in Ciskei went ahead.

Over a period of several years Transkei gradually progressed to the point at which it was declared a fully independent sovereign republic. This came into effect on 26 October 1976. Chief Mamogale did not wait thirty years after all, for his territory became the republic of Bophuthatswana on 6 December 1977. Venda followed on 13 September 1979 and Ciskei became a republic on 4 December 1981. In the case of Transkei, the establishment of a separate postal service lagged some way behind the attainment of independence, South African stamps continuing in use until the following year; but in the case of the other bantustans, a fully-fledged postal service, complete with distinctive stamps, was seen as part of the trappings of sovereignty and came into effect automatically once independence was proclaimed.

The stamps of all four countries were designed and printed at the South African Government Printing Works in Pretoria. There was a certain uniformity, therefore, both in the numbers of stamps issued and

The stamps of the black homelands—like those of South Africa itself—bear the sheet numbers and letters which help when sorting the stamps into proper sequence.

in the policy governing their frequency and design. Each country started with a set celebrating independence, closely followed by a distinctive definitive series pursuing a specific theme—flowers (Venda), tribal totems (Bophuthatswana) and birds (Ciskei). Transkei was the odd man out by embarking on a definitive series which comprised a mixture of scenery, occupations and landmarks, including a view of the Bunga, or parliament building, in the capital Umtata.

Very few stamps from these countries were commemorative in the strict sense. In the early period Transkei issued several stamps marking the inauguration of Transkei Airways and the first anniversary of Radio Transkei (both 1977), but the others had few anniversaries worth recording, other than fifth and tenth anniversaries of independence.

By and large, however, stamps were released in thematic sets of four. Some of these sets developed quite a following in their own right. Bophuthatswana, for example, issued an Easter quartet each year and gradually built up the story of the Passion and Cruxifixion with appropriate Biblical quotations. Transkei had several sets devoted to medicinal plants and fishing flies, but its most popular annual issue portrayed heroes of medicine drawn from all over the world. Venda's best-seller was the annual set featuring the history of writing through the ages and covering many lands. Bophuthatswana's annual set reproducing antique maps was beginning to look very promising, when it became a casualty of the changing political scene in South Africa.

New definitive sets were issued at five-yearly intervals, with additional denominations as and when South African postal rates were increased. The four countries soon settled to a regular routine of four sets of four stamps apiece per annum. These stamps were modestly priced and covered the basic postal rates. Very occasionally they were augmented by a miniature sheet.

A particularly helpful feature of these stamps (also found on stamps of South Africa itself) was the code number and letter printed in the margin. Thus sets were lettered A, B, C or D, and individual denominations numbered 1, 2, 3 and 4, which, together with the year of issue, made the sorting of stamps into the proper sequence a very easy matter.

The sets dealt with all manner of subjects, from tribal headdress to holiday hotels, waterfalls and dams, traditional crafts and indigenous grasses. Over the seventeen years in which stamps from the black homelands were issued, they built up into a very colourful display reflecting life in the rural heartland of southern Africa. They were accompanied by attractive first day covers and often maximum cards, with appropriate pictorial handstamps.

Following the general elections which swept the ANC to power under Nelson Mandela in May 1994 it seemed that the homelands, symbols of that hated policy of separate development, would disappear. Sure enough, a mass demonstration at the frontier of Bophuthatswana in which the crossing barriers were uprooted, was swiftly followed by the peaceful reabsorption of the republics into South Africa as a whole, and at the end of June the stamps were quietly phased out.

One interesting point remains to be resolved. The *Stanley Gibbons Catalogue* continued to list the stamps of South Africa in the part I sectional catalogue (British Commonwealth) as a matter of convenience to collectors, even after South Africa left the Commonwealth in 1961. Oddly enough, however, the stamps of the four homelands were not included in this arrangement as they were deemed to be independent republics. For that reason they were listed in the appropriate volumes of the *Simplified Stamps of the World Catalogue*. Now that South Africa has rejoined the Commonwealth Gibbons will bow to the inevitable and transfer the stamps of Bophuthatswana, Ciskei, Transkei and Venda to the "red" book.

Palestine

In June 1967 Israel fought a brief war with its Arab neighbours. It had been preceded by an intensification of terrorist activities by the Syrian-backed Al Fatah organisation against Israeli targets. To combat this terrorism the Israeli defence forces were mobilised and put on full alert. President Nasser of Egypt retaliated by moving his troops eastward into the Sinai Desert. The Egyptians delivered an ultimatum to the UN forces patrolling the Gaza Strip: evacuate immediately so that the Egyptian army could move up to the Israeli border. The UN threatened to pull out of the Middle East altogether, and Nasser promptly responded by closing the Straits of Tiran, thus denying Israeli ships access to the Red Sea. While Nasser was being lauded throughout the Arab world as its saviour, King Hussein of Jordan concluded a pact with his old adversary. He even permitted an Iraqi tank division to cross Jordan to get to the West Bank.

Israel was now ringed by implacable enemies, bent on her total destruction. Sceptical of Anglo-American assurances of support, the Israelis struck back with a suddenness and ferocity which took the Arabs completely by surprise. A pre-emptive strike began on the morning of 5 June, destroying the air force of the United Arab Republic in less than three hours. Mastery of the air proved decisive and the Arab land forces, left without air cover, were powerless to withstand the Israeli armoured onslaught. The ensuing campaign was a textbook Blitzkrieg which turned a ragged withdrawal into an utter rout. Within four days the Israelis had reached the east bank of the Suez Canal.

When Jordan joined in the fray the Israeli air force promptly destroyed the Jordanian air force—and the air forces of Syria and Iraq for good measure. After three days of fierce fighting the Israelis had complete control of Jerusalem and the West Bank. By the conclusion of hostilities on 10 June Israel was occupying territory inhabited by 750,000 Arabs on the West Bank, and another 300,000 in the Gaza Strip. When Syrian artillery foolishly began a bombardment of Israeli positions on 9 June, the Israelis seized the opportunity to neutralise the Golan Heights. Impregnable positions, which had seemed unassailable, fell into Israeli hands in a matter of hours.

The Six-Day War left Israel in control of a vast territory, with secure natural frontiers, but over a million hostile Arabs. At that time the population of Israel itself was 2,624,000. Jerusalem was now re-united and Israel itself seemed more secure from external attack; but the war left a bitter legacy of hatred which festered over the ensuing quarter of a century. Although Israel subsequently relinquished Sinai to Egypt and eventually concluded a treaty of peace, it was only in 1994 that a similar treaty with Jordan brought to an end a state of war which had existed for 46 years.

Meanwhile the problem of coping with the large and ever-growing Arab population was to bedevil Israeli politics for more than two decades. Ironically it was Itzhak Rabin, the general who engineered victory in 1967, who had the task of bringing hostility to an end. As Prime Minister, he initiated a dialogue with the PLO leader, Yasser Arafat, which culminated in the peace accord of 1994.

By this agreement Israel conceded autonomy to the Arabs of the West Bank, around the city of Jericho, and their comrades in Gaza. A government, to be known as the Palestinian Authority, was established in these territories and allowed to form its own police and defence force. It was inevitable that, as part of the deal, the Palestinians should assume control of their own postal services and begin issuing distinctive stamps. It is a reflection on the situation over the past quarter of a century that, although a third of the population of Israel was Arab, not a single Arab or Arabic motif has ever appeared on an Israeli stamp.

The contract to print stamps for the Palestinian Authority was won by the Bundesdruckerei in Berlin which has now produced a number of stamps in offset lithography. The postal service was inaugurated on 15 August 1994, with two sets of

Yitsbak Rabin, Bill Clinton and Yasser Arafat clinch the Peace Agreement on the miniature sheet isued in 1994.

stamps. One, intended for use on official correspondence, had a uniform design showing the eagle emblem and comprised 50, 100, 125, 200, 250 and 400 mil denominations. Unsure of what currency to adopt—the Israeli sheqel being no longer acceptable—Palestine has now reverted to the currency which was in use until 1948 when Israel seized its independence from the British mandate. So far as I am aware, however, at the time of writing no actual mil currency has been introduced, so that the new stamps are presumably sold in Israeli currency.

The second set consisted of five high-value stamps, forming the first part of a definitive series for general use. These stamps had a common design featuring the green, black and red Palestinian flag. Two weeks later, on 1 September, the lower denominations were released. The 5, 10 and 20m stamps depicted the Palestinian Memorial on the West Bank of the Jordan, while the 30, 40, 50 and 75m stamps depicted the Church of the Holy Sepulchre in Jerusalem. The choice of this motif is rather surprising given that it is not only a Christian rather than a Moslem holy place, but it is located in Jerusalem, the Israeli capital. Clearly the Palestinians have not lost sight of their long-cherished ambition to recover the old Arab quarters of the Holy City.

This was confirmed by the top value, 1000m, which showed the Dome of the Rock, in Jerusalem, one of the most sacred sites in all Islam.

A commemorative issue appeared on 1 October and consisted of a miniature sheet containing a single stamp denominated 750 + 250m. This showed Itzhak Rabin and Yasser Arafat, with President Clinton looking on. The flags of Israel and Palestine appeared below. According to reports in the philatelic trade press, however, it would appear that the stamps of Palestine have gone off at half-cock. No agreement for the transmission of mail between Gaza and Jericho had actually been made with Israel, nor had the Palestine Authority applied to the Universal Postal Union for recognition of its stamps. Thus the exact status of the new stamps is unclear.

During 1995 a further set of stamps was introduced, reproducing the designs of the Palestinian stamps of 1927–45. The appearance of Rachel's Tomb and David's Tower in Jarusalem on the new stamps was regarded unfavourably in Israel itself as underscoring Palestinian ambitions to recover all the West Bank territory seized by Israel in 1967.

In the course of the year several important Arab towns in the West Bank were handed over to the Palestinians as part of the implementation of the peace process, and the new stamps introduced there.

BRITISH POSTMARKS
OF THE YEAR

Technically the most important event of 1995 has been the extension in the use of ink jet machines. These have been in use for several years and have crept in very stealthily. At first they were used to apply alphanumeric codes to pieces of mail processed in the new generation of sorting and cancelling machines employing Optical Character Recognition equipment. These OCR marks were fairly unobtrusive, appearing on the left-hand side of the front of envelopes. Subsequently more elaborate ink jet marks appeared on the reverse and gave the office name or code together with the time and date of processing. From this it was but a short step to including a one-line inscription, such as PLEASE USE YOUR POSTCODE or A HAPPY CHRISTMAS.

At the same time, one was suddenly becoming aware of the fact that these ink jet marks were by no means confined to the United Kingdom. They began appearing on the front of covers from Canada and the United States. At first these marks were fairly simple, giving the time, date and place of posting in a single line. When I first came across them, they were on permit mail from Washington and Ottawa and no harm was done; it seemed that they were intended to identify and time items which did not normally have a postmark. How wrong can one be! Soon it was all too apparent that ink jet machines were being used, particularly in Canada, to cancel adhesives on mail, and in addition to the usual inscription a heavy horizontal band was being applied to make sure that the stamps were well and truly cancelled. In recent months the philatelic press in North America has been lamenting the intrusion of the ink jet printer in this manner, to the detriment of stamps, especially commemoratives. The postal authorities have so far been deaf to all entreaties from collectors; the operational requirements of the postal service take precedence over philately, it seems.

So often we have found that trends, fashions and crazes that start on the far side of the Atlantic are not long in becoming established in Britain. It seems that the ink jet canceller, complete with slogan and dater die, is coming here as well. One such machine was tested on live mail at Gloucester in November 1993 and produced quite a passable slogan, with a square dater in the transposed position to minimise the obliterating effect on stamps, with the slogan on the left. The BT slogan, not unlike that used in conventional cancelling machines, was apparently computer-generated in the space of 30 minutes! The dater bore the office name across the top, with the time, date and year in three lines below. The cryptic inscription at the foot of the box is IJP SCM, signifying Ink Jet Printer Stamp Cancelling Machine. An interesting feature is that the time was programmed to change automatically minute by minute while the machine was in use.

At the conclusion of the Gloucester trial the machine was installed at Darlington where it was used with a pattern of seven unbroken wavy lines and a square dater box in the normal position, though a Christmas slogan was substituted from 29 November onwards. A third trial took place at Birmingham in April, using a commercial slogan (for Ty-phoo Tea) and a square dater in which, unusually, the office name was rendered in upper and lower case lettering. The machine was used with red ink on April 11–12, 1994 and then in black ink on April 14, so examples of these postmarks are likely to be very elusive. The machine was subsequently tested at Milton Keynes on May 4 and 5, though it is understood that most of the items processed were internal sample mail. Subsequently a more extensive trial was carried out at Swindon from August 1994 onwards, including strikes in red ink on bulk postings, and a version of the "snowman" Christmas slogan in December. The machine has not been without considerable teething troubles, but it seems certain that once these problems have been resolved ink jet cancellers will eventually take over from the Universals and Krags which have given such good service for 80 years.

Politics have had an effect on the postmarks seen on mail from British servicemen stationed in Germany. For almost half a century units of the British Army and RAF have been stationed at bases in West Germany and West Berlin. With the end of the Cold War and the unification of Germany, the presence of foreign troops has been scaled down very considerably. During 1994 troops of the four powers, (USA, UK, USSR and France) were withdrawn. In fact, when I was in Berlin early in 1994 the only troops I saw on the streets were Ukrainian. This has meant the closure of the field post office facilities at many of these bases. Britain, however, still maintains a presence in western Germany and during the year new postmarks were introduced. Previously mail from the field post offices was cancelled with a handstamp or machine mark merely indicating the FPO number. Now, meter-style cancelling machines have been introduced which bear the name of the German town round the top, with the FPO number at the foot. British stamps and postal stationery continue to be used at these offices. The meter indicium consists of twin black bars with a 000 value across the centre, this being used to obliterate the stamps. More recently, the machine used at Osnabruck omits the value 000 and has an additional wavy line on the left, while Bruggen and other bases are now using dies with the value shown as 00. Several dies do not incorporate the location of the field post office, the dater dies merely having BFPO round the top and the number at the foot.

During the year the relentless march of automation brought further cancelling dies with the letters CFCL or CFCT at the foot. These initials identify the use of Culler Facer Cancellers, the suffixes L or T denoting leading edge or trailing edge respectively. In some offices, however, the initials CFC are followed by a number instead. Tyneside not only has dies with CFC at the foot, but pairs of initials at the sides identifying the places whose mail is thus concentrated (e.g. Newcastle and Sunderland). Other machines have the initials SCM at the foot, denoting Stamp Cancelling Machine (which one might have thought was self evident). Machines used in the London North Western District Office have the initials R.M. (Royal Mail) and N.W. flanking the name at the top, with CFC at the foot.

Another sign of the times is the disappearance of long-familiar names, to be replaced by generic names covering even larger areas. The latest casualties were London W1 and Paddington, names which have been around for generations. Because all the mail in western London is now processed at Paddington, the western district office having closed in April 1994, it was thought more politic to introduce the generic name of West London. Handstamps thus inscribed were introduced at Paddington in March pending the re-organisation.

Some generic names are confined to mail processed on Sundays. In this category come Royal Mail Midlands and South East Division, the latter covering Kent. It seems strange that the county name was not used in this instance and, in fact "South East Division" is the first generic name which does not include an actual geographical location. Can this be the prelude to postmarks inscribed South England or North Britain, perhaps?

On February 14, 1994 Ambleside, Windermere, Kendal and Sedbergh lost their identities, becoming mere numbers in Lancashire South Lakes, a new generic found in both handstamps and machine cancellations.

In April 1994 new machine dies came into use at Doncaster which now handles mail from Lincoln as well. The name of the former continues to appear, at the foot of the circle, but round the top is a curious arrangement: the letters DN and LN separated by a lengthy single arc. Bournemouth and Poole, one of the earliest generic names dating back before the war, was replaced in July 1994 by Dorset and South West Hants which has now begun to appear on rubber handstamps as well as, in a slightly abbreviated form, on machine dies. In June 1995 London North came into operation, following the amalgamation of the North West and North 1 districts, and this inscription may now be found in both machine dies and rubber handstamps. Even Krag and Roddis continuous impression machines, mainly used for prepaid bulk postings of bulky packets, have been recorded with LONDON NORTH set in two lines. London's South East district office closed later in the year, merging with London South West to become London South. By late 1995, therefore, London's mail was being processed at five Automatic Processing Centres— Mount Pleasant, and North, South, East and West London.

By contrast, Scotland appears to have lost its generics. Machine dies inscribed EDINBURGH

LOTHIANS FIFE BORDERS had been in use since 1982 but with the upgrading of Edinburgh's MLO (mechanised letter office) to become an APC (automatic processing centre) in June 1995 and the absorption of the Central area based on Perth, dies simply inscribed EDINBURGH have been re-introduced. Consequently, the PERTH DUNDEE ANGUS dies were withdrawn from use on August 18, 1995.

Of course, towns and villages up and down the land retain their identity so far as the handstamps used at post office counters are concerned, and on guaranteed delivery envelopes and certificates of posting they are as collectable as ever. During 1994 there was a great extension in the use of the Reiner self-inking datestamps which tend to give a much clearer impression than the conventional handstamps. By contrast, a rash of strange packet handstamps was reported in use at Swansea in the first half of the year. These were undated, set in four lines and apparently made up from loose type in Printy stamps. Christmas is a time when there is an upsurge of handstamping to relieve pressure on the cancelling machines, and then all manner of oddities and antiques are brought into service. The oddest example to come to light this year was a large oval from Glasgow which obviously was converted from some specific function by having an inscription cut out of the upper portion.

A large diameter rubber datestamp was introduced at Northampton for use on unpaid and underpaid mail. The circular rim and inscription NORTHAMPTON SURCHARGE DUTY were struck in blue ink but the date across the centre appeared in red ink. This was hailed as Britain's first bicoloured postmark, ignoring the special handstamps used in 1965 and 1970.

Rubber handstamps seem to be getting larger and larger all the time. Bournemouth has a pair of paid handstamps measuring 55mm in diameter. The West London APC has capped this, however, with paid handstamps 57mm in diameter.

There have also been recent developments in paid machine dies. West London has special dies employed on bulk postings of mail from the BBC TV Centre at Shepherd's Bush. Initially such mail was cancelled with an improvised die in which a portion of the slogan had been erased, but by July this had been replaced by a die specifically designed for the purpose, with ROYAL MAIL POSTROOM SERVICES set in three lines. About the same time, a paid machine die was introduced at the Foreign Section with a new-style central slug in the wavy line obliterator, inscribed 1ST PAID AIRMAIL in two lines set at right angles to the lines.

As regards slogans, there was a remarkable upsurge of commercial advertising—something which only a few short years ago would have been anathema to the Post Office but which, in these more enlightened times, seems to be positively welcomed. Interestingly, the main reason why the Post Office refused to permit such advertising was the fear of giving offence to rival businesses who would object to having their mail cancelled with names and trademarks not their own. No such opposition seems to have arisen since the policy was abandoned. Indeed, if the rash of double-gazing slogans is anything to go by, Royal Mail are now positively encouraging all rival companies to vie with each other in this medium.

This commercialism is now going hand in hand with more colourful postmarks, red, green and blue inks having been seen in slogans of 1994–95 as well as the more usual black. Through the year we were

urged to get popcorn poppin', use Coldseal, Aluwhite, Glevum or KLG double-glazing, play Sonic 3 (a Sega computer game), support National Continence Week, tune into innumerable local radio stations, shop at Marks & Spencer's and Sainsbury's, drink Perrier water or Ty-phoo tea, travel on Le Shuttle, enjoy more fruit and veg, join the Matalan Discount Club or Britannia Music & Video Club, and make our mark with Zanders Zeta Mattpost versatile business papers. There was even a nationwide campaign in May and June 1995 with a special offer on Colonel Sanders Kentucky Fried Chicken, complete with a picture of the bearded colonel himself. Time was, not so long ago, when such portraiture was frowned upon lest it sully Her Majesty's features—but in these highly commercialised times, anything goes.

Royal Mail's partiality seemed to be evident in slogans urging us to collect stamps and read the Philatelic Bulletin, while subsequently we were warned that Coins Cause Chaos! On closer inspection this turned out to be not so much against the sister hobby of numismatics, but a warning about putting coins into envelopes which can do untold damage to sorting and cancelling machines. The incidence of what Royal Mail officially terms "dogbite" must have escalated of late, to judge by the rash of slogans urging people to keep their dogs indoors or under control when the postman calls.

In general, however, the quality of machine cancellation was deplorable. Many slogans had minuscule lettering which was unreadable in practice or clogged with ink, while other machines were underinked and the slogans too faint for legibility. A postmark collector who has access to the mail coming into a large firm tells me that he manages to salvage only about 3 per cent of incoming items in collectable condition. I hope that Colin Richardson of Exeter was better served when he embarked on the ultimate philatelic ego trip, sponsoring a slogan cancellation on February 27, 1994 to celebrate his 40th birthday.

Pictorial handstamps for what can broadly be described as special events (covering a multitude of sins these days) continue to proliferate. With nine issues of commemorative and special stamps in 1995, together with the Greetings in Art booklet, a National Trust prestige booklet and the Spitfire booklet, there were more opportunities for sponsored handstamps than ever before. Time was when a new stamp issue would have first day handstamps from the Philatelic Bureau and one other designated office appropriate to the issue, but these days every issue is accompanied by a host of souvenir covers, both from private sponsors and from large companies specialising in this business, with the result that an event can attract anything up to two dozen different postmarks. These are not only aimed at the local postal historian who has perforce to have everything pertaining to his town or district, but, increasingly, at the thematic stamp collector for whom mint stamps are no longer enough and who requires all the special postmarks associated with his theme as well. At the same time, there is a tendency towards more and more quasi-commemorative handstamps coinciding with new stamps, even although the event commemorated has no bearing on the stamps themselves. A good example of this was the Blick handstamp of June 6, 1995 celebrating 70 years in time recording, neatly exploiting the *Time Machine* stamp in the H. G. Wells series released that day.

Handstamps which were not connected directly or indirectly with new stamp issues were comparatively few. One which caught the eye, however, was used at Birmingham on May 12, 1994 and celebrated the 70th anniversary of the birth of the late, lamented Tony Hancock. Oddest commemoration of the year, however, was the elaborate armorial handstamp celebrating 147 years of the Norfolk Show. Let's hope that the sesquicentennial will not be forgotten in three years time.

Illustrations to this feature are taken from the British Postmark Bulletin, by courtesy of Royal Mail. The Bulletin is published fortnightly by Royal Mail, 22 Finsbury Square, London EC2A 1NL. For a subscription costing £10 (UK and Europe) or £21.75 (rest of the world), write to the British Philatelic Bureau, 20 Brandon Street, Edinburgh EH3 5TT.

LOOKING BACK

150 YEARS AGO

Although adhesive postage stamps had been in use since May 1840, the concept had only spread to three other countries in the first five years. Brazil became the first country in the Western Hemisphere to follow Britain's lead, introducing the celebrated Bull's Eye stamps in 1843. In the same year two of the Swiss cantons, Zurich and Geneva began issuing their own stamps. Stamps had actually appeared in the USA in 1842, but these were confined to a private local service, operating in New York City. This was only the first of numerous local services that flourished in many towns and cities until 1863 when the US Postal Service took over local collection and delivery.

Thus many people, especially in the commercial sector, would have been quite familiar with adhesive stamps on their mail long before the first stamps were issued for nationwide use in 1847. As an interim measure, however, Congress passed an Act in March 1845 regulating the postal rates within the USA and permitting postmasters to issue their own stamps pending a general series. This Act came into effect on 1 July 1845. Letters could be sent up to 300 miles for 5 cents, or beyond that for 10 cents. At first these rates applied to single letters (i.e. those which consisted of a single sheet whose outer page served as the wrapper). Double letters (including those with a separate envelope) were charged double rates, but in practice any packet weighing less than half an ounce was treated as a single letter, and so the British system of charging postage by weight came into use.

The first US post office to take advantage of the new regulations was New York whose stamps were introduced on 15 July 1845. George Washington, who had been portrayed on the first of the local stamps three years earlier, was the subject of the 5c stamp, engraved and printed in intaglio by Messrs Rawdon, Wright & Hatch. The stamps were black on bluish paper, and as a security precaution, were initialled by the postmaster Robert H. Morris or his clerks Alonzo Castle Monson and Mercena Monson. Interestingly, Morris advertised that stamped envelopes were also available, but so far none has ever come to light.

James Madison Buchanan, postmaster of Baltimore, Maryland, produced 5 and 10c stamps in 1845. Unlike the professionally produced stamps of New York, Buchanan used slips of paper with his signature engraved in a

The famous Basle Dove, which was actually only issued for use within the city boundaries.

horizontal frame with the value underneath. John M. Wimer of St Louis, Missouri also released 5 and 10c stamps in 1845, followed shortly by a 20c value. All three denominations featured the civic arms flanked by two bears, hence the popular name of St Louis Bears by which these stamps are known.

In 1846 the idea spread to other parts of the country and stamps were issued by the postmasters of Alexandria (Virginia), Annapolis (Maryland), Boscawen (New Hampshire), Brattleboro (Vermont), Lockport (New York), Millbury (Massachusetts), New Haven (Connecticut) and Providence (Rhode Island). Meanwhile sales of the original New York 5c stamp were extended to Albany, Boston, Philadelphia and even Washington, so that they assumed the character of a national issue. It is said that this was done on the express command of the US Postmaster General, Cave Johnson, but confined to letters addressed to New York. It appears to have been an experiment discontinued after a short time. These stamps continued in use until August 1847 when they were superseded by the general issue for the USA as a whole.

Also in July 1845, Basle became the third canton in Switzerland to adopt ahesive stamps. It should be borne in mind that, prior to 1848, each canton was a miniature republic, quite independent of the others, and it was only after a brief war in November 1847 that the Swiss Confederation acquired real central power, eventually including control of the postal services.

In point of fact, the famous Basle Dove was not intended for use throughout the canton of Basle, but was restricted to a local service operating within the city itself. It differed from the US local stamps, however, in that it was authorised by the municipal authorities, but it explains the caption STADT-POST-BASEL (Basle Town Post). Twenty stamps were sold for 5 batzen but individual stamps had a value of 2½ rappen, denoted in the lower corners.

The principal motif was the civic arms, showing a white dove on a plain red shield, a letter in its beak. This stamp is of great interest for several reasons. It was the first stamp to be printed in a country other than that which issued it, having been printed by Krebs of Frankfurt-am-Main, Germany. It was the world's first stamp to be printed in combined processes, involving embossing and letterpress. Like the stamps of Zurich and Geneva, which were bicoloured, the Basle Dove had a penchant for colour, but was the first tricoloured stamp—black, carmine and blue. Examples in black, vermilion and green are colour proofs.

Under the new federal Constitution drawn up in 1848 notice was served that the cantonal postal administrations might continue for the time being, "until the definite regulations of the Postal Department come into force". Both Zurich and Geneva subsequently issued stamps bringing them into line with the new federal regulations and postal rates, but they were phased out when the Swiss federal stamps were adopted in May 1850.

100 YEARS AGO

28 February 1895 Majunga

Madagascar, the world's third largest island, became the prey of European commercial and political interests in the course of the nineteenth century. French, British and Norwegian missions vied with each other in converting the heathen Malagasy and in their wake came the traders and merchants. These encroachments were not accepted without some resistance. When in 1846 the Malagasy tried to curb the foreign powers the French and British sent a joint expedition to bombard the island into submission. Thereafter foreign consulates wielded increasing influence on the native administration. Government remained in the hands of Queen Ranavalona II who had come to the throne in 1868, but relations between the Malagasy and the French deteriorated rapidly in 1882. In vain the Queen sent emissaries to Europe to negotiate with the French and secure treaties with Britain and Germany. In May 1883 the French government sent a harsh ultimatum to the Queen. When she failed to meet their demands, the French sent a punitive expedition which bombarded the port of Tamatave. Tamatave and several other seaports were occupied but though the war dragged on desultorily for several months no attempt was made to occupy the capital Antananarivo in the interior.

By a treaty of December 1885 the Queen was forced to accept a French Resident and agree to France controlling the island's external relations. Some territory round the bay of Diego Suarez was ceded to France for use as a naval base. The word "protectorate" was studiously avoided in the treaty, and the Queen was allowed to retain her position. As part of the external relations, the French established post offices at which French stamps were sold for outgoing mail. The first distinctive stamps were the general colonial series surcharged with new values, released in 1889, followed two years later by stamps inscribed MADAGASCAR.

The treaty lasted for nine years, but successive Residents found themselves frustrated by the wily Queen who continued to govern at Antananarivo, and raised a large army trained by British officers. Inevitably this led to considerable tension and towards the end of 1894 the French government delivered another ultimatum, demanding that France should have exclusivity in foreign relations and the right to garrison the entire island with troops if need be. When the Queen refused, the French community left the island. As soon as all civilians had been evacuated, the French forces struck.

In a well-planned operation the French occupied all the seaports, but there remained the major problem of subjugating the interior. In January 1895, therefore, after a heavy bombardment, an army led by General Metzinger landed on the north-west coast at Majunga or Mojanga, then the second seaport of Madagascar, with a population of some 14,000. Majunga became the French base for operations against the interior, the French forces growing to more than 8400 under Major-General Duchesne. It was not until the end of September that the Malagasy were forced to admit defeat, but the "pacification" of the island, by General Gallieni, took several years.

A shortage of 15 centime stamps, used to prepay postage on soldiers' letters home, led to a number of provisional surcharges at Majunga from 28 February onwards. At first 25c and 1fr stamps of the general colonial series were surcharged 0.15 in pen and ink. This was found to be unsatisfactory, so the original pen-marks were washed off and the stamps overprinted 15 in various founts of type. These new values were applied by hand and may therefore be found in different positions—horizontal, vertical or sideways. The stamps were sold one at a time, and no pairs, blocks or multiples are known to exist. Examples are scarce, especially on soldiers' envelopes.

20 March 1895 Uganda

The powerful central African kingdom of Buganda was penetrated by European missionaries in the 1870s and traders soon followed. The country was at first left to its own devices but in the 1880s the major European powers carved out spheres of influence and began establishing protectorates. Fearing that some hostile power might gain control of the headwaters of the Nile, Captain (later Lord) Lugard urged the British government to take Buganda under its protection. In November 1893 Colonel Colville took over command of British troops at Kampala and the following year helped the Kabaka of Buganda defeat the King of Bunyoro. A line of forts was erected to keep the peace and on 19 June 1894 a British protectorate was formally declared over Buganda and extended on 3 July 1896 to Bunyoro and Busoga.

The Rev. Ernest Millar typed Uganda's first stamps.

Rev. Rowling's stamps were printed by letterpress.

The protectorate was known as Uganda and when peace was restored trade flourished. In this peaceful atmosphere a postal service was planned by Deputy Commissioner George Wilson. At that time, however, there was no such thing as a printing press in Uganda so Wilson enlisted the help of the Rev. Ernest Millar of the Church Missionary Society at Mengo who had recently imported a Barlock typewriter from England. Millar's diary reveals that Wilson approached him on 14 March 1895 and two days later Millar typed out a sheet of stamps using the thin paper on which he normally wrote his sermons. On 19 March Millar called at the fort in Kampala and delivered the first consignment. The stamps came into use the following day.

The design was extremely simple, just the letters UG (Uganda Government) at the top, with the numerals of value in the centre and framed by hyphens at top and bottom and apostrophes at the sides. The stamps were imperforate and ungummed, the adhesive being supplied from tree resin. The stamps were denominated 5, 10, 15, 20, 25, 30, 40, 50 and 60 cowries, these shells being used as currency at the rate of 200 to the Indian silver rupee.

New stamps, varying in width, were typed out in April, May and November. Originally stamps were typed with a black ribbon but by November Millar had acquired a new machine using a violet ribbon. The same colour was used for a set issued in June 1896 with a more elaborate design. In this issue the digits 96 appeared at the top, flanked by V and R, while the country name appeared in full across the foot. The Uganda Cowries were superseded in November 1896 by stamps produced on a printing press by the Rev. F. Rowling at Lubwa's in Usoga, and denominated in annas and rupees.

In turn, they were replaced by stamps recess-printed by De La Rue and bearing the Von Angeli portrait of Queen Victoria. A shortage of the most commonly used denominations was filled in February 1902 by overprinting the corresponding values of East Africa (Kenya) with UGANDA. The postal services of Kenya and Uganda were amalgamated later that year and distinctive stamps replaced by a joint issue the following year. Sixty years would elapse before Uganda re-emerged as a stamp-issuing entity, following the grant of self-government in 1962.

1 July 1895 Inhambane

For centuries Portuguese traders had maintained bases in the vast east African territory known as Mozambique. The fortunes of this territory waxed and waned, but in the scramble for Africa in the nineteenth century Portuguese interest in the area was renewed and an attempt was made to link it with Angola in west Africa. This ambition was foiled by Cecil Rhodes whose British South Africa Company drove northwards and occupied what is now Zimbabwe.

The boundaries of Mozambique were defined by international arbitration in 1891, and as a result the territory, then renamed Portuguese East Africa, was re-organised into two provinces named Mozambique and Lourenco Marques. Mozambique province was subsequently sub-divided into the districts of Mozambique, Zambezia, Gaza and Inhambane. Stamps inscribed MOCAMBIQUE had been introduced throughout the whole of Portuguese East Africa in 1876 and continue to the present day, but in the 1890s the area which they served was considerably reduced. Lourenco Marques and Zambezia had their own stamps from 1893 onwards. A large tract was granted to a chartered company whose own stamps were issued from 1892 till 1942, and within its territory separate issues were made in Quelimane and Tete from 1913 onwards.

The distinctive stamps of Inhambane were introduced on 1 July 1895 and consisted of stamps of Mozambique overprinted with the district name, and a second inscription celebrating the 700th anniversary of St Anthony. These stamps exist in various perforations and several have been recorded with inverted overprints. Eight years elapsed before they were replaced by something more permanent, the colonial keyplate design portraying King Carlos with the name in two lines at the foot. When Portugal became a republic in 1912 the stamps of Inhambane were diagonally overprinted REPUBLICA. The following year the currency was changed and for this purpose stamps of Africa, Macao and Timor were surcharged and overprinted REPUBLICA INHAMBANE in two lines.

In 1914–15 the Ceres colonial keyplate series was adopted. Belatedly, the Carlos series was re-issued in 1917 diagonally overprinted REPUBLICA and continued in use until 1920 when all of the provincial and district stamps were replaced by the general issue of Mozambique.

August 1895 The Black Flag Republic

Today the island of Taiwan or Formosa constitutes the territory of the Nationalist Chinese Republic, but a century ago it was briefly held by a rebel Chinese government. The island, off the coast of south China, had a large and quite distinct aboriginal population but from the seventeenth century onwards was subject to large-scale migration of Hakkas from Canton and Hoklas from Fukien who displaced the primitive inhabitants, known to the Chinese as *Sheng-fan* (wild savages). In 1874 the island was invaded by the Japanese in retaliation for the murder of a shipwrecked crew, the Chinese government being unwilling, or unable, to punish the culprits. War was averted through British mediation. In 1884 the French bombarded the forts at Keelung as a reprisal for the Tongking dispute and a blockade of the island was maintained till the spring of 1885.

Serious trouble erupted, however in 1895, at the conclusion of the Sino-Japanese War. The Japanese soundly defeated the Chinese who were compelled, by the Treaty of Shimonoseki, to hand over Taiwan. The resident Chinese governor, Tang Ching-sun, refused to comply with this order, or recognise the cession, and declared an independent republic with himself as president. He even toyed with the idea of transferring the island to British protection but Britain refused.

A formal ceremony ceding the island had to be held aboard a ship offshore, as neither Chinese mainland nor Japanese officials dared land in face of the implacable hostility of the Taiwanese. The Japanese were left to take possession of the island as best they could but eventually

The stamps of Inhambane saw a number of changes in a relatively short period.

Crudely printed stamps were issued under the authority of the warlord Liu Yung-fu.

they landed a military force and occupied the capital Taipei. Tang and his entourage were arrested and deported to mainland China, but a large part of southern Taiwan remained in rebel hands.

Resistance to Japanese rule was led by the notorious Black Flag warlord Liu Yung-fu, under whose authority stamps were issued in August 1895. The stamps were crudely printed from various dies showing the tiger emblem of the Black Flag republic, and the individual values were applied by hand. Some fifteen stamps, and a number of minor varieties, were issued in a period of three months before the Japanese succeeded in subjugating the island. On 15 October Takow was bombarded and resistance collapsed, Liu and his followers escaping into the mountains and thence back to China. Thereafter, Japanese stamps were in use till 1945 when the island reverted to China.

10 November 1895 Zanzibar

The sultanate of Zanzibar, comprising the islands of Zanzibar and Pemba off the east African coast, became an important trading centre and base for expeditions into the heart of the Dark Continent in the middle of the 19th century. A post office under Indian administration was opened there in 1868 but closed a year later. This office was re-established on 1 October 1875 as a postal agency in special relations with the Indian Post Office and using ordinary Indian stamps. It continued until 10 November 1895 when responsibility for the postal service was transferred to British East Africa (Kenya). There were also French and German post offices in Zanzibar using the ordinary stamps of these countries. The French office, however, also used French stamps overprinted ZANZIBAR until it was closed in 1904.

On 10 November 1895 contemporary Indian stamps with the name of the sultanate overprinted went on sale, to be followed in 1896 by stamps of British East Africa similarly overprinted. The first truly distinctive stamps appeared in September 1896 and were recess-printed by De La Rue with a portrait of Sultan Seyyid. A new series portraying Sultan Hamoud was issued in 1899. The stamps of his successor, however, depicted the state emblem instead in deference to the commands of the Koran which forbade portraits.

Under Sultan Ali bin Hamoud (1908) portrait stamps were re-introduced, but a horizontal design featuring a harbour scene was used for the seven highest values. Ali abdicated in 1911 but two years elapsed before stamps portraying his successor, Sultan Kalif were released. During his long reign the stamps underwent a number of changes, a greater degree of pictorialism being gradually adopted. In 1936 the first commemorative set celebrated the Sultan's Silver Jubilee, and eight years later the bicentenary of the Al-Busaid dynasty was marked by stamps showing an Arab dhow. The first fully pictorial series, with a portrait of the aged Kalif inset, appeared in 1957. The same designs, but with a portrait of Sultan Seyyid Sir Abdulla, appeared in 1961.

Sultan Sir Abdulla died suddenly in 1963 and was succeeded by his son Sultan Seyyid Jamshid whose portrait was included in the design of the stamps celebrating the grant of independence on 10 December that year. The celebrations were short-lived, for the Afro-Shirazi party rose in revolt against the Arab-dominated regime. Both commemorative and definitive stamps were overprinted JAMHURI (republic) and released on 17 January 1964. Three months later President Karume agreed to unite Zanzibar with Tanganyika to form a United Republic, renamed Tanzania in 1965.

Until 1967, however, Zanzibar continued to have a separate postal administration and various sets of rather garish stamps, printed in East Germany, reflected the political character of the Afro-Shirazi government. Ironically, the very last sets of 1966–67 were printed by De La Rue, the firm which had printed Zanzibar's first stamps seventy years earlier. Since the middle of 1967 only stamps inscribed Tanzania have been in use.

The Sultans of Zanzibar.

50 YEARS AGO

19 March 1945 Allied Military Government of Germany

After the setback of the Ardennes counter-offensive in December 1944 the Allies fought back and by the end of January 1945 had regained most of the territory lost in the Battle of the Bulge. The next few weeks were spent in consolidating gains and preparing for the onslaught on Germany itself. On 23 February the Allied offensive in the west was resumed. Driving towards the Rhine eight Allied armies swept up all the industrial towns and cities on the West Bank of the Rhine and on 7 March one column crossed the river by the railway bridge at Remagen, the "bridge too far" which the retreating Germans had somehow failed to destroy. Aachen (Aix la Chapelle) became the first major city in the Reich proper to fall into Allied hands. Something approaching normality was restored by 19 March when the postal service resumed, albeit on a limited, local basis.

For this purpose the Allies had prepared a set of stamps in advance and those denominated 5, 6, 8 and 12pf were placed on sale initially, with other values from 1pf to 1Rm eventually added. The stamps had a simple design by W. A. Roach, with a capital M in German script in a central oval denoting military administration. Across the top appeared the inscription AM POST (Allied Military Post) while the country name DEUTSCHLAND appeared at the foot. The numerals of value occupied the upper corners.

This series was unusual in that it was printed in three different countries, using two different printing processes. The original series was produced by the Bureau of Engraving and Printing in Washington using the offset process. Subsequently, printings were made by Harrison and Sons in England using the photogravure process, and finally the responsibility of producing the stamps passed to a German firm, G. Westermann, which used the offset process. Many denominations (including all those over 25pf) were confined to the German printing, but all three versions of the AM Post stamps have different characteristics, such as perforation, paper and gum. These stamps remained valid for postage until 7 November 1946, although they had been largely superseded by stamps inscribed *Deutsche Post* (German Post) which had been adopted in the British, American and Soviet zones of occupation in January of that year.

9 June 1945 Soviet Zone of Germany

Unlike the Anglo-American forces in western Germany, the Soviets had no immediate plans to restore the postal services, yet within a month of the Nazi capitulation restricted services, often operating on a fairly local basis, had been resumed. A fundamental difference between the Anglo-American and Soviet zones is that in the latter responsibility for getting the services going again devolved on the regional postal administrations (*Oberpostdirektion* or OPD). The first to resume services, complete with distinctive stamps, was Berlin and Brandenburg whose stamps, designed by Goldammer, were released on 9 June 1945. A different design was used for each of the seven denominations from 5pf to 30pf and of these all but the top value featured the Berlin Bear, either in a purely

The Allied Military Government issued stamps prepared in advance of the occupation.

A large number of towns and districts issued their own stamps to fill the gap left by the collapse of the Third Reich.

Locally-produced stamps, particularly in the Soviet Zone, varied considerably in quality.

heraldic form (5, 8 and 20pf) or engaged in reconstruction work. The 30pf showed an oak sapling in leaf amid the ruins of the city, symbolising rebirth.

On 23 June OPD Dresden, covering east Saxony, began a local service and issued a 12pf stamp inscribed POST at the top, with the equivalent in Cyrillic at the foot. As the use of Russian contravened a Four-Power agreement, this stamp was hastily withdrawn and replaced by a similar design with an ornament across the foot. Subsequently separate issues appeared in Mecklenburg-Vorpommern under OPD Schwerin (28 August), West Saxony under OPD Leipzig (28 September), Saxony Province under OPD Halle (10 October) and Thuringia under OPD Erfurt (10 October). These stamps continued to be valid for postage after the introduction of the Deutsche Post numeral series in January 1946 and were not withdrawn from use until the end of October that year.

In addition, many towns, especially in the Soviet zone, issued their own stamps, pending the resumption of the OPD services, to fill temporary gaps when stamps were in short supply, or latterly to raise money for local reconstruction funds. In many cases the Hitler Head definitives of the Third Reich were overprinted or had the Fuehrer's features blotted out. The local productions varied considerably in technical and design qualities, from the crude hand-printed stamps of Frankenau and the typewritten stamps of Eckartsberga to the photogravure pictorials of Meissen. Many other towns used a wide range of handstamps inscribed *Gebuhr Bezahlt* (charge paid), and these are of considerable interest to postal historians.

15 June 1945 Venezia Giulia and Istria

This area at the head of the Adriatic, formerly part of the Habsburg Empire, had been in Italian hands since the end of the First World War and included the port of Fiume which had been seized by Gabriele d'Annuzio in 1919. By 1944 the area was part of the Italian Social Republic, the puppet state ruled by Mussolini under German auspices,

but by the end of that year much of the Istrian peninsula was in the hands of Tito's partisans. On 30 April 1945 they entered Trieste and two days later the remnants of the Wehrmacht surrendered to New Zealand forces.

At the end of the war control of Venezia Giulia and Istria was disputed between Yugoslavia and Italy and pending a decision the area was placed under joint Allied military administration. By virtue of conquest, the Yugoslavs controlled the ports of Trieste and Fiume and in these towns stamps of the erstwhile Italian Social Republic were overprinted FIUME or TRIESTE with their Serbo-Croat equivalents (RIJEKA and TRST) and the dates of their seizure. At the same time various Italian stamps were overprinted ISTRA for use in Istria and Pola (Pula) but not issued at that time. Four of them were released a month later, resurcharged with new values.

On 9 June an agreement was signed in Belgrade whereby Trieste and the roads and railways from there to Austria via Gorizia, Caporetto and Tarvisio, as well as the town of Pola, should be under the control of the Supreme Allied Commander. The rest of Venezia Giulia would be under Yugoslav control. This arrangement came into effect on 12 June. Trieste, Pola, Gorizia and the Isonzo Valley thus came under Anglo-American control. On 22 September contemporary Italian stamps were released with a two-line overprint A.M.G. / V.G. denoting "Allied Military Government, Venezia Giulia". These continued until October 1947 when they were superseded by similar stamps overprinted A.M.G. / F.T.T. signifying "Free Territory of Trieste".

In the Yugoslav zone stamps inscribed in Serbo-Croat and Slovene were released on 15 August 1945. By the Treaty of Paris, signed on 10 February 1947, all former Italian territory in Venezia Giulia and Istria was annexed by Yugolavia, except for Gorizia and the town and district of Trieste which was to constitute a Free Territory. The use of Yugoslav military stamps in Istria thus came to an end on 11 February 1947.

2 September 1945 Vietnam

Two thousand years ago the kingdom of Annam and Tongking, then known as Namviet, was annexed to the Chinese Empire. By 939 AD Ngo Quyen succeeded in asserting his independence and over the ensuing centuries Annam was a semi-independent kingdom under Chinese suzerainty. In 1802 Nguyen Anh of Annam, with French help, overran Tongking and proclaimed himself Emperor of Vietnam. Too late, however, he discovered that his erstwhile helpers had territorial designs of their own. Cochin China was ceded to France in 1862–74 and in 1883 a French protectorate was established over Annam and Tongking. These territories, together with the protectorate of Cambodia (1863) were consolidated into the Union of Indochina, Laos being added in 1893. After the fall of France in 1940, Indochina was occupied by the Japanese. For some time civil administration remained in the hands of the Vichy French, but on 9 March 1945 the Japanese declared that French rule was at an end. The Emperor Bao Dai of Annam was appointed by them as titular head of the autonomous state of Vietnam, but on 14 August Japan surrendered and nine days later Bao Dai abdicated.

The Viet Minh began as a nationalist guerrilla movement, waging war on the Japanese from 1941 onwards, under the leadership of a Soviet agent named Nguyen Ai Quoc who changed his name to Ho Chi Minh ("he who enlightens"). By August 1945 the Viet Minh was a large, well-equipped and well-trained force and in the vacuum left by the Japanese surrender they rapidly took control in Tongking. At Hanoi, on 2 September, Ho Chi Minh proclaimed the independence of the democratic republic of Vietnam.

Contemporary stamps of French Indochina were released with an overprint signifying "Vietnam Democratic Republic—Independence, Freedom, Happiness—Postal Service". Subsequently some stamps were surcharged to raise funds for famine relief or war wounded. Towards the end of the year the definitives were re-issued surcharged in a new currency based on the dong of 100 xu.

Bowing to the inevitable, the French recognised

Ho Chi Minh, who proclaimed the independence of the democratic republic of Vietnam on 2 September 1945.

Vietnam on 8 March 1946, as an independent state within the Indochinese Federation. In the ensuing months there were several further charity issues, made by simply surcharging various definitives, but the only distinctive stamps of Vietnam were the set of three released on 13 May 1946 bearing the portrait of Ho Chi Minh. Two denominations were released the same day surcharged in aid of national defence.

Relations with the French deteriorated in 1946 and culminated in bloodshed when Ho refused to evacuate his forces from the port of Haiphong. The port was bombarded by the French cruiser *Suffren* and over 6000 Vietnamese were killed. Ho counter-attacked on 19 December but was defeated and forced to withdraw his forces into northern Tongking. Thereafter stamps of Indochina continued in the areas under French control, while crudely printed, ungummed stamps (often denominated in quantities of rice, the basis of the economy) were issued by the Viet Minh in the areas under their command. These are regarded as the forerunners of North Vietnam which emerged as a political entity after the defeat of the French at Dien-Bien-Phu in 1954.

October 1945 Indonesia

There were parallels between French Indochina and the Dutch East Indies. Both were colonial empires which had suffered defeat or humiliation at the hands of the Japanese. The spectacle of the former colonial masters humbled by an Asiatic power was an object lesson to the subject peoples in both countries. In the Indies, however, there was an important difference in that the Japanese planned to establish a semi-autonomous regime under local leaders (as in the Philippines), and thus the administration led by Achmed Soekarno was not originally a guerrilla movement.

The sudden collapse of Japan following the atomic bombs was swiftly followed by the surrender of Imperial Japanese forces in the Indies. Holland itself had been under Nazi occupation and was in no position to resume control of the Indies as a whole. In those islands which had previously fallen to American and Australian troops Dutch rule was restored with relative ease, but in Java, Madura and Sumatra, held by Japan till the very end of the war, the Dutch never regained control. In the interim these islands were administered by British and Indian forces, ironically assisted by units of the Imperial Japanese Army who retained their weapons.

Soekarno was not minded to relinquish the control which had been granted by the Japanese. On 17 August 1945 Soekarno proclaimed the independent Republic of Indonesia. Various stamps of the Japanese occupation were unofficially overprinted in handwriting "Republik" but it was not until October that stamps with a printed inscription were released in Java and Madura. These were stamps of the former Dutch Indies overprinted in two lines REPOEBLIK INDONESIA with the original inscription obliterated. Subsequently stamps of the Japanese occupation were similarly treated. At the same time

Indonesia, from overprints to independence.

various unoverprinted stamps of the Dutch and Japanese administrations had the inscriptions obliterated by pen and ink or brush or pencil to validate them for postal use.

The first distinctive stamps appeared on 1 December and were typographed at Djokjakarta. One showed a charging bull while the other featured a bull and the new national flag. The stamps celebrated the declaration of independence. Early in 1946 stocks of the former Netherlands Indies and Japanese occupation stamps were overprinted with a large framed handstamp inscribed REPOEBLIK INDONESIA P.T.T. which covered three stamps, so that only a portion of the overprint appears on individual stamps. During 1946 further typographed stamps were released with various symbolic motifs.

By the end of 1946 British and Japanese forces were replaced by Dutch troops who then began the reconquest of areas in rebel hands. Meanwhile republican stamps began appearing in Sumatra in 1946, including some portraying Soekarno. The use of republican stamps continued sporadically until December 1948 when the Dutch captured Soekarno and most of his cabinet. A compromise, brokered by the United Nations, was the United States of Indonesia which issued stamps in 1950, but by August, the fifth anniversary of the original republic of Indonesia, the forces of Achmed Soekarno gradually liberated territory held by the Dutch.

19 October 1945 British Military Administration of Malaya

Before the Second World War the British sphere of influence in south-east Asia consisted of the Straits Settlements (the three crown colonies of Singapore, Malacca and Penang), the Federated Malay States (Negri Sembilan, Pahang, Perak and Selangor), the unfederated states of Johore, Kedah, Kelantan and Trengganu, the territory of the British North Borneo Company and the independent sultanates of Brunei and Sarawak. Japanese troops landed in Borneo and the Malayan peninsula in

December 1941 and within weeks had defeated British and Commonwealth forces, although the island fortress of Singapore held out till 15 February 1942.

For almost four years the entire area was under Japanese military administration. At first there was a spate of local occupation issues but eventually ordinary unoverprinted Japanese stamps were in general use. From November 1943 the four most northerly Malay states were under Thai administration, distinctive stamps being used in 1943–45.

Following the defeat of Japan in August 1945 the whole of Malaya and British Borneo came under British Military administration, pending the restoration of civil authority. Prewar stamps of the Straits Settlements were overprinted B.M.A. MALAYA in two lines and introduced on 19 October. The series eventually ran from 1c to $5 and consisted of eighteen denominations, together with a number of prominent colour varieties. These stamps were phased out in 1948–49 when each state of the Malayan postal union resumed its own stamps, using uniform designs.

4 November 1945 Taiwan

After the surrender of Japan in August 1945 the island of Taiwan was returned to Chinese rule on 25 October, under the terms of the Cairo agreement of 1943. A Chinese postal service came into operation on 4 November using various stamps of the Japanese occupation overprinted with Chinese ideograms to signify "Taiwan Province, Chinese Republic". These were supplemented by a number of Japanese stamps similarly overprinted, with surcharges in Chinese currency, which appeared in June 1946.

Because the currency on the Chinese mainland was now depreciating rapidly, it was necessary to continue with separate issues for Taiwan. In the latter half of 1946 many Chinese stamps were released on the island surcharged in local currency. These were followed in 1947 by several commemoratives as well as a definitive series, identical to the mainland issues except for the figures of value and the four characters denoting Taiwan. Two Chinese stamps of August 1947, celebrating the second anniversary of the return of Taiwan, were put on sale on the island without an overprint, the $500 being sold at $7 local currency and the $1250 at $18. By February 1948, however, the inflation raging on the mainland was beginning to affect the Taiwanese economy and there was a spate of surcharges to create higher and higher denominations. During 1948 and 1949 the only new stamps to appear in Taiwan were temporary surcharges and revaluations to cope with the exigencies of the inflation.

Taiwan ceased to be a mere province, and assumed the role of *the* Republic of China, in November 1949 when Chiang Kai-shek and the remnants of his Nationalist army were forced to flee before the Communist advance. Henceforth the stamps used on the island were inscribed "Republic of China", although no English equivalent to the Chinese characters actually appeared until 1953.

PHILATELIC TERMS

The following glossary of terms used in philately and postal history is intended only as a brief summary. For fuller details the reader is recommended to *Philatelic Terms Illustrated* by James Mackay and *Fundamentals of Philately* by L. N. and M. Williams.

Abnormals Twelve British stamps by De La Rue (1862–80) from plates which were not put into general production. Only six sheets of each were printed, one being retained as the imprimatur (qv) and the others either destroyed or perforated and distributed to post offices.

Accepted Design the artwork (qv) approved by a postal administration and passed to the printer for production.

Accessories the indispensable aids to stamp collecting: albums, mounts, tweezers, watermark detector, perforation gauge, magnifier and callipers for measuring overprints.

Accidental Grill indentation on Turkish stamps (1870–71) perforated by sewing machine, the marks being made by the claws intended originally to move cloth through the machine.

Accountancy Mark handstamp applied to international letters prior to 1875, denoting the charge to be recovered from the addressee. British marks, for example, may be found with values in centimes, groschen or US cents, depending on the routing of the letter.

Acknowledgment of Receipt popular but incorrect term for Advice of Receipt (qv).

Additional Halfpenny a tax on letters to, from or within Scotland (1813–39) if conveyed by a vehicle with more than two wheels. Many post offices in England and Ireland as well as Scotland had special handstamps to denote this tax.

Adhesive common term for a postage stamp in the form of a gummed label, as opposed to stamps impressed on postal stationery, or handstruck on mail prepaid in cash.

Admirals popular name for the definitive issues of Canada (1912), Rhodesia (1913) and New Zealand (1926) portraying King George V in the full-dress uniform of an Admiral of the Fleet.

Adsons New Zealand stamps (1893) with advertisements printed on the back.

Abnormal 10d from Plate 2

Advertisements both commercial and public service announcements have appeared on postal stationery since the Mulready (qv) wrappers of 1840. They have been extensively used in the interleaves of booklets, the backs of letter-cards (New Zealand) and telegram forms (UK). Booklet panes (margins or se-tenant labels) often carry advertising.

Advertising Labels non-postal labels used by businesses to advertise their products and services, largely superseded by slogans on meter marks (qv).

Advice of Delivery international service since 1891, denoted by the letters AR on stamps (Chile, Colombia, El Salvador and Montenegro), providing the sender with notification of delivery to the addressee.

Aerogramme lightweight letter sheet pioneered by Iraq (1933) and now universally used for airmail, usually with an impressed stamp.

Affixing Machine device for sticking stamps on mail, developed in the USA (1907). Special coil stamps (qv) were often used in this connection.

Airgraph message microfilmed for transmission by air, then enlarged on arrival and printed for despatch to the addressee, a facility for servicemen overseas (1941–45). See also *V Mail*.

Air Letter Sheet British term for aerogramme.

Airmail any form of correspondence transmitted by air.

Airmail Label sticker affixed to mail intended for transmission by air, usually printed in blue and often inscribed *Par Avion* in French, with the local equivalent.

Air Stamp   stamp inscribed specifically for airmail.

Airport Dedication   covers, handstamps and cachets marking the opening of an airport, particularly fashionable in Canada and USA.

Airway Letter Stamp   semi-official stamp used by airlines providing a letter service, often accelerating mail which would otherwise have gone by road or rail.

Albino   colourless, deficient in pigment or defective in printing.

Album   book designed to house stamps, stationery, booklets, FDCs, etc, first produced by Lallier in France (1862). Albums may be fixed-leaf or loose-leaf, the latter with either peg-fitting, springback or multi-ring binders.

ALF—see *Automatic Letter Facing*

All-over Watermark   watermark covering the entire sheet, so that only a portion of it may appear on indvidual stamps.

Alphabet Letters   letters in the corners of British line-engraved stamps (1840–80), four different alphabets (or lettering styles) being used.

Anaglyph   two-colour printing producing a three-dimensional effect when viewed through special spectacles, confined to the 25 and 60 lire stamps of Italy marking admission to the UN (1956).

Anaglyptography   printing process conveying the impression of three dimensions by the use of parallel contour lines. Good examples are Austria 1 and 2g (1890) and the George V stamps of Australia (1913–21).

Anhyphenate   inscription in which compound words are run together without a hyphen, e.g. GB 6d (1869) with SIXPENCE instead of SIX-PENCE and South African stamps inscribed SUIDAFRIKA instead of SUID-AFRIKA. See also *Hyphenated*.

Aniline Colour   used philatelically to denote aqueous inks with a distinctive bright colour and showing through on the back of stamps.

Approvals   selections of stamps sent by dealers and clubs by mail to prospective customers, usually mounted and priced in small booklets. See also *Exchange Packet*.

Arc Roulette   type of separation using curved cuts to produce a scalloped effect. French (*percé en arc*).

Archer Roulette and Perforation   pioneering attempts at separation invented by Henry Archer (1853–54).

Armoured Car Mail   correspondence transmitted between Rishon-le-Zion and Jerusalem (1948) using armoured cars to avoid Arab ambush. Covers were distinctively cacheted and special stamps were provided for the service.

Army Post   Egyptian stamps thus inscribed were used by British forces in the Canal Zone (1936–51) on mail sent at concessionary rates.

Arrangement   the orderly presentation of stamps, laid out and written up on the album page.

Arrow Block   block of stamps with an arrow in the sheet margin.

Artwork   artist's painting or drawing serving as the basis for a stamp design.

ATM   abbreviation for *Automatenmarken*, German for "automatic vending machine stamps", or Automatic Teller Machine (qv).

August Printing   term for the first designs of the US stamps of 1861 which may, in fact, have been essays (qv) as they differ in some respect from the later printings.

Authorised Delivery Stamp   issued by Italy since 1928 indicating the fee on mail delivered under licence by private courier services.

Authorised Non-Profit Organisation Stamp   issued by the USA since 1979 to prepay special rates on mail of charities. Such stamps are characterised by odd amounts, e.g. 3.1c or 5.9c.

Automatic Letter Facing   system for the handling, sorting and facing (getting envelopes right-side up) mail by electronic machines pioneered at Southampton in 1957. Distinctive cancelling dies with alphanumeric codes at the foot denoted mail thus sorted. For this purpose graphite lines and later phosphor bands (qqv) were introduced.

Automatic Machine Perforation   distinctive perforation (very large holes or slots) applied vertically to horizontal coils in New Zealand and the USA (1906–12) by various companies providing affixing machines.

Automatic Stamps   gummed slips or labels dispensed by coin-operated machines. The value is printed on the stamp by punching a key-pad. Frama (Switzerland) and Klussendorf (Germany) manufacture the equipment and stamps for many countries.

Automatic Teller Machine   machine originally used by banks for dispensing cash to customers after normal hours, but adapted in the USA and Australia to dispense special small sheets of self-adhesive stamps.

Baby Type   Spanish colonial keytype portraying Alfonso XIII as an infant.

Back of the Book   term for special purpose stamps (official, express, newspaper, parcel) and postage due labels, often grouped in catalogues at the end of the main list of ordinary stamps.

Backprinting   any inscription or device printed on the back of a stamp. See *Adson* and *Discount Postage*.

Backstamp   postmark applied to the back of an envelope, either in transit or at the delivery office.

Balloon Post   mail transmitted by balloon: USA (1859 and 1877), the sieges of Paris (1870–71), Metz (1870) and Przemysl (1914–15), and in more recent years in connection with balloon races. See also *Zeppelin.*

Bandalette   alternative name for Dominical Label (qv).

Bande   French term for a newspaper wrapper (qv).

Banknote Paper   paper bearing partially printed banknotes, used for the stamps of Latvia (1920) and the Ukraine (1993).

Banknote Stamps   US stamps produced by the American, Continental and National Bank Note Cos. (1870–79).

Bantams   South African stamps (1942–44) printed in a reduced size to save paper.

Bar Cancel   obliteration in the form of bars.

Bar Code   pattern of vertical lines and bars which can be scanned electronically and read by computer, found on stamp booklets (UK), sheet margins (New Zealand), registration labels (Japan) and parcel labels (UK).

Bar Cut   groove or nick deliberately cut into the obliterating bars of some British double and combined stamps (notably at Edinburgh, 1881–95) to identify the stamper.

Barred   stamps in which the portrait of a deposed ruler has been obliterated by bars, e.g. Hitler (Germany, 1945–46), Farouk (Egypt, 1953) and the Shah (Iran, 1979).

Battleship Revenue   US documentary and proprietory revenue stamps of the Spanish American War period (1898) depicting a battleship.

Batonne   French for "ruled", describing paper with a watermark of prominent parallel lines.

Bicycle Posts   services by bicycle, using distinctive stamps, e.g. Coolgardie (1893), Fresno and San Francisco (1894) and Coralit, Italy (1944).

Bilingual Pair   pair of stamps in which a different language appears on each stamp, mainly South Africa (1926–51).

Bilingual Stamp   stamp with inscriptions in two languages, e.g. French and English (Canada), English and Afrikaans (South Africa), French and Flemish (Belgium) and many countries using a non-European script, with the equivalent in English or French.

Bipartite   stamps or labels perforated or rouletted down the middle so that the halves can be easily separated, e.g. Italian parcel stamps and Roumanian postage due labels.

Bisect   stamp cut in two so that each half can be used as a stamp.

Bishop Mark   datestamp devised by Colonel Henry Bishop (1661) indicating the day and month of posting, the first dated postmark in the world.

Bite   white spot in an impression due to a small piece of paper (perforation cut-out) adhering during printing. See also *Confetti Flaw.*

Bizonal   stamp issued in the Anglo-American occupation zones of Germany, 1945–49.

Black Bar   marginal marking on some sheets of British stamps to assist checking in the Stores Department.

Black Jack   nickname for the US 2c stamp (1863) portraying Andrew Jackson.

Black Print   proof printed in black and affixed to sheets describing each new issue of Austrian stamps.

Blackout Cancel   Canadian wartime postmark with the name removed for security reasons.

Blanc   name for the French keytype designed by Joseph Blanc and used for stamps of 1900–29.

Bleed-off   printing running off at the edges into the perforations instead of having a colourless surround.

Bleute   French for "blued", denoting a blue tinge caused by chemicals in the paper or ink.

Blind Perforation   perforation where the holes are not punched out, due to blunt or missing pins.

Blitz Perforation perforation by Waterlow and Sons of stamps usually printed by De La Rue whose premises were temporarily out of action due to German air raids. As Waterlow used a different gauge, the resultant stamps are quite distinct.

Block unsevered group of four or more stamps, containing at least two parallel rows in any direction.

Blockade Mail covers to and from the Confederacy (usually Texas or South Carolina) during the American Civil War which evaded the Union naval blockade.

Blocked Value a stamp forming part of a set on general sale, but itself severely restricted. Effectively this curbed philatelic traffic in the set, and was practised by the German Democratic Republic (1955–82).

Blue Safety Paper paper containing prussiate of potash, added to the printing ink to make it more fugitive. This chemical tended to diffuse through the paper producing a blue tinge. See *Bleute* and *Ivory Head.*

Blued Paper paper with an overall bluish tinge caused by chemicals in the paper used by De La Rue for British high value stamps (1881–84).

Boardwalk Margin an abnormally wide margin, usually in cases where perforation is omitted from stamps adjoining the selvedge (qv), and not to be confused with Wing Margins (qv).

Bogus a label purporting to be a stamp but which is completely fictitious. Many examples have been produced for political propaganda (qv) but others are intended to deceive collectors.

Bold Type lettering thicker and darker in colour than normal, often used in registration labels.

Booklet blocks or small panes of stamps bound together in card covers, often with interleaving bearing advertising. Introduced by Luxembourg (1895).

Booklet Pane block or strip of stamps issued in booklets, often imperforate on the outer edges or having one or more labels or coupons (qqv) attached, or having stamps of different denominations side by side.

Booklet Stamp stamp produced specifically for distribution in booklets, differing in watermark, perforation, format or design from corresponding stamps issued in sheets.

Bordeaux Print a stamp lithographed at Bordeaux (1870–71) instead of being produced by letterpress at Paris, during the Franco-Prussian War.

Boule de Moulins metal ball containing bundles of letters floated down the Seine into Paris during the siege of 1870–71. Many were shot and sunk by German marksmen, then salvaged during dredging operations many years later.

Braille system of printing by means of raised dots enabling the blind to read by touch. A Braille inscription is incorporated in the British £10 stamp of 1993.

Branch Post Office in Britain usually abbreviated as B.O., denoting a branch of a head post office, offering the full facilities of the head office in a district or suburb. In the USA a Branch Post Office is one located outside the limits of the city to which it is attached.

Broken Letter break or malformation in inscription caused by damage or wear on printing plate, type forme or cylinder.

Brunswick Star experimental postmark of Edinburgh (1863–71) associated with trials of the Pearson Hill cancelling machines, the name being derived from the order of chivalry whose rays it simulated.

Bulk Posting facility offered to businesses whereby large mailings of identical matter can be prepaid in cash and then handstamped or machine cancelled to indicate that no further charges are necessary. Low rates of postage are offered for large mailings of low-priority printed matter.

Bulk Rate Stamp low-denomination stamp issued specifically for bulk mailings, e.g. US half-cent stamps (1922–54) and many of the fractional denominations of more recent years.

Bull's Eye nickname for the first stamps of Brazil (1843).

Bureau Precancel precancels printed by the US Bureau of Engraving and Printing, the letterpress overprint being added at the time of printing the stamps by intaglio.

Bureau Print printing of stamps from the Bureau of Engraving and Printing, as opposed to versions produced by other printers.

Burelage intricate pattern of lines or dots as an underprint to the main design, as a security feature. Good examples include the first stamps of Denmark (1850) and the French 50fr airmail (1936).

Bus Parcel Stamp   stamp issued by a bus company to prepay carriage of parcels. Most are private or local issues, but stamps inscribed AUTOPAKETTI BUSSPAKET have been issued by the Finnish post office since 1949 for this purpose.

Bypost   Scandinavian for "town post" inscribed on many local issues of Denmark and Norway.

Cachet   device, other than the postmark, applied to mail to indicate the mode of posting, some special circumstance, or special handling. Private cachets are often applied to tourist mail.

Calendering   process of ironing paper to give it a gloss prior to printing.

Camel Postman   nickname for the first stamps of Sudan (1898–1931).

Campaign Cover   item posted by forces on active service, with distinctive postmarks, regimental cachets, censor marks or manuscript endorsement.

Cancellation   obliteration or defacement of an adhesive or impressed stamp to prevent re-use.

Cancelled   security endorsement, either manuscript or overprinted, to prevent stamps being used postally. Stamps marked CANCELLED or its equivalent in other languages, were often sold off cheaply as remainders (qv).

Cancelled to Order   postmarked stamps which have not been used postally and often still have the gum on the back.

Cape Triangular   nickname of the three-cornered stamps issued by the Cape of Good Hope (1853–64).

Capped Numerals   numerals on US 2c stamps of 1890–93 with flaws resembling caps.

Cardboard   usually confined to postal stationery (postcards and lettercards) or proof impressions. This material was used to print stamps of Russia and Ukraine circulated as small change, during and after the First World War.

Carlist Stamp   stamp issued under the authority of Carlos VII, pretender to the Spanish throne (1873–74).

Carriers' Stamps   stamps issued by carrier and freight companies in general, but more specifically applied to the issues of the US carriers (1842–63).

Carton   fine card usually confined to postal stationery.

Cartouche   small oval or circle containing a portrait or heraldic device.

Cartridge Paper   thick, hard rough paper originally used in the manufacture of cartridges but used for some stamps: Trinidad 1d (1853) and Russia Volga Famine set (1921).

Cash on Delivery   international service under UPU regulations, providing for the recovery of costs of goods from the recipient. Distinctive labels with a triangular design are used in many countries for this purpose.

Catalogue Value   price indicated in a stamp catalogue for mint and used stamps, usually based on a dealer's selling price.

Catapult Mail   a ship-to-shore service by light aeroplane catapulted from the deck, to speed up trans-Atlantic mails. France (1928) and Germany (1929) offered this service, denoted by specially overprinted French stamps or cacheted covers.

Cavallini   Italian for "little horsemen". The nickname for handstruck stamps on Sardinian letter sheets from 1818.

Censorship   the examination of mail to check on subversion or breaches of security, usually in wartime; denoted by special resealing labels and cachets.

Census Marking   mark applied by cancelling machine to mail as part of a periodic check on the volume of mail handled. In Britain the mark takes the form of a diamond, with or without wavy lines or a slogan.

Centre Lines   thin vertical and horizontal lines found on sheets of American stamps to assist in cutting sheets into halves and quarters. The block of four stamps where these lines intersect is called a Centre Line Block.

Centred   the position of a stamp design relative to its margins and perforations, ideally with an equal margin all round.

Certificate of Posting   slip stamped with the date of posting and retained by the sender as proof that an item has been posted.

Certified Mail   mail for which a receipt is given to the sender and required from the addressee, pioneered in the USA which issued a special 15c stamp for the purpose in 1955.

Certifying Stamp   cachet applied to official mail to certify that it is on government business and thus entitled to pass through the post either free of charge or subject to some inter-departmental account.

Chain Lines   prominent vertical lines in the watermark found on laid paper at right angles to the fine lines.

Chalk-surfaced Paper   highly-surfaced, chalk-coated paper adopted by De La Rue in 1902 for many British and colonial stamps to prevent attempts to wash off the postmark.

Chalky Paper   very white paper introduced for British stamps in 1962 producing a much clearer and more vivid impression.

Chalon Heads   name for the classic stamps of New Zealand, Tasmania and Ceylon bearing the portrait of Queen Victoria by Sir Edward Chalon.

Charge Marks and Labels   devices applied to unpaid or underpaid mail to show infringement of the regulations and the amount of deficit and fine to be recovered from the addressee.

Charity Label   non-postal label sold by charities, political parties, religious and other bodies to raise funds.

Charity Stamp   postage stamp bearing a premium in aid of some good cause. As a rule the amounts of postage and the charity premium are indicated separately, usually recognised by numerals separated by a plus sign.

Check Letters   letters punched into the lower corners of British line-engraved stamps (1840) and repeated in reverse order in the upper corners (1858–1902). Also found on stamps of Victoria (1850–57).

Cheque Stamp   fiscal stamp (1855–1971) embossed on cheques to denote the stamp duty. Such stamps were printed on sheets and overprinted for postal use in British Central Africa (1898).

Cherry Blossoms   name for Japanese stamps (1872–74), from their chief motif.

Children's Stamps   (a) stamps sold with a premium for child welfare, e.g. *Pro Juventute* (Switzerland) or *Voot Het Kind* (Netherlands); (b) stamps designed by children; (c) miniature versions of stamps included in toy post offices and occasionally found postally used by accident.

Chop   small circular or oval seal bearing Japanese ideograms, used to overprint stamps of countries occupied by Japanese forces in World War II.

Christmas Charity Posts   private delivery services organised by scouts, youth and church groups in Britain since 1981 and authorised by Parliament between 25 November and 31 December each year. The stamps, stationery and postal markings of these posts now constitute a large group.

Christmas Seal   charity label (qv) devised by Einar Holboell of Denmark in 1904. The idea spread from Scandinavia to America in 1907 and is now world-wide. Although non-postal, many seals are issued by the post offices in a number of countries.

Christmas Stamp   distinctive stamps for use on greetings mail. Apart from Canada's 2c of 1898 inscribed XMAS, these stamps were pioneered by Austria (1937) and Hungary (1943).

Chromolithography   form of lithography (qv) involving two or more colours. Not extensively used for stamps other than El Salvador (1897) and the Soroka zemstvo (qv) issue (1879), but common on labels at the turn of the century.

Cigarette Paper   very thin paper, confined to stamps of Latvia (1919) and some Polish PoW issues of World War II.

Cigarette Tax Stamp   fiscal stamp issued by South Africa, used for postage due purposes in 1922.

Cinderella   anything resembling a government-issued postage stamp, but actually something else—a local, telegraph or fiscal stamp, a label or a bogus stamp.

Circular Datestamp   (abbreviated as "cds") postmark in single or double circular form, either handstruck or forming the dater of machine cancellations.

Circular Delivery Stamp   a stamp produced by a private company. Several firms arose in the 1860s, offering a cut-price service for the delivery of circulars, samples and printed matter.

Classic   any stamp issued before about 1880, as well as some rarities of a more recent period.

Clean-cut Perforations   perforations that are sharply incised and have the punched discs of paper removed.

Cleaned   the chemical removal of postmarks or manuscript marks to pass off a used stamp as mint.

Cleaned Plate   the removal of clogged ink from a printing plate will produce a very much sharper impression than that before cleaning, and philatelists distinguish between these states.

Cliche   electrotype or stereo used in the letterpress process.

Climax Dater   rubber datestamp used at minor post offices in the UK from 1885 to 1935. Coloured inks were used till 1911, adding to the appeal of these elusive postmarks.

Co-extensive Lines   thick lines in the sheet margins with breaks corresponding with the perforation rows.

Coffee-house Mail   in the 18th century coffee-houses were often used as unofficial post offices whither mail was addressed for collection.

Cogwheel Cancel   circular numeral obliterator with distinctive projections. This type was used in Bavaria (1850–69).

Coil pair from Sweden

Coil a stamp issued in a continuous roll either for sale through slot machines or for use in office dispensing machines. Often differs from sheet stamps by being imperforate on two opposite sides, or having a sideways watermark.

Coil Join pair of coil stamps linked by a narrow strip of marginal paper, the coil being made up of rows from sheets.

Coil Leader strip of paper at the beginning of a coil of stamps, fed into the machine, either perforated but blank, or having printed matter in the colour of the stamp.

Coin Date French term meaning "dated corner", denoting the dates printed in the lower corners of French sheets.

Collateral Material drawings, photographs, press-cuttings and ephemera mounted on the album page to expand the information on or background to the stamps and covers.

College Stamp stamp issued by the Oxford and Cambridge colleges (1871–86) for inter-collegiate messenger services.

Collotype photographic printing process widely used at the turn of the century in book illustration but confined to the Poltava zemstvo stamp of 1912 and the souvenir sheet for the 1950 London International Stamp Exhibition.

Colour Changeling a stamp which has changed colour due to chemical or climatic action.

Colour Fake a stamp whose colour has been deliberately altered by chemical action to convert a common to a rare shade.

Colour Proof impression of a stamp in the approved colour, made before general production.

Colour Trial proof taken of a stamp in a wide range of colours to assist the postal authority in selecting the most suitable colour.

Coloured Paper any paper other than white. It may be coloured right through or tinted on the front with a white back.

Coloured Postmark it is an international convention that black ink should be used for cancelling stamps, and red ink for bulk postings prepaid in cash or meter marks. Any exception to these rules is regarded as a coloured postmark and ranges from the use of green or blue in British slogans of the 1990s to the two- or three-coloured handstamps fashionable in Czechoslovakia in the 1930s.

Comb Perforation perforation in which the pins are arranged in a comb pattern, so that the top and sides of a stamp are perforated at a single blow. This produces perforations with clean intersecting holes and regular corners. See *Line Perforation*.

Combination Cover cover bearing the stamps of more than one postal authority, the stamps of each prepaying the postage for a different part of the journey. See also *Mixed Franking*.

Combined Stamp circular datestamp combining an obliterating element (thick arcs or bars at the sides) with the name and date of posting.

Commatology pseudo-scientific term devised in the USA to signify the study of postmarks.

Commemorative Label adhesive label intended to mark an anniversary or celebrate some event. First used about 1845, they peaked around the turn of the century, but have since been largely superseded by Commemorative Stamps.

Commemorative Stamp a postage stamp which marks an anniversary or current event. The USA pioneered commemorative stamped stationery (1876), while German local posts issued the first adhesives (1887). The first government issue appeared in New South Wales in 1888.

Commemorative Postmark mark associated with a special event, for which a temporary post office is provided. The earliest instance appears to have been the Exposition Universelle at Paris (1855), followed by the International Exhibition in London (1862). Many modern marks are merely Special Event Handstamps (qv) without postal facilities, other than the provision of a special posting box or reposting facility.

Commercial Propaganda stamps designed to promote national products have been widely issued since Costa Rica publicised its coffee industry in 1923. Stamps actually advertising branded goods are relatively scarce, although Canada has had the McDonald's logo on the sheet margin of stamps sponsored by that fast-food chain (1990), the Isle of Man has produced advertising labels as part of a tourist issue (1994) and Britain has issued 25p stamps in a miniature sheet with the logo of Boot's (1994).

Commonwealth Reply Coupon reply coupon designed for use in Britain and Commonwelth countries.

Compartment Line irregular line in margins of sheets produced by the letterpress process, notably Australia (1914–23) and New Zealand (1909–26).

Composite Sheet sheet in which the picture is spread across the entire sheet, so that each stamp bears only a part of the motif.

Composite Stamps stamps in which the motif is spread over two or more adjoining stamps.

Compound Envelope postal stationery envelope bearing more than one embossed or impressed stamp.

Compound of Perforation and Roulette stamps perforated horizontally and rouletted vertically, or vice versa.

Compound Perforation perforation involving two or more different gauges, e.g. British and Irish stamps perf 15 x 14.

Compound Roulette pierced separation in which the gauge or pattern is not the same on all four sides, e.g. Yugoslav "Chainbreakers" (1919) with zigzag and straight-line roulette.

Compulsory Postage Due Label postage due label affixed to mail which has failed to use compulsory tax stamps. Special labels have been issued by Portugal, Roumania and Yugoslavia.

Compulsory Registration the registration of packets detected in transit as containing coins or other valuables. Such packets are then registered and the fee, plus a fine, is charged to the recipient on delivery. Special handstamps inscribed COIN REGISTERED and warning labels are known in this connection.

Compulsory Tax Stamps charity stamps whose use is compulsory, either at certain times of year or for more extended periods. Pioneered by Portugal which issued several different types (1911–28), they have been widely used since then. The most notable example is the Refugee Fund stamps of Cyprus from 1974 to date, differing since 1977 only in the date printed at the foot.

Computation of Official Postage adhesive stamps issued by Germany for Prussia (1903) and Baden (1905) and by Thailand (1963–64) and quasi-meter marks in Britain (1981–82) to determine the volume of mail being treated as official correspondence.

Computer-designed Stamp stamps known to have been generated by computer include a set of five from the Netherlands (1970) and the Brazilian definitive of 1985. It is suspected that many stamps of the 1990s have been originated by computer, but the technology is now so sophisticated that this aid to artistry is more difficult to detect.

Computer-printed Label label arising as a computer print-out, found on postage paid impressions (qv) from Britain, and explanatory or redirectional labels in the USA and Britain.

Computer Stamp stamp produced by micro-processor machines which weigh parcels and packets and calculate the postage, denoted by a gummed label giving the amount as well as the date and place of posting. Such stamps were pioneered in South Africa and Australia and have spread to Canada, Hong Kong, Singapore, New Zealand, USA and Zimbabwe. See also *Counter Printed Stamp.*

Concentration Camp Mail covers and cards from the Nazi concentration camps, distinguished by special postmarks, cachets, censor marks and even stamps, e.g. the Theresienstadt parcel stamp (1943) and the Lodz ghetto stamps. Several camps were later used for displaced persons and organised their own mail services complete with stamps. See also *Internee Mail* and *Prisoner of War Mail.*

Concessionary Parcel Stamp stamps issued by Italy since 1953 for use by companies operating local parcel delivery services. Inscribed *Trasporto Pacchi in Concessione,* they denote the fee paid to the government for permission to operate services. Germany (1942–44) and the USA (1968) issued stamps denoting concessionary rates for servicemen's parcels.

Concessionary Postage Label label without postal validity as such, but denoting a tax on letters which the Italian Post Office has permitted private companies to deliver since 1928. See *Authorised Delivery.*

Condensed Type lettering in a narrower style than normal, often used for long inscriptions in registration labels.

Condition in unused stamps, full gum with no trace of a mout, in both mint and used stamps well-centred margins, no blunt or pulled perforations, no surface rubbing or thinning on the back, no tears, and a light cancellation.

Condominium joint administration of a territory by two or more powers. Andorra, under joint French and Spanish rule, has separate stamps for each post office; but the New Hebrides, under Anglo-French rule, had identical stamps, inscribed in English and French respectively.

Confetti Flaw small circular albino patch in the design of a stamp, caused by a piece of paper (usually a perforation cut-out) adhering to the surface during printing, and later falling off.

Consular Mail mail transmitted from consulates acting as postal agencies, often using distinctive cancellations. Stamps inscribed B.C.M. were used on British Consular Mail from Madagascar (1884–87).

Continuous Line   otherwise known as a Jubilee Line (qv), it appears as a thick line running round the sheet margins of British stamps. See also *Co-extensive Line*.

Continuous Overprint   multiple, over-all overprint appearing without regard to position on each stamp, e.g. Spanish republic (1931) and the posthorns of the Anglo-American zone of Germany (1948).

Control Letter   letter in the sheet margin of British stamps (1881–1947) for accountancy purposes.

Control Mark   mark applied by firms to stamps to prevent pilferage, by overprint, underprint or perforation (qqv). See also *Perfin*.

Control Number   number engraved in the sheet margins of stamps from Canada and the USA as a means of controlling the use of plates released from the vaults for printing.

Control Overprint   overprint on stamps as a precaution in cases of theft. Stamps from legitimate stocks are then overprinted in some way to distinguish them from those which have been stolen.

Copperplate Engraving   another name for intaglio (qv).

Cork Cancel   obliterator crudely carved from a bottle cork.

Corner Block   four or more stamps from the corner of the sheet, showing the plate number, traffic lights or other marginal markings.

Corner Card   inscription in the top left-hand corner of envelopes and postcards, mainly in Canada and the USA, and often including pictorial advertising.

Cottonreels   nickname for the first stamps of British Guiana, on account of their circular shape.

Counter Coil Pair   pair of stamps from dispensing machines used by counter clerks in New Zealand, divided by a gutter bearing a numeral.

Counter Printed Stamp   stamp with a pictorial motif, but details of value and office of posting inserted at the point of sale. Pioneered by Australia (1993).

Counterfeit   a forgery intended to defraud the post office.

Counterfoil   part of a stamp or label retained by the sender as a receipt.

Coupon   label attached to a stamp, often with a pictorial motif. See also *Tab*.

Coupon Paper   grey granite paper (qv) used for wartime food coupons in Germany but subsequently utilised for stamps of Latvia (1919).

Courier Service   express service operated by government departments for official and forces' mail. Distinctive stamps for this purpose were produced by the German Democratic Republic.

Cover   envelope or wrapper for letters and packets.

Cowries   nickname for the first stamps of Uganda (1895) whose values were expressed in cowrie shells.

Cracked Plate   printing plate showing cracks caused by uneven pressure, resulting in stamps with white or coloured lines interrupting the design.

Crash Cover   cover salvaged from the wreckage of crashed trains or aircraft, often bearing marks of fire or damage and labelled or handstamped with an explanation.

Creased Transfer   paper transfer in the lithographic process, creased when laid down for printing and resulting in compression or distortion of the impression.

Cross   common heraldic symbol. Anonymous labels bearing a white cross on a red ground were used for postage due in Switzerland (1883–1924). Many stamps were overprinted during World War I with a red cross to raise funds for the Red Cross.

Cross Hatching   crossed lines incised in intaglio to create toned or shaded areas.

Cross Roulette   form of separation known also as *perce en croix*, used in Tasmania and Madeira.

Crowned Circle   postmark, usually struck in red, containing the words PAID AT followed by the name of a British colony or overseas postal agency, used in the 19th century before the advent of adhesive stamps in these countries.

CTO   abbreviation for Cancelled to order (qv).

Cubierta   Spanish for "covered", denoting large labels affixed to insured letters in Colombia (1865–1909).

Culler Facer Canceller   automatic machine used in British sorting offices for segregating different classes of mail, facing them right way up and cancelling them. More advanced than the ALF and FCT machines (qqv). Postmarks often include the letters CFC and a numeral.

Curly Head   nickname for the Spanish colonial keytype stamps portraying King Alfonso as a boy.

Currency Stamp   postage or fiscal stamp pressed into service as small change during economic crises and wartime. Such stamps were either encased (qv) or affixed to pasteboard, often coin-shaped. See also *Fractional Currency*.

Current Number   number inserted by De La Rue on the plate margins of British and colonial stamps, denoting the order in which the plates were manufactured.

Customs Inspection   the examination of packets by

customs officials. Distinctive labels and handstamps are used, both to indicate that examination has taken place, and to raise charges on dutiable items. See *Franc de Droits*.

Cut Cancellation   a cancelling device which cuts through stamps and postal stationery to prevent re-use.

Cut-out   postal stationery stamp cut from the original card or envelope and affixed by gum to another packet.

Cut Square   imperforate stamp with a circular, oval or polygonal outline, cut to form a rectangle.

Cut to Shape   imperforate stamp, as above, but cut close to the design.

Cylinder Number   number identifying the cylinder from which a photogravure stamp is printed. On British stamps these numbers generally appear in the lower left-hand margin of the sheet.

Cyrillic Alphabet   system of letters derived by St Cyril from the Greek alphabet and used in Russia, Bulgaria, Yugoslavia an other Slav countries.

Damaged Mail   items damaged in the post range from crash and wreck covers (qqv) to those which have suffered careless handling in cancelling machines, or have been burned in pillar-box fires caused by vandals. Various explanatory and sealing labels as well as handstruck cachets are used.

Dandy Roll   wire-gauze roller which impresses paper pulp with its texture. The brass or wire bits attached to the dandy roll give paper its watermark (qv).

Datapost   an express service of the British post office, introduced in 1971 and guaranteeing next-day delivery anywhere in the UK.

Date Cut   vertical cuts in the Jubilee lines (qv) below stamps printed at Somerset House (1911–12) providing a kind of code to the sequence of manufacture.

Dated Corner   see *Coin Date*.

Dated Stamp   stamp which incorporates a date in its design. Since 1987 the Universal Postal Union requires all commemorative or special issues to include a date, often in the margin.

Datestamp   instrument for applying a dated postmark to mail and postal documents.

Dead Country   collectors' term for a country which no longer exists politically, and therefore no longer issues distinctive stamps.

Dead Letter   postal term for a packet which cannot be delivered and is therefore returned to the sender.

Death Masks   nickname for the Serbian stamps (1904) celebrating the centenary of the Karageorgevich dynasty. When viewed upside down they allegedly depict the death mask of King Alexander, murdered the previous year.

Decoupage   French term for the adjustment of the pressure on printing plates by means of cut-outs or built-up overlays. Misalignment produced very light or very dark portions in the impressions.

Dedication Cover   souvenir marking the inauguration of post offices, airports and similar installations.

Deep Etching   additional etching in photo-engraving to emphasise lines, and in long production runs to compensate for wear.

Deep Etch Offset   form of lithography (qv) using plates on which the printing areas are etched below the surface to compensate for wear, or prevent blurring on rough paper.

Deferential Cancellation   obliteration in such a manner that the portrait on the stamp is not defaced.

Definitive Stamp   a stamp forming part of the permanent series.

Delacryl   form of lithography patented by De La Rue and used for stamp production in the 1960s.

Delayed Mail   mail subject to delay in transit and thus denoted by means of explanatory labels and handstamps.

Deliberate Error   error perpetrated by a postal administration to defeat philatelic speculation. Greece (1937) and the USA (1962) resorted to this practice when stamps with an inverted overprint or background respectively were discovered.

Delivery Tax Stamps   postage due labels issued by Spain (1931), later authorised for use as postage stamps.

Demonetised   withdrawn from use and no longer valid for postage, sometimes overprinted to note this fact.

Denomination   the face value expressed on a stamp.

Departmental Stamp   stamp printed (USA, 1873–79) or overprinted (South Australia 1868–74, UK 1882–1904 and Argentina 1913–38) specifically for the use of a government department. See also *Life Insurance Stamp*.

Diamond Roulette   also known as *perce en losanges*, a form of separation producing diamond shaped holes.

Dickinson Paper   paper with a silk thread enmeshed, devised by John Dickinson and used for British postal stationery (1841) and embossed stamps (1847–48).

Die original piece of metal on which a stamp design is first engraved, and from which reproductions are made to form the printing unit.

Die-cutting process for cutting paper by means of variously shaped dies under great pressure. Originally applied to envelopes and Victorian scraps, it has been more recently used to simulate perforations in many self-adhesive stamps (qv).

Die Proof impression taken on special paper or card from the die.

Die-stamping alternative term for embossing (qv).

Diplomatic Mail distinctive stationery, labels and handstamps applied to mail transmitted by diplomatic bag.

Directional Mark or Directory Mark (USA) a cachet applied to undeliverable mail to denote its disposal, usually by return to sender.

Discount Postage stamps printed, underprinted or overprinted to indicate sale at a discount off face value. Overprinted stamps have been issued by Turkey and Belgium. British stamps sold at a discount are denoted by a D or star printed on the back, while Sweden has issued special stamps in booklets since 1979.

Disinfected Mail mail from plague-infested countries fumigated with smoke, disinfected with vinegar or slit open to release the pestilential air, and usually handstamped with an explanatory cachet, or the postmark of a lazaret or quarantine station.

District Overprints security overprints on stamps of Mexico (1856–83). In addition to the names of every state from Aguascalientes to Zacatecas, stamps were usually overprinted with the number of the sub-district. German stamps issued in the Soviet zone of occupation were overprinted with district names and numbers in 1948 at the time of the currency reform, pending the release of stamps overprinted for general use throughout the zone.

Dockwra Marks handstamps (mostly triangular) used in connection with the London Penny Post operated by William Dockwra (1680–82) and later taken over by the Post Office.

Doctor Blade flexible steel knife which removes surplus ink from the printing cylinder in rotary presses. Faulty operation causes the blade to jump, leaving a flaw in the form of a colourless line flanked by lines of colour.

Dog Team Mail mail transmitted in the Yukon and Alaska by dog teams during the winter months, often denoted by pictorial cachets.

Domestic Mail mail posted and delivered within the same country.

Dominical Label tab (qv) attached to Belgian stamps (1894–1914) or printed as a separate label in Holland, requesting the post office not to deliver mail on a Sunday.

Double Geneva nickname for the cantonal stamps of Geneva (1843) on account of the fact that the 5c stamps (for local mail) were printed in pairs with an inscription across the top signifying the cantonal rate of 10c. The stamps were actually sold for 8c and therefore rank as the world's first discount stamps (qv).

Double Impression a stamp in which all or, more usually, part of the design is doubled owing to a slight shift in the paper during printing.

Double Letter letter prior to 1840 consisting of two sheets of paper and therefore charged double postage. As the wrapper counted as a separate sheet envelopes were rarely used until after the introduction of Uniform Penny Postage.

Double-lined Letter outline letter mainly found in paper-maker's watermarks, but also favoured by Royal Mail, e.g. in the underprint on discount stamps.

Double Paper security paper patented in the USA and used in the production of some stamps of the 1873 series. It consisted of two thin sheets bonded together. Any attempt to clean off the cancellation would destroy the surface.

Double Print stamp printed twice. Swedish 20 ore stamps (1876) were originally printed in very pale orange which faded so badly that sheets were recalled and printed a second time in bright vermilion. On sheets which were inaccurately lined up both impressions are visible.

Double Stamp Post Office term for the handstamps combining a dater and an obliterator. Often, though erroneously, called a Duplex (qv) by collectors.

Downey Head nickname for the British halfpenny and penny stamps of 1911–13 reproducing a portrait of King George V from a photograph by W. and D. Downey.

Drop Letter a packet delivered to an address in the same postal delivery area as the office in which it was posted. In some countries (notably the USA) such letters were transmitted at special low rates of postage.

Dropped Letter a letter in a typeset inscription or overprint which has dropped out of alignment.

Dry Print a stamp with a weak or thin impression due to the paper being too dry for the intaglio process.

Dumb Cancellation obliteration bearing no indication of the office of origin. Many of the earliest cancellations, such as the Maltese Cross (qv), come into this category. In more recent times such devices as Black-out Cancels (qv) have been used in wartime for security reasons.

Duplex Cancellation   postmark from an implement in which the dater and obliterator are integrated and not separate elements as in double stamps (qv).

Duplex Paper   paper having different colours on either side of the sheet.

Duty Plate   the plate which prints the duty (i.e. the value) in stamps printed at two operations, the portrait being printed by the Head Plate (qv).

Early Impression   stamps from the beginning of the printing run, with sharp lines and deep colours.

Economy Gum   type of gum used in Germany immediately after World War II in which the adhesive was applied in a pattern of blobs—sufficient for the stamps to stick but cutting the amount of gum required by half. Known as *Spargummi*.

Electric Eye Mark   marginal mark on sheets of stamps to ensure perfect perforation, alignment being controlled by a device known as an electric eye which scans the marks.

Electrotype   cliche (qv) for letterpress printing, produced by pressing the die into wax or soft lead on which a shell of copper is deposited by electrolysis The thin copper shell is then backed with lead.

Elliptical Perforation   elongated, elliptical hole in a line of normal perforations, found on British National Insurance stamps (since 1966), extended to Savings stamps (1968–73), Telephone and television stamps, and then postage stamps in 1993. Since then this security device has spread to the stamps of the Netherlands and other countries.

Embossing   stamping in relief to produce a raised impression, usually colourless, with a coloured surround. Mainly used for postal stationery but also used for stamps, notably early Portugal, German states and the Gambia.

En Epargne   French for "in relief", describing the printing plate used in letterpress (qv) printing.

Enamelled Paper   highly glazed paper coated with zinc white and glue producing a very glossy surface, used for stamps of Portugal and colonies.

Encased Postage Stamp   stamp inserted in a small mica-faced metal disc and used in lieu of small change. First used during the American Civil War but also in France, Germany and other European countries at the end of World War I.

Engine-turning   intricate pattern of lines engraved by the rose engine on dies used for banknotes, share certificates and stamps printed by intaglio. Also known as *guilloche.*

Engraver's Proof   proof taken from the die (qv) by the engraver to check the progress of his work. Such proofs may be found in sets showing progressive development of the design.

Entire   envelope, card or wrapper in complete condition.

Entire Letter   a complete folded letter sheet with the letter inside and outer wrapper intact.

Envelope   wrapper or cover for letters, with the four corners of the sheet folded across the back. Ready-cut and folded envelopes developed in the 1840s.

Epreuve de Luxe   French term for "luxury proof" signifying limited editions of die proofs produced by the government printing works originally for presentation purposes but nowadays for sale to collectors.

Erasure   the removal of part of the design or inscription in a stamp, overprint or postmark to modify it. Stamps of Corrientes an Australia's first postage due labels are good examples. The countries which emerged from the Habsburg Empire in 1918 often erased the German placename from bilingual postmarks.

Erinnophily   pseudo-scientific term (from German *Erinnerung,* commemoration, and Greek *philos,* love) denoting the collecting and study of commemorative labels (qv).

Error   a stamp which has something wrong in its design, either a misspelling in the inscription, or some detail in the picture. Technical errors include the inadvertent use of the wrong paper, watermark or colour, the inversion of part of the design or the overprint, the omission or doubling of the overprint, the entire or partial omission of the perforation, and the inversion or reversal of the watermark.

Esparto Paper   paper made from esparto grass, used to print New Zealand stamps.

Essay   design for a stamp which has either been rejected or only adopted eventually after substantial modification and thus differing in some respect from the adopted design.

Etiquette   French for "sticker" and thus implying any kind of label, although usually confined to airmail labels.

Europa Stamps   stamps issued since 1956 with the word EUROPA on them. Originally confined to the European Coal and Steel Community, they were taken over by the European Conference of Posts and Telecommunications (CEPT) in 1960. Uniform designs were used till 1974 but common themes are now employed.

Examiner's Label   label used to reseal packets subject to inspection by customs or censors.

Examiner's Mark   mark, often cryptic in appearance, applied to letters and packets which have been checked by postal inspectors in transit.

Exchange Club   group formed specifically for the exchange of stamps among its members, approval books (qv) being circulated in parcels known as exchange packets.

Exchange Mark   a mark applied in Canada or the USA on mail going between these countries. Such accountancy marks (qv) date from 1792 and continued until 1874, taking note of the difference in the value of Canadian and American currency.

Exhibition Label   non-postal label produced in connection with an exhibition or fair. First used in 1845, they were very popular prior to the advent of commemorative stamps and even today have a certain vogue.

Exhibition Postmark   postmark used at a temporary post office attached to an exhibition. The earliest examples date from 1855 (Exposition Universelle, Paris). Particularly popular are the postmarks in connection with philatelic exhibitions.

Exiled Government Post   postal service operated by various European governments forced into exile as a result of the occupation of their country during both world wars. Should not be confused with bogus (qv) stamps of "free" Albania, Croatia, Roumania, Moluccas and Nagaland which performed no postal function.

Expedition Stamp   stamp provided for use by scientific, military or exploration expeditions. First supplied by New Zealand (1908 and 1911) for the expeditions to King Edward VII Land and Victoria Land, led by Shackleton and Scott respectively.

Experimental Duplex   trial handstamps in the UK (1853–60) with dater and obliterator fully integrated. Many distinctive designs were used before a uniform pattern emerged.

Experimental Roulette   trial separation devised by Henry Archer (1847–48) prior to the invention of perforation (qv).

Explanatory Label   label used by postal administrations to explain the reason for non-delivery or delay in transit.

Explanatory Mark   postal marking or cachet giving reasons for delay, damage, surcharge or non-delivery of mail.

Exploded Booklet   stamp booklet dismantled in order to display the individual panes, interleaves and covers. Even the staples are retained, so that the booklet may be reconstituted if need be.

Express Airmail   special stamps for air express services, issued by Canada, Colombia, Italy and the USA.

Express Label   adhesive label, usually printed in deep red, indicating express mail. More recently international labels for the Express Mail Service (EMS) are printed in blue and orange.

Express Newspaper and Printed Matter Post   service offered by prewar Czechoslovakia which issued distinctive stamps for the purpose.

Express Parcel   stamps inscribed for this purpose were issued by the Vatican in 1931.

Express Stamp   stamp designed specifically for express mail, notably in Canada, China, Italy, Mauritius, Mexico, Russia, Spain and the USA.

F   a letter engraved on the plate to indicate that it has been chemically hardened and ready for use. Usually trimmed off the margin of printed sheets but occasionally found alongside the plate number (qv) on American stamps.

Facer Canceller Table   equipment designed for the automatic sorting and stamping of mail. Machine cancellations often include the initials FCT and a numeral.

Facsimile   an imitation of a genuine stamp but usually printed on different paper and usually marked in some way to denote it status. Thus distinct from counterfeits and forgeries (qqv) designed to deceive postal authorities and stamp collectors.

Faidherbe   a French colonial keytype, so-called from the portrait of Louis L .C. Faidherbe, general and colonial administrator.

Fake   a genuine stamp which has been altered or repaired to transform it into a much more valuable stamp—by removing the postmark, by regumming the back, by changing the colour chemically or by reperforating it.

Fancy Type   printer's type in a decorative style, used in overprint and typeset stamps (qqv).

Farley's Follies   US stamps (1934–37) issued imperforate on the authority of Postmaster General James Farley, thus named by collectors whose protests eventually forced the USPO to make such printings freely available to the philatelic market.

Fastpost   New Zealand service offering accelerated domestic overnight delivery and overseas airmail for an additional fee.

Field Post   postal service for troops serving in wars, campaigns and even peacetime manoeuvres, using distinctive postmarks and even stamps.

First Day Cover   a souvenir cover bearing stamps postmarked on the first day of issue.

First Day Postmark   special postmark applied to stamps on the first day of issue.

First Flight   flight marking the inauguration of a mail route, usually marked by souvenir covers, cachets, postmarks and labels, and sometimes also by special stamps.

Fiscal Stamp   stamp intended for revenue purposes, as opposed to those designed for postal or telegraphic use. See *Postal Fiscal*.

Fixed Values   applied to meters and automatic stamp machines offering a limited range of values.

Flag Cancel   machine cancellation originating in the USA (1894) with an obliterator showing the Stars and Stripes. The idea spread to Canada, France, Germany, Italy and New Zealand and from it arose the seven wavy lines in Universal cancelling machines.

Flamme Illustrée   French term signifying "pictorial slogan", widely used for tourist publicity postmarks since 1950.

Flatbed Printing   originally all stamps were printed on flatbed presses, but the distinction became important when rotary high-speed presses were introduced. In Britain's Seahorse high values, for example, one can distinguish the flatbed printings (22mm high) of 1913–15, from the later stamps (22.75 or 23mm high), printed on rotary presses using curved plates.

Flat Plate   plate designed for use in a flatbed press.

Flaw   accidental blemish on a stamp, arising in the course of production. Such blemishes, if constant, are termed varieties (qv).

Floating Safe Mail   mail transmitted in special fire-proof safes aboard ship, designed to float to the surface should the ship sink. The Netherlands and Dutch East Indies issued Marine Insurance stamps (qv) for this purpose.

Flown Cover   cover whose postmark, stamps, cachet or inscription indicate that it has been transmitted by airmail.

Fluorescence   the emission of electromagnetic radiation, which may be caused by constituents of the printing ink, but more usually by optical brightening agents in the paper. In North America such papers are known as hi-brite, in Britain FCP (fluorescent coated paper).

Foil Stamp   stamp printed on paper laminated with metal foil, pioneered by Hungary in 1955.

Foreign Mail Stamp   stamp issued specifically to prepay the postage on mail going overseas, e.g. Turkey (1901) and Haiti (1906–19). See also *Porte de Mar*.

Forerunner   stamp or label used provisionally pending the introduction of authorised stamps of a new country. Many British colonies used British stamps prior to c. 1860 when they adopted their own stamps (see *Used Abroad*). Stamps of Sarawak used in Brunei before 1907 and NZ stamps used in Pitcairn before 1940 are classed as forerunners. JNF and other fund-raising labels, temporarily used as stamps during the interim between the withdrawal of the British mandate and the emergence of Israel, also qualify.

The infamous Stock Exchange forgery.

Forgery   the deliberate imitation of a stamp to deceive. Those intended to defraud the postal authorities are classed as counterfeits (qv) but sometimes called postal forgeries.

Format   the shape or layout (horizontal or vertical) of a stamp.

Forme   term in letterpress or typeset printing (qqv) for the cliches (qv) locked into a frame ready for printing.

Forwarding Agent   merchant or businessman, part of whose operations was a service to clients forwarding goods and merchandise from one seaport to another, or from a port to an inland town. This service included the handling of mail, and many distinctive cachets (qv) have been recorded.

Fractional Currency   small notes circulating in place of coinage in the USA during and after the Civil War. They reproduced postage stamps of the equivalent face value.

Fractional Stamp   a stamp cut into two, three, four, six or even eight, for use as a stamp of proportional value. See also *Bisect*.

Frakturschrift   style of printing used in Germany till about 1940, common in overprints and stamp inscriptions, sometimes known loosely as Gothic or Teutonic script.

Frama Label   popular, if inaccurate, name for the automatic machine stamps (qv) produced by the Frama Company of Switzerland. See also *Royal Mail Postage Label*.

Frame   the part of the stamp which encloses the portrait, vignette or other motif.

Franc de Droits   French for "Free of Dues", inscribed on certain customs labels (qv) to indicate that the sender has paid the duty prior to posting, and thus relieving the addressee of any further charges.

Franchise Stamp   sometimes called a private stamp, but in fact a stamp supplied for the use of a particular individual or organisation granted the privilege of free or reduced-charge postage, notably in Spain and Portugal. See also *Military Franchise Stamps*.

Frank   a mark or handstruck postage stamp applied to mail to denote transmission without charge to sender or recipient.

Freak   any kind of abnormal stamp caused by transient accident in production, e.g. paper folds and creases, faulty perforation, inadequate inking, misalignment of colours and (on postal stationery) misplacement of impressed or embossed stamps.

Free Front   cut-out front of an entire letter (qv) showing the name and address, together with the endorsement of the sender, date of posting and signature entitling the sender to frank (qv) the letter. Collecting free fronts was a popular pastime of autograph hunters in the 19th century, but nowadays these collections are a fruitful source of handstruck franks.

Free Mail   correspondence transmitted free of charge. Apart from mail sent under the franking privilege, it includes mail to and from troops on active service, from prisoners of war (qv) and disaster areas, and the return to sender of undeliverable letters and packets.

Fresh Entry   the substitution of a new entry on an engraved plate for an unsatisfactory or defective original, often resulting in a partial double impression.

Fugitive Ink   ink containing chemicals or aqueous solvents which will fade, change colour or disappear if any attempt is made to wash or clean off the postmark or pen cancellation.

German Type   see *Frakturschrift*.

Glazed Paper   highly calendered paper without any special coating such as is found in enamelled paper (qv) with which it is sometimes confused.

Glider Mail   mail carried by glider or sailplane, first attempted in Germany, 1923. Motor-assisted gliders were used to carry mail from Lympne to Hastingleigh, England later in the same year. Special stamps were issued by Cuba (1935) for mail carried by strings of gliders towed by aircraft. Since the 1970s mail has often been carried by hang-glider.

Goat's Eyes   nickname for the second series of Brazil (1844–46).

Goldbeater's Skin   a thin, tough, translucent, resin-impregnated paper used for the 1886 parcel stamps of Germany. They were printed on a collodion surface on the reverse side, the gum being applied over the printing, so that any attempt to remove the cancellation would destroy the surface.

Grand Consommation   trade name for a type of rough, greyish paper used temporarily for printing French stamps during the First World War.

Granite Paper   paper with coloured fibres enmeshed in it.

Graphite Line   vertical black line of Naphthadag (qv) on the back of some British definitives, 1957, associated with early trials of automatic sorting equipment at Southampton.

Gravure   American term for photogravure (qv).

Greetings Label   label affixed to greetings mail, originating in 1904 with Christmas Seals (qv) but now including Easter, New Year and other festivities. In recent years labels have been included in booklets of greetings stamps (qv) or associated with special stationery (Canada).

Greetings Stamp   stamp for use on greetings mail. Such stamps were pioneered by local delivery companies in Germany (1900) and adopted by postal authorities in the 1930s. See also *Christmas Stamp*.

Greetings Stationery   special envelopes, aerogrammes or postcards with pre-printed stamps, intended for seasonal greetings. New Year cards were pioneered by Germany (1900), Christmas aerogrammes by Australia (1957) and general greetings envelopes for birthdays and congratulations by New Zealand (1988).

Grille   a security device in the form of small square dots embossed on some stamps of the USA and Peru, intended to break the paper fibres and enable deeper penetration of the postmark.

Guaranteed Delivery   service introduced by Royal Mail (1993) with distinctive labels and stationery.

Guerrilla Stamp   stamp issued by guerrilla forces. Pioneered by the Black Flag republic in Taiwan (1895) and Aguinaldo's forces in the Philippines (1898).

Guide Arrow   a marginal mark on stamp sheets indicating the centre point of the sheet or pane.

Guide Lines and Dots   fine lines or dots marked on the plate as a guide to the engraver or operator of the transfer roller. Usually these marks are erased after the plate is laid down, but occasionally they remain wholly or partially visible in the unprinted portion of stamps or in the sheet margins.

Guilloché   alternative term for Engine-turning (qv).

Gum   the adhesive material found on the back of stamps. Certain British stamps may be found with gum arabic, PVA or PVAD gum. Some German stamps have horizontal or vertical graining in the gum, distinguished by collectors. See also *Economy Gum, Original Gum* and *Regummed*.

Gum Breaker Bars   lines on the gummed side of stamps, breaking up the pattern of the gum and preventing the stamps from curling.

Gum Device an imitation watermark on the gummed side of stamps (notably from Germany, Czechoslovakia, Liechtenstein and Switzerland).

Gutter the space between stamps occupied by the perforations. An interpane gutter is the space between two panes of stamps, a common feature of British surface-printed stamps and re-introduced in 1973 for commemorative stamps, encouraging the collecting of gutter pairs and blocks.

Hair Lines diagonal white lines crossing the outer corners of stamps printed from the reserve plates made by De la Rue (1863).

Half Lengths stamps of Victoria, Australia 1850 bearing a half-length portrait of Queen Victoria.

Half-tone Process a photo-mechanical method of showing light and shade by dots of varying size and proximity, used for some stamps of Kishengarh, Latvia, Saudi Arabia, Iran and the Netherlands.

Hand-made Paper paper made by hand in moulds, and thus in separate sheets, deckle-edged and often varying in thickness, quality and consistency even within the same sheet.

Hand-painted colour applied by hand to a stamp after printing, notably in the bi-coloured high values of Germany (1900).

Handstamp implement used to stamp or cancel mail by hand, often used loosely to denote handstruck stamps and postmarks.

Handstruck Postage Stamp a mark made by a handstamp direct on to a postal packet to denote the prepayment of postage. Such stamps were pioneered by William Dockwra (qv) in 1680–82 and were widely used even after the advent of adhesive stamps in 1840. In this category may also be included adhesive stamps produced by handstamping pieces of paper to be affixed to packets, e.g. Bermuda postmasters' stamps (1848–61), stamps of Bhor and Indore, and many provisional issues from Russia and the Ukraine since 1991.

Harrow Perforation a method of perforating entire sheets at a single stroke, the pins being arranged in a criss-cross pattern.

Hawid Strip clear plastic strip with adhesive backing, used to hold mint stamps on the album page without actually sticking a hinge or mount (qqv) to the back of the stamp.

Health Stamp charity stamp (from New Zealand and Fiji) raising funds for children's sanatoria and holiday camps.

Helecon zinc sulphide compound in the printing ink or paper of Australian stamps to facilitate electronic sorting, segregating and cancelling of mail.

Helicopter Mail mail carried by rotary wing aircraft, pioneered by England (1934) and widely used in more recent years for feeder airmail services. Distinctive labels, cachets and stationery have been provided in this connection.

Heliogravure French term for Photogravure (qv).

Hidden Date minuscule date inscribed in some part of the design in most Canadian stamps since 1935.

High Value Packet parcel of banknotes or high-security documents transmitted by the British Post Office on behalf of the clearing banks (1930–73) and distinguished by red labels inscribed HVP

Highway Post Office postal service in rural areas of the USA since 1941 using postmarks inscribed HPO. Similar services now operate in many other countries.

Hinge thin, transparent gummed slip used for affixing stamps to the album page, alternatively known as a mount.

Holed stamp which has been pierced or punched with a hole or holes, a common form of telegraphic cancellation in Spain. See also *Perfin*.

Hologram a device creating a three-dimensional effect in different colours when angled to the light. Pioneered by Austria on a stamp of 1988 and since used philatelically by Finland, New Zealand, Canada, the Isle of Man and Tonga, and on postal stationery of the USA.

Honour Envelope envelope used by British forces in World War II, bearing a double-lined green cross and an inscription, signed by the sender, stating "I verify on my honour" that the contents contain nothing but personal matters. Such active service envelopes were not censored at unit or regimental level but could be examined by the base censor.

Hooded Datestamp handstamp in which part of the inscription appears in a concentric semi-circle above the main design, used for registered, late fee and royal household mail in Britain.

Hotel Post service operated to and from hotels located in remote areas, notably the Swiss Alps and the Carpathian districts of Hungary and Roumania where many hotels even provided their own distinctive stamps. Many other hotels have, or had, their own post offices whose marks are much sought after.

HVP—see *High Value Packet*.

Hyphen Perforation a form of separation in which the paper is cut out in long narrow strips instead of round holes. Often confused with rouletting (qv) but differing in that the paper is actually cut out instead of merely pierced.

Hyphenated inscription in which compound words or names are joined by a hyphen, e.g. SIX-PENCE on British stamps (1865) and SUID-AFRIKA on South African stamps, distinguishing them from similar but anhyphenate (qv) stamps.

Ident code letter or number printed during the automatic handling of mail and identifying the sorter.

Imitation Perforation simulated denticulation surrounding stamps and labels. In printed form this appears on stamps of Sirmoor (1891), Djibouti (1894–1902) and Obock (1893–94). In recent years it also occurs die-cut on self-adhesive stamps which are actually imperforate.

Imitation Stamp stamp produced officially in imitation of an obsolete original, usually to complete a series for presentation purposes.

Imperforate a stamp having no perforations or roulette (qv).

Imperforate Between two or more stamps normally perforated, but lacking perforations between them.

Imperial Reply Coupon form of international reply coupon (qv) intended for use within the British Empire.

Impressed Watermark an imitation watermark impressed by die-stamping, notably on Swiss stamps of 1862.

Imprimatur Latin for "let it be printed", denoting stamps from the first sheet off the press normally retained for record purposes.

Imprint name of printer or issuing authority inscribed on the sheet margin.

India Paper thin, soft, absorbent paper normally used for taking proofs (qv).

Indicium that part of a meter mark or postage paid impression (qqv) indicating the value or postal rate.

Inflation Stamps stamps with astronomical face value, notably Austria, Germany and Poland (1923), Greece and Hungary (1945–46), China (1949) and Bolivia (1986).

Ink-jet Slogan an inscription applied by ink-jet printer to covers during automatic sorting and handling. Originally appearing on the reverse and later at the foot of covers, but since 1993 applied as a cancellation in Canada and experimentally also in England. It may be recognised by the dotted pattern in lettering.

Inland Mail Stamp stamps intended for domestic mail. Madagascar (1895) and Liberia (1897) issued stamps thus inscribed.

Inserted by Hand the correction of defective overprints by the addition of letters or accents in manuscript.

Instructional Label label bearing an inscription drawing attention to the nature of a packet requiring special handling, or the class of mail.

Instructional Mark handstruck or machine mark denoting the need for special handling or acceleration of mail.

Insured Mail a facility adopted by the British Post Office in 1878, granting compensation for loss in transit through the post, later adopted by the UPU internationally and denoted by red or pink labels inscribed *Valeur Declarée* (French for "declared value").

Intaglio Italian for "in recess", the proper name for the printing process known to collectors as recess-printing, in which the image is cut into grooves below the surface of the die or plate.

Integral Stamp US pre-cancel over 6c in value, requiring the initials of the poster and the month and year of use to be included in the overprint, either by machine or handstamp.

Intelpost a facsimile transmission service for documents pioneered by the British Post Office for use by the general public.

Interleaf paper inserted between the panes of stamps in booklets, usually bearing advertising matter.

Intermediate Perforation refers to stamps produced by Perkins Bacon in the 1860s, using a perforator which was showing signs of wear. It thus distinguishes stamps from the clean-cut originals and the very rough later states.

International Reply Coupon a slip issued by countries of the UPU enabling people to exchange them at post offices abroad for a stamp of the appropriate airmail rate. It is a method of prepaying return postage without having the trouble of obtaining foreign stamps to do so.

Internee Mail mail from persons interned during time of war. Special franking labels were provided by Switzerland for the use of French troops interned in that country during and after the Franco-German War of 1870–71 and distinctive stamps, stationery and postmarks are associated with Ruhleben (Germany), Bando (Japan) and Knockaloe (Isle of Man) during World War I.

Interpanneau   French for "gutter" (qv). An interpanneau pair consists of two stamps with a blank label between them.

Interpostal Seal   circular adhesive label sealing the flaps of envelopes and denoting transmission by post free of charge. The term is applied specifically to labels of the Khedival Post of Egypt, but similar labels, with scalloped edges, were used in the Netherlands and the German states till about 1905.

Inter-Provincial   a stamp inscribed for use in one territory but valid for postage in another, due to political union. Stamps of the South African colonies (1910–13) and Australian states (1902–13) come into this category, and examples with the postmarks of other colonies are much sought after.

Interrupted Perforation   a method of strengthening strips of stamps used in automatic vending machines, where gaps are created in the line of perforations by removing certain pins. Used by Danzig and Holland.

Invalidated   no longer valid for the prepayment of postage. See also *Demonetised.*

Inverted Centre   a stamp in which the central motif is upside down in relation to the frame.

Inverted Frame   a stamp in which the frame is upside down in relation to the centre. Stamps of Western Australia (1854) and Brazil (1891) come into this category, as the frame is inverted relative to the frame of the adjoining stamp.

Inverted Overprint   a stamp whose overprint is upside down in relation to the stamp itself.

Inverted Watermark   a watermark upside down in relation to the image on the stamp, a frequent occurrence in booklet stamps where the panes are printed alternately upside down.

Irregular Perforation   perforation which is out of alignment or of mixed gauge in one or more lines at the sides of the same stamp.

Italic Lettering   a fount of type in which the letters slope upwards towards the right, used in overprints for decorative effect.

Ivory Head   nickname for British stamps (1841–57). Prussiate of potash added to the printing ink creates a blue effect, darker where the printing is densest and lighter where the lines are wider apart, on the Queen's portrait. Viewed from the back, this shows up as a pale head on a blue background.

Japanese Paper   a soft, fine paper made from mulberry bark, used for the earliest stamps of Japan.

Joined Paper   paper with a slight overlap where two strips of stamps have been joined by the sheet margins, or where two reels of paper have been joined for continuous printing.

Joint Line   a coloured line between coil stamps, where the curved plates on a rotary press meet.

Journal Tax Stamp   stamp prepaying a tax on newspapers and often permitting free transmission by post. Handstruck red stamps on British newspapers up to 1855 served this purpose, while adhesives were issued by Austria and France.

Jubilee Line   a line of printer's rule in the sheet margin, designed to strengthen and protect the printing plate, so-called because it first appeared on British stamps of 1887, the year of Queen Victoria's Golden Jubilee.

Jusqu'a Mark   a mark found on airmail of the interwar period, meaning "as far as" followed by the name of a terminal. Used in connection with mail which was only flown over a part of its journey and completed it by surface transport.

Key Plate   the plate on which the general design of colonial stamps was printed, the name of the colony being inserted by variable duty plates (qv).

Key Type   term for uniform designs used in the stamps of many colonies. Pioneered by De La Rue in 1879 and retained as late as 1956 (Leeward Islands), but later adopted by Spain (1887), Portugal (1897), France (1892–1908) and Germany (1900–16).

Killer   a very heavy obliteration, virtually blotting out the stamp.

Kiloware   used stamps on piece, sold by weight.

Kocher Stamp   Swiss stamp of the Tell Boy type printed on to the advertising labels of A. Kocher et Fils of La Chaux de Fonds (1909).

Label   a slip of paper with an adhesive back and some form of printing on the front. Effectively anything which does not denote the prepayment of postage is classed as a label, including accountancy, postage due and to pay labels which are listed in stamp catalogues.

Labelled Stamp   a stamp with a label attached, either for advertisement or as a decorative feature. See *Dominical Label, Coupon* and *Tab.*

Laid Paper   paper showing a pattern of fine watermarked lines close together, from the parallel wires in the mould.

Last Day Cover   a souvenir posted on the last day of a service (by air, sea or rail) or before the closure of a post office, or the termination of an issue of stamps.

Late Fee Postmark   handstruck mark applied to mail posted after the normal hours of collection, usually in connection with a TPO (qv), denoting the payment of an additional fee.

Late Fee Stamp   a stamp issued in connection with the late posting facility. Victoria issued stamps inscribed TOO LATE (1855–57) while various Latin American countries issued stamps inscribed RETARDO.

Lay-out Line   fine line on steel-engraved plates to assist the lay-out of the impressions. Usually erased before hardening, but occasionally left and therefore appearing on the printed stamps.

Lecocq Press   a French machine which printed Peruvian stamps in a continuous strip.

Letter Card   a form of stationery consisting of a double card folded over, with a perforated and gummed strip for sealing the edges. Pioneered by Belgium (1882).

Letterpress   the correct term for the process often known to philatelists as surface printing or typography, in which the design is in relief.

Letter Sheet   a double sheet of writing paper with an impressed or embossed stamp on the outer side forming the wrapper. Pioneered by the Cavallini (qv), Sardinia (1818) and embossed at Sydney, New South Wales (1838). See also *Mulready*.

Life Insurance Stamp   stamp issued by New Zealand since 1891 for use by the Government Life Insurance Department, and invariably depicting a lighthouse.

Ligature   two or more letters joined or run together, e.g. æ, œ or ff.

Line Block   an illustration block used in letterpress.

Line Engraving   a method of engraving lines in recess for the intaglio process (qv).

Line Perforation   form of perforation in which rows of stamps are punched in single lines, horizontally then vertically. Such stamps can usually be identified by their irregular ragged corners.

Literacy Fund Stamp   compulsory tax stamp (qv) to raise money for a literacy campaign, issued by Haiti and Mexico.

Lithography   a printing process originally involving designs drawn on limestone slabs, though nowadays zinc or even paper plates are used. It works on the principle that oil or grease repels water. See also *Deep Etch Offset* and *Offset Lithography*.

Local Carriage Label   a term devised by the Philatelic Traders' Society in Britain to describe a label which purports to prepay the transmission of parcels and packets from various offshore islands to the mainland.

Local Provisional   a provisional stamp or overprint made under authority of the local postmaster.

Local Stamp   a stamp whose validity is confined to a certain district, town or country, or over certain routes where no government service exists. It includes the issues made by carriers and freight companies.

Loose Letter   a letter from an incoming ship put into the post at the port of arrival. Special postmarks thus inscribed were used at Australian ports.

Lottery Stamp   stamp valid for postage but combining an element of chance. Norway (1964) issued a lottery ticket which had a portion that could be used as a stamp, whereas more recently Japan issues stamps that are serially numbered for a prize draw.

Love Stamp   a stamp intended for use on greetings cards, usually in connection with St Valentine's Day. Such stamps were pioneered by the USA (1973) and adopted by Ireland (1985).

Lozenge Roulette   alternative name for Diamond Roulette.

Luminescence   the light or glow emitted by a stamp when activated by either short- or long-wave ultra-violet light.

Machine Cancellation   obliteration of stamps by mechanical means, dating from 1857 when Pearson Hill invented a machine for this purpose.

Machins   nickname for British definitive stamps since 1967 from the effigy of Queen Elizabeth sculpted by Arnold Machin.

Mailomat   a form of automatic stamp in Canada and the USA using postage meters adapte for use as coin-operated machines. Such marks can be recognised by the letters PO at the sides of the dater.

Makulatur   German term for Printer's Waste (qv).

Maltese Cross   nickname for the quatrefoil obliterator used 1840–44 to cancel the first British stamps.

Mandates   popular term for stamps issued by Belgium, Britain, France and Australia for former enemy colonies assigned to them by mandate of the League of Nations as trust territories.

Manilla Paper   a coarse, strong paper originally made from Manilla hemp, usually pale brown in colour. Used in making envelope and wrappers.

Manuscript Overprint and Surcharge   the alteration of a stamp's purpose, value, place of issue or validity by pen and ink.

Manuscript Postmark   any postal marking made in handwriting, ranging from a simple pen cancel (qv) to the name and date written across the stamp. Not uncommon on British registration receipts and parcel labels (1883–1904) before Climax Daters (qv) were supplied to even the smallest post offices.

Map-Backs   stamps of Latvia (1918) printed on the backs of German war maps and thus showing a portion of the map on the reverse.

Maple Leaves   nickname for the definitive series of

Canada (1897–1902) on account of the maple leaves in the corners.

Margin   the paper bordering the printed image on a stamp, or the selvedge (qv) of the sheet itself.

Marginal Advertising   advertising matter printed on the margins of sheets (Germany, 1923) or booklet panes (France, New Zealand, South Africa).

Marginal Guide Marks   lines, dots, arrows and other marks in the margins of sheets, usually to guide the printer in perforating and trimming the sheet. See also *Black Bar, Electric Rye Mark* and *Arrow Block.*

Marginal Inscription   any printing in the sheet margin: the printer's imprint, the control, current, plate or cylinder numbers, colour dabs, cumulative value of each row, the date of issue or even a descriptive title of the stamp issue.

Marginal Watermark   a watermark designed to appear only in the sheet margin, often the name of the papermaker.

Marine Insurance Stamps   stamps inscribed *Drijvende Brandkast* (floating safe) issued by the Netherlands and East Indies in 1921 in connection with a special service to protect valuable packets from shipwreck.

Maritime Mail   mail brough ashore from warships and other naval vessels and therefore entitled to exemption from postal charges, lower rates of postage or some other form of preferential treatment.

Master Die   the die used to generate secondary dies, punches and transfer rollers in the production of printing plates.

Matched Pair   originally applied to British Penny Blacks and Penny Reds printed from the identical plate but in different colours, but also applicable to any other pair of stamps or postmarks which possess some common factor.

Matrix (plural matrices)   a mould used in the production of stereotypes (qv) for the letterpress process.

Maximum Card   a picture postcard bearing a stamp and postmark relevant to the picture on the card. Conversely many postal administrations now produce postcards reproducing new stamps which can be affixed on the reverse side. See also *PHQ Card.*

Medallions   collectors' term for the stamps of Belgium 1849–50.

Merson   French keytype (1900–27), from the name of the designer, Luc-Olivier Merson.

Metal Currency Stamp   a stamp denominated in silver or gold currency, as opposed to the debased paper money in general use. Peruvian stamps overprinted *Plata* (silver) in 1880 and Greek stamps inscribed or overprinted AM (*Axia Metallike*, metal value) are prime examples.

Metallic Ink   copper, silver and gold inks have been used in overprints and even the production of entire stamps, a practice begun by Switzerland in 1867. See also *Foil Stamp.*

Metered Mail   mail on which the postage is denoted by marks applied by a postage meter. The system was pioneered by Norway, New Zealand and the USA in 1904, and made international in 1922. Meter marks are usually applied in red ink, though other colours are sometimes used, and some machines now have a facility to provide a slogan (qv) in a second colour (green, purple or blue).

Meter Tape   gummed paper, often with a security underprint, used for meter stamps affixed to parcels and packets too bulky to be put through the machine itself.

Military Franchise Stamp   a stamp allowing troops on active service to send mail free of postage, or at a reduced rate, first used by Brazil during the war against Paraguay (1865–70) and widely used ever since.

Military Posts   services organised for the use of armed forces on campaign and manoeuvres. Such services, with distinctive postmarks, stamps and labels, date from the Napoleonic Wars and continue to this day.

Millesime   a number denoting the final digit of the year of printing, found in the interpane gutters of many French and colonial stamps.

Miniature Sheet   a small sheet containing a single stamp, pair, block or set of stamps, with wide, inscribed and decorative margins, pioneered by Luxembourg (1923). Sometimes the stamps in miniature sheets differ from those in normal sheets, either in perforation (or the lack of it) or colour, or face value. See also *Sheetlet* and *Souvenir Sheet.*

Mint   a stamp in its original state, unused and with full gum if thus issued.

Mirror Print   a proof from a die made in relief for stereotypes and therefore a negative image of the issued stamp.

Missionaries   the first stamps of Hawaii, so-called because they were mainly used on mail from missionaries writing home to the USA.

Mission Mixture   used stamps sold by weight, so-called because they were often collected by religious organisations to raise money for charity.

Mixed Founts   the use of several different founts of type in overprints or typeset stamps (qqv).

Mixed Franking   collectors' term for items bearing stamps of two or more different countries or regimes, usually during an interim period.

Mixed Perforation   defectively perforated stamps which have been patched on the reverse and reperforated, usually resulting in compound perforations.

Mixed Printing   the use of more than one printing process in the production of a stamp, e.g. combinations of intaglio and photogravure (Austria), lithography and letterpress (Britain Inigo Jones set of 1973), or intaglio and letterpress (Britain Commonwealth Parliamentary Conference 1973).

Mobile Post Office   a vehicle equipped for use as a post office, mainly used at showgrounds, but also intended as a temporary office in wartime to replace bombed premises.

Moiré   a pattern of close wavy lines resembling watered silk. Printed on the back of Mexican stamps (1872) and overprinted on British Honduras (1915–16) for security purposes.

Money, Stamps as   see *Currency Stamps, Encased Postage Stamp, Fractional Currency* and *Postage Currency.*

Money Letter   a letter containing coin or banknotes. Prior to the introduction of inland registration in 1841, such letters were endorsed in red ink and handled carefully in transit at no extra charge.

Mottled Print   spotty print due to poor distribution of ink.

Mouchon   French keytype (1900) named after the designer, Eugene Louis Mouchon.

Mount   Originally a synonym for hinge (qv) but in recent years applied to gummed-back, acetate-faced pieces designed to hold a single stamp, pair or block without the necessity to attach anything to the back of the stamp. See also *Hawid Strip.*

Mounted Mint   unused stamp showing traces of stamp hinges on the back.

Mourning Stamp   a stamp issued at a time of national mourning for a head of state, and either entirely printed

in black, or with a heavy black border. First issued by German local posts in 1888 but not adopted by a government postal administration till 1923 (Warren Harding 2c, USA).

Movable Box   a posting box on the deck of cross-Channel steamers plying between England and France. The contents would be emptied at the port of arrival and cancelled, irrespective of the stamps, with English marks inscribed MB, or French marks inscribed BM (*Boite Mobile*).

Movable Type   design wholly or partially made up of loose slugs of type. More often, values in movable type may be inserted into a standard cliche to create different denominations.

Mulready   pictorial letter sheet or wrapper issued by Britain in 1840 and derived from the name of the artist William Mulready who designed it. The pompous design was much lampooned and parodied at the time, giving rise to numerous caricatures.

Multilingual Postmark   a postmark inscribed in two or more languages, prevalent in the Austro-Hungarian Empire where German or Hungarian were often matched by Czech, Slovene, Polish or Serbo-Croat names, and in countries using Arabic or native scripts as well as French or English.

Multilingual Stamp   a stamp inscribed in two or more languages and / or scripts. Some commemorative issues (notably from Denmark, Sweden and South Africa) have inscriptions in many languages. Switzerland and South West Africa have had stamps issued simultaneously in three different languages.

Multiple   any number of unsevered stamps in blocks or strips but less than a full sheet.

Multiple Watermark   a watermark device repeated all over the sheet, so that each stamp may show several devices in whole or part.

Multipositive   the image produced by the "step and repeat" process from a master negative, and then transferred to the printing cylinder for photogravure (qv).

Multivalue   applied to meters and vending machines producing labels of any value desired, as opposed to those offering a limited number of fixed values (qv).

Multivalue Coil Strip   strip dispensed by coin-operated slot machines, offering a number of different stamps making up the value of the coin. More recently applied also to *Readers' Digest* coil strips (qv).

Mute Cancellation   alternative term for Dumb Cancellation (qv).

Mutilation   the cancellation of stamps or postal stationery by cutting, tearing or punching out a portion of the design.

Name Tablet   that part of the keyplate (qv) in which the name of the territory is inserted.

Naphthadag   trade name composed of Naphtha and DAG, an acronym from Deflocculated Acheson's Graphite, indicating the black substance used for Graphite Lines (qv).

Native Paper   locally handmade paper, tough and fibrous and varying considerably in thickness and texture, particularly in stamps of the Indian states.

Naval Mail   mail carried by or landed from naval ships, usually though not always in time of war. Very occasionally distinctive stamps have been used (e.g. the German *Vineta* provisional), but more often special postmarks, e.g. German *Marineschiffspost* and the French and US Navy marks. Stamps produced aboard ship include those for Rouad Island (1915), Mount Athos (1916) and Bouvet Islands (1934). See also *Submarine Mail.*

New Issues   stamps newly available to the public. Some dealers offer a new issue service to their customers.

Newspaper Stamp   a stamp intended for the prepayment of postage on newspapers and periodicals.

Newspaper Tax Stamp   a stamp denoting the payment of a tax on newspapers and periodicals, used by many governments as a method of controlling the press. Such a tax was imposed in Britain (1712–1855) and indicated by means of red stamps printed in the top right-hand corner of the front page. Adhesive stamps were issued in Austria and France. In many cases payment of the tax exempted newspapers from postage, so such stamps constitute a form of postage stamp.

Nightrider   an overnight service of the British Post Office, confined to the London area, and using distinctive labels and postmarks.

Non Value Indicator Stamp (NVI)   term coined by Royal Mail for a stamp which bears no actual monetary inscription, but shows the class of postage instead. First used in postal stationery but extended to adhesive stamps in 1989. See also *Undenominated Stamp.*

Not For Use   overprint on 1d stamps of Natal (1910). One stamp in each booklet of 30, sold for 2s 6d, was thus overprinted to recoup the cost of the booklet.

NPM Card   picture postcard published by the National Postal Museum, London, illustrating stamps and subjects of postal interest.

Numbered Stamp   a stamp bearing a serial number as part of the design or printed on the back. Many railway letter stamps of Britain were serially numbered by overprint on the face, while stamps of Spain and colonies from 1875 onwards had numbers on the back. Some modern coil stamps (France, Germany, Sweden among others) are numbered on the back of every tenth stamp.

Numeral Cancellation   obliteration incorporating a number as a means of identifying the post office pioneered by the UK in 1844.

Obligatory Stamp   alternative name for Compulsory Tax Stamp.

Oblique Roulette   also known as *percé en lignes obliques,* a form of separation used in Van Diemen's Land (Tasmania).

Obliteration   any form of postmark designed to cancel the stamp and prevent re-use.

Obsolete   no longer on sale at the post office counter, but still valid for postage.

Occupation Stamp   a stamp overprinted or specially printed for use in territory occupied by military forces during or after a war. First issued by the German Federal Commissioners in the duchy of Holstein (1864) and continuing right down to Bosnia at the present day.

Off Centre   inaccurate perforation resulting in unequal margins round a stamp or even cutting into the design.

Official Mail   correspondence of government departments, members of parliament, officials of state and royal households, subject to special handling and often exempt from postage. Distinctive stamps and stationery have often been issued for this purpose as well as special postmarks and certifying stamps. In certain countries (notably the USA) a penalty for improper use is prominent on both stamps and stationery.

Official Paid   inscription on postmarks and stationery used in connection with official mail in Britain. Special stationery, with a crown logo, was in use from 1903 till 1983.

Official Stamp   a stamp intended for use on official mail, either as an overprint on ordinary stamps, or specifically designed for the purpose. See also *Departmental Stamp.*

Off Paper   term in advertisements indicating used stamps which have been soaked off their backing paper.

Offset Lithogrpahy   a modern variant of lithography in which the image is transferred from the cylinder to a blanket roller which, in turn, is transferred to the paper.

Omnibus Issue   an issue of stamps made by a number of countries simultaneously to commemorate the same person or event. Uniform designs were used from 1898 (Vasco da Gama quatercentenary, by Portugal and colonies) to 1967 (UNESCO, British Commonwealth) but since then different designs in a common theme have been preferred.

On Paper   term in advertising denoting used stamps offered for sale adhering to bits of envelopes or wrappers.

Ordinary Paper   plain wove paper, as distinct from watermarked, tinted or chalk-surfaced papers (qqv).

Original Gum   a stamp which still possesses all or some of the gum present at the time of issue. Often abbreviated to O.G. In auction catalogues and dealers' lists.

Outline Letters lettering in colourless outline, as opposed to solid lettering.

Out of Register denotes one or more colours in printing out of alignment with the others, and resulting in a blurred impression.

Overall Multiple Watermark a network pattern watermark covering all stamps in a sheet.

Overland Mail a postal service operating between two seaboards, linking sea routes over land, notably the service across Egypt by Thomas Waghorn to accelerate mails from Britain to India, but also the trans-continental stage-coach service of the USA in the 1860s. Special labels thus inscribed were also used on mail carried across the desert between Baghdad and Haifa by Nairn Transport Ltd (1923).

Overprint any inscription or device added to the face of a stamp subsequent to the original printing.

Oxidised see *Sulphuretted*.

Packet Letter a letter brought ashore from a packet (a ship maintained by the government or carrying mail under Post Office contract). Special rates applied, and distinctive postmarks thus inscribed were used.

Paid Postmark a postmark, usually struck in red, denoting that postage has been pre-paid.

Pair two unsevered stamps.

Palimpsest term denoting the erasure (qv) of part of a design, where vestiges of the original can still be seen below or alongside the revised inscription.

Pane a sub-division of a sheet of stamps, often separated by a gutter (qv), or the block of stamps forming a leaf in a booklet.

Parliamentary stationery.

Paper Error a stamp printed on paper of the wrong colour, quality or watermark.

Papermaker's Watermark a watermark incorporating the papermaker's name, brand name or trademark, sometimes appearing in the sheet margin but more usually in the centre and therefore spread over several stamps.

Paquebot French word derived from "packet boat", adopted by the Universal Postal Union in 1894 to denote mail posted on board ship and taken ashore for onward transmission. The word is often found in postmarks applied to such mail.

Parachute Mail a form of airmail using free-fall parachute to deliver packets to remote areas where aircraft cannot normally land.

Paraph an ornamental flourish or manuscript cypher, overprinted on stamps of Puerto Rico (1873–76) or Mexico (1914).

Parcel Label label used at post offices in the UK (1883–1918), each office being given labels with its own name and postal designation. Superseded by rectangular handstamps in the larger offices and by small anonymous labels at sub offices.

Parcel Postmark a postal marking used in connection with the parcel post, either distinctive in pattern or specifically inscribed for the purpose.

Parcel Stamp a stamp prepaying the postage on parcels.

Parcelforce name for the Royal Mail parcel service, using distinctive labels and handstamps thus inscribed.

Parliamentary Stamp a stamp intended for the use of members of parliament, notably from Spain (1895–98) and the Council of Europe since 1950.

Parliamentary Stationery special envelopes and cards designed for the use of members of parliament. Introduced in the UK (1840) on the abolition of the franking privilege (qv) and now used in most countries.

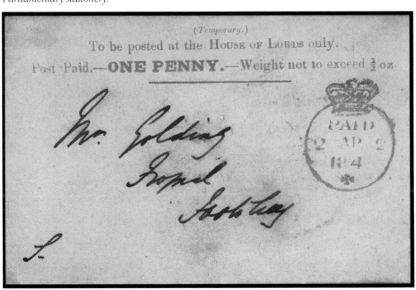

Part Impression   a stamp which has received only a part of the printing due to a fault arising during production, either from underinking or a paper fold.

Part Perforation   an irregularity caused by missing, blunt or defective pins in the perforation, or from the perforator missing a row or rows.

Patriotic Cover   envelope decorated with pictures and slogans of a patriotic nature, popular during the American Civil War (1861–65) and extensively used in both world wars and other conflicts since then.

Peace and Commerce   French and colonial keytypes introduced in 1876.

Peace and Navigation   French and colonial keytpes adopted in 1892.

Pelure   French word indicating very thin, hard and durable semi-transparent paper, used for stamps of New Zealand, Serbia and Russia.

Pen Cancelled   a stamp marked with pen strokes to prevent postal re-use.

Penalty Mail   official mail bearing a warning that a penalty will be imposed for improper use. Stationery bearing a penalty clause has been issued by the USA, South Africa and Norway, while the USA has had stamps thus inscribed since 1983.

Penmarked   a stamp defaced by pen and ink for fiscal purposes.

Penny Black   nickname for the world's first adhesive postage stamp, issued by the UK in May 1840.

Penny Post   a postal service handling letters and packets within a certain limited area for a penny each. Pioneered by William Dockwra (qv) in London (1680), penny posts spread to Dublin (1773) and Edinburgh (1774), and other provincial towns from 1800 to 1839, when a uniform post was substituted. Many local services in the USA incorporated the words PENNY POST in their title and issued stamps thus inscribed.

Percé   French for "pierced", used to describe a form of roulette (qv).

Perfin   term meaning stamps perforated with the initials of firms, organisations and government departments.

Perforation   type of separation in which small holes are punched out of the paper between rows of stamps.

Perforation Gauge   a method of measuring the perforations, invented by Dr Jacques Legrand. "Perf 14" means 14 holes in the space of two centimetres.

Permit Mail   bulk posting of printed matter which the USPO has permitted private companies to despatch since April 1904, with various types of handstruck or printed impressions denoting prepayment of postage. This system eventually spread to many other countries. The term derives from the permit number incorporated in the mark. See also *Postage Paid Impression*.

Personal Delibery Stamp   a triangular stamp issued by Czechoslovakia or Bohemia and Moravia in connection with a personal delivery service. Two types of stamp were issued; those in red with the letter D in each corner denoted a fee paid by an addressee who required all his mail to be delivered to him personally, while those in blue, inscribed V, were affixed by the sender to ensure personal delivery to the addressee.

Phantom   a synonym for Bogus (qv).

Philatelic Handling Label   an instructional label (qv) requesting the post office to cancel stamps lightly and handle mail carefully as it is intended for a stamp collector. Distinctive labels for this purpose have been issued by many European countries.

Phonopost see *Recorded Message*.

Phosphor   popular term for a substance overprinted, added to printing ink or impregnated in the paper of stamps to facilitate electronic sorting and cancellation.

Phosphor Dots   pattern of dots applied to mail, translating the postcode (qv) from an alpha-numeric sequence to a medium which can be read by sorting equipment.

Photography   method of stamp production seldom used. It was employed for the 1d and 3d stamps of Mafeking (1900), the Regensburg air stamps (1912), the Mount Athos series (1916) and the Figueroa air stamp of Chile (1919).

Photogravure   printing process (known also as gravure, heliogravure or rotogravure) involving the use of photography to create a printing cylinder. The design is screened and broken up into patterns of dots etched into the cylinder for printing in the same manner as intaglio (qv). First used for stamps of Bavaria (1914).

Photo-lithography   a process developed in the late 19th century for printing multicoloured labels and first used for stamps of Bavaria in 1911. It is the preferred medium for stamps produced by Leigh-Mardon of Australia.

PHQ Card   postcard since 1973 reproducing a British commemorative or special stamp, deriving its name from the initials of Postal Headquarters.

Pictorial Postmark   a postmark incorporating a picture in its design. Surprisingly, some of the earliest known marks have a pictorial element, although this medium has been greatly expanded in both slogans (qv) and special event handstamps (qv) in recent years.

Pigeon Post   mail service using carrier pigeons to

transmit special flimsies or microfilmed messages. Distinctive stamps have been produced in New Zealand for the purpose.

Pillar   ornament in columnar form, filling the gutter and sheet margins of many British letterpress stamps.

Pin Roulette   also known as *percé en pointes*, a form of roulette in which holes are puncture in rows. Most examples of pin roulette are achieved by sewing-machine.

Plagiarism   artistic theft which, in philatelic terms, arises when the design of a stamp in one country is copied by a stamp of another. Examples range from the stamps of Corrientes (1856) based on the French Ceres design (1849) to Afghanistan's imitation of the US "Atoms for Peace" stamp (1955). Mexico, New South Wales and Australia all issued postage due labels derived from an American design of 1879.

Plate Flaw   blemish on a stamp caused by damage to the printing plate. When the damage is repaired the result is known as a Retouch (qv).

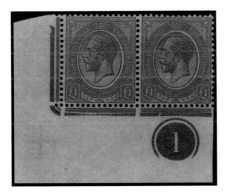

Plate Number   numeral inscribed in the sheet margin to identify the plate used in printing.

Plate Proof   an impression taken from the plate prior to general production to check details.

Plebiscite Stamp   a stamp issued for use in a district pending a decision on its political future by referendum of the inhabitants. Such stamps were issued in several parts of Europe after World War I and also in Peru for the Tacna-Arica plebiscite.

Plug   portion of a printing plate plugged into the main design, usually where stamps are printed from the same plate ad different values are created by inserting suitably engraved plugs into the appropriate spaces.

Pneumatic Post   a method of transmitting messages by pneumatic tubes. This system was installed in Paris, Berlin, Vienna and several Italian cities and used distinctive stamps, labels postmarks and stationery.

Poached Egg   nickname for a photogravure label used by the British Post Office for testing vending machines. See *Testing Label*.

Political Propaganda   the use of postage stamps, meter marks and labels to promote a political message. This medium was exploited in the USSR, Nazi Germany and many countries of the communist bloc, notably Cuba, North Korea and North Vietnam.

Polyvinyl Alcohol Gum   almost invisible substance (PVA) used as adhesive from the late 1960s. Polyvinyl Alcohol Dextrin (PVAD) has a pale blue-green to distinguish it from the earlier PVA gum.

Porte de Mar   Spanish for "carried by sea", inscribed on Mexican stamps (1875–79) for use on mail going to Europe and denoting the fees paid to ship-owners.

Positional Block   a block exhibiting a variety known to occur on a particular stamp in the sheet, or with marginal paper attached bearing arrows, guide lines, imprint or other markings which enable the collector to assign the block to a particular position in the sheet.

Post Offices Abroad   post offices and postal agencies maintained by the major powers in many parts of the world outside their own territory but using their stamps without any distinguishing overprint. British stamps were widely employed, not only in many British colonies, but also in the main ports of Latin America and the Ottoman Empire. Austrian, French, German, Indian, Italian, Japanese, Polish, Roumanian, Russian and US stamps have also been used in this manner at various times, distinguished only by the postmarks.

Post-a-Book   service of the British Post Office whereby booksellers undertook to post books purchased by customers, distinguished not only by special stationery but also by self-adhesive stamps of a design subsequently used for Royal Mail Postage Labels (qv).

Postage Due Label   a label which does not prepay postage, but which is affixed to unpaid or underpaid mail, or items infringing postal regulations and therefore liable to a fine, so that the delivery postman can recover the amount from the addressee. Such labels, usually inscribed "To Pay" are also used to collect customs duty on packets and parcels from abroad.

Postage Currency   name inscribed on some issues of US Fractional Currency (qv), during and after the American Civil War.

Postage Paid Impression   a mark, handstruck or printed, applied to bulk postings of mail prepaid in cash. This system was adopted by the UK in 1966. Such marks indicate the class of posting, the name of the office of posting and a serial number. Impressions used on mail posted at more than one office have PHQ (Postal Headquarters) instead of a town name. See also *Permit Mailing*.

Postal Charge Label   stamp of Papua New Guinea thus overprinted (1960) for use to collect fees and customs duty, in the same manner as a postage due label (qv).

Postal Concession Label   label sold through NAAFI canteens for the use of servicemen and their families stationed in Egypt, permitting transmission of mail at reduced rates. Sometimes termed NAAFI seals, they were in use from 1932 to 1936.

Postal Fiscal   a stamp originally intended for revenue purposes but subsequently authorised for postal use.

Postal Forgery   a forgery perpetrated to defraud the postal revenue.

Postal Frank   term denoting accountancy labels produced by the British Vice Consul in Antananarivo, Madagascar. These labels were subsequently removed and replaced by stamps of Madagascar or Reunion for onward transmisison.

Postal History   the study of the origins and development of the postal services in all aspects, though usually referring to the study and collecting of postmarks, postal stationery and entire letters.

Postal Marking   any mark, either handstruck, applied by machine or handwritten, of a postal nature appearing on a piece of mail.

Postal Mechanisation   the process of speeding up the handling, sorting and cancelling of mail by mechanical means, but specifically the use of machines such as Transorma (qv) and electronic equipment since 1957, reflected in phosphor dots, tagging (qqv) and distinctive postmarks. See *Automatic Letter Facer, Culler Facer Canceller, Facer Canceller Table, Postcode, Sefacan* and *Zipcode*.

Postal Seal   circular label, often scalloped and embossed, used to seal the flaps of envelopes and also denote exemption from postal charges. Widely used in Austria, Germany and the Netherlands for official mail. See also *Interpostal Seal*.

Postal Stationery   any form of envelope, postcard, lettercard, wrapper, aerogramme, telegram form or reply card issued by a post office and usually bearing impressed or embossed stamps.

Postal Telegraphs   stamps originally issued for telegraphic use but subsequently permitted for ordinary postage.

Postal Union Colours   standard colours laid down by the UPU in 1880 for the basic international rates: green (printed matter), red (postcards) and blue (letters). The stamps prepaying these rates were supposed to conform to this colour scheme, but it was gradually abandoned in 1953.

Postbus Ticket   ticket for use on a postbus. Many of these services use adhesive stamps with appropriate cancellations.

Postcard   type of postal stationery made of cardboard, generally transmitted at a much lower rate than letter mail. It was introduced by Austria (1869) and quickly followed by other countries.

Postcard Stamp   an adhesive stamp overprinted with the national arms for use on postcards issued by the Orange Free State (1889–97).

Postcard Tax Stamp   stamp overprinted "Controle"

and issued by Persia in 1904 to denote a tax on picture postcards sent by post.

Postcode   a group of numbers, or combination of letters and numbers, in which all addresses can be encoded for processing in automatic sorting machinery. Germany pioneered two-digit (1942) and four-digit (1961) codes, since adopted by many other countries. Britain pioneered alphanumeric codes (1959–73). See also *Zip Code*.

Postmark   any mark, manuscript, handstruck or applied by machine, connected with the postal service and found on matter sent through the post.

Postmasters' Stamps   stamps issued by the postmasters of certain towns to facilitate the prepayment of postage, notably in the USA (1845–47), in the Confederate States during the Civil War and in Germany at the end of World War II.

Postnote   type of stationery used in Britain (1982) resembling an aerogramme (qv) but on stouter paper and intended for domestic mail.

Pre-adhesive   a piece of mail sent through the post before the introduction of adhesive stamps. Sometimes loosely termed "pre-stamp", although it may actually bear a handstruck postage stamp.

Precancel   a postage stamp intended for bulk postings and bearing some kind of handstruck or machine-printed cancellation.

Premieres Gravures   French for "first engravings", denoting the original version of the US 1861 series, later versions being slightly altered.

Premium Offer   goods or services offered free or at a discount as a sales incentive. In the philatelic context it applies to stamps, booklets or postal stationery given in exchange for wrappers or tops collected from certain branded goods.

Presentation Pack   a philatelic souvenir containing a set of stamps and descriptive text, introduced by the British Post Office for the Shakespeare stamps (1964).

Pre-stamp Cover   popular but inaccurate term for entires or wrappers predating the introduction of adhesive stamps but often bearing handstruck stamps (qv).

Prestige Booklet   a stamp booklet sponsored by a company or organisation, containing special panes of stamps with descriptive text alongside, and usually including unusual combinations of stamps in a mixed-value pane, pioneered by the British Post Office in 1969 and since adopted by many other postal administrations.

Printed Matter   circulars, samples and other types of commercial papers transmitted by post at special reduced rates. Many countries issue stamps and wrappers specifically for this purpose.

Printed on Back   a stamp which has an inscription or design printed on the back, e.g. Greece (1861–80) with numerals of value, Swedish stamps with a posthorn (1886–91), serial numbers on stamps of Spain and colonies, coils of Germany, France and Sweden with control numbers, the burele (qv) pattern on Queensland stamps, and graphite lines (qv) on British stamps (1957). Many countries have issued stamps with a descriptive text on the reverse, a practice pioneered by Portugal (1895).

Printed Watermark an imitation watermark adopted as a cheap substitute for security paper, e.g. Argentina (1922), El Salvador (1935) and New Zealand (1925).

Printer's Imprint name of the printer in the bottom margin of the stamp or in the sheet margin.

Printer's Ornament and Rule decorative elements used in the production of typeset stamps (qv) or in the setting of overprints.

Printer's Waste defective, malformed or doubly printed stamps, usually scrapped during production but occasionally coming on to the philatelic market.

Printex printing process patented by Motley & Miller of England, applying photography to letterpress (qv). Though used to print the so-called Ideal Stamp labels at the philatelic exhibition of 1912, it was overtaken by photogravure and never used for actual stamps. There is no connection with the Maltese printing firm of the same name.

Printing an edition or production run of stamps. It is often possible to distinguish between various printings by subtle changes in shade, quality of paper, etc.

Prisoner of War Mail correspondence to or from prisoners of war, from the Napoleonic Wars to the present day, distinguished by special postmarks, stationery, cachets and even stamps.

Private Control inscription overprinted or underprinted on stamps by firms to prevent pilferage or improper use by their employees. See also Perfins.

Private Label a label without postal validity or significance, affixed to mail to advertise companies and their products, or provide tourist publicity.

Private Perforation the unofficial perforation of stamps which were generally issued imperforate. Examples have come from France, Switzerland and Greece. New Zealand and the USA supplied imperforate coils to firms who perforated them to fit their affixing machines (qv).

Private Postmark a postmark permitted in Belgium, Germany and the USA for the use of firms, organisations and even private individuals. They may be recognised by the fact that they advertise company products and services and include a license number.

Private Stamp see *Franchise Stamp*.

Privilege Envelope an envelope giving preferential postal treatment to a charitable organisation, pioneered by Prussia (1867) for a war charity which was allowed to send packets for a flat rate of 4pf irrespective of size and weight.

Proof an impression taken during the preparation of the master die or printing plate prior to the production of stamps.

Propaganda Forgery a forgery used for the purpose of circulating subversive propaganda in postcard or leaflet form, in enemy or enemy-occupied countries.

Propaganda Leaflet a leaflet bearing a propaganda message, often dropped from aircraft over enemy, occupied or even neutral countries in time of war.

Propaganda Stamp a stamp designed to promote a campaign and get a message across to the public. Many exhortatory stamps in recent years have urged people to pay their taxes, increase production, grow more food, care for the environment, cut down on waste, give up smoking and prevent accidents.

Provisional Label a label, handstruck or manuscript, in use during a temporary shortage of printed labels, notably parcel and registration, or overprinted to convert one kind of label to another use.

Provisional Stamp a stamp bearing an overprint to convert its purpose or validity, or a surcharge (qv) to alter its face value. This category also includes all kinds of makeshifts prepared at a local level, including handstruck or manuscript stamps, pressed into temporary service during a shortage of government stamps.

Publicity Envelope Stamp an Italian definitive stamp overprinted B.L.P. (*Buste Lettere Postali*) and issued in 1921–23 for sale at a discount in aid of an ex-servicemen's organisation.

Publicity Slogan Postmark a machine cancellation publicising tourist and commercial facilities in a particular town or district.

PVA, PVAD abbreviations for Polyvinyl Alcohol and Polyvinyl Alcohol Dextrin gum (qv).

Quadrille Paper paper watermarked with crossed lines forming a pattern of small squares.

Quadripartite Label a postal label consisting of four parts, notably Chinese express labels (1909).

Quarter the fourth part of a divisible stamp, issued by Mecklenburg-Schwerin (1856) and Brunswick (1857). Each quarter could be used on its own to prepay the local printed matter rate, but the whole stamp prepaid the letter rate.

Quartz Lamp a lamp emitting ultra-violet light, producing fluorescence (qv) and extremely useful to the philatelist checking the inks and papers used in stamp production, as well as repairs and faking in damaged stamps.

Railway Air Services airmail services operated on behalf of railway companies in Great Britain, 1933–39, using distinctive stamps and envelopes.

Railway Company Stamp local or semi-official stamp issued by railway companies to prepay the postage on letters and parcels carried by rail.

Railway Letter Stamp a stamp prepaying an additional fee on a letter sent from station to station by rail. This service was introduced in Britain in 1891, each company issuing its own stamps. They were phased out in 1922 but since 1957 many of the preserved lines have issued their own stamps, mainly as fund-raisers.

Railway Parcel Stamp a stamp prepaying the charges on parcels carried from station to station by rail. Such stamps have been recorded from 1846 onwards in Britain, and have been issued in many other countries in more recent years.

Railway Stamp a postage stamp issued by a government postal service specifically for letters and parcels handled by the state railways. Such stamps have been issued by Belgium, Bavaria, Bulgaria and France.

Rainbow Trials a series of colour trials produced by the British authorities in 1840–41 to test various coloured inks, paper and postmarks. They were in the design of the Penny Black (qv) but were distinguished by having the top right-hand corner blank, and omitting the check letters (qv) from the lower corners.

Readers' Digest Coil Strip a multi-value coil strip issued by Britain or South Africa on behalf of the *Readers' Digest.*

Receipted Parcel a parcel service of the British Post Office in the 1980s, superseded by Trakback (qv).

Recess Printing see *Intaglio* and *Line Engraving.*

Recorded Delivery a service of the British Post Office, similar to Certified Mail (qv) in the USA, involving special labels since 1961.

Recorded Message Stamp a stamp issued by Argentina (1939) to prepay the postage on messages recorded

on discs for transmission by post. Britain, Ireland and Taiwan have operated similar services with distinctive postmarks, labels and stationery.

Redrawn denotes a new printing of a stamp whose design differs in some respect from the original, while retaining its principal features.

Re-engraved a stamp produced from a plate which has had wear and tear repaired or the image strengthened by entering new lines.

Re-entry duplication of part of a line-engraved stamp design to remedy a faulty first impression, or where the original impression has not been wholly erased (qv).

Regional Postcard a picture postcard issued by the various regional postal boards in the UK (1971–86) and usually featuring a subject of philatelic or postal interest.

Regional Stamp a stamp issued for use in a particular region of a country, although usually valid for postage throughout the entire country.

Register Marking any marking in the sheet margin, in the form of lines, dots and arrows, placed there as an aid to colour registration in multicolour printing.

Registered Envelope a special envelope, pioneered by Britain (1878) for registered mail, and distinguished by crossed blue lines and stout linen-backed paper.

Registered Postmark a postmark designed specifically for registered mail, often of a distinctive oval or hooded shape (qv) to make such packets more prominent.

Registration Label a label bearing the name of an office and a serial number, pioneered by Germany and Scandinavia about 1873 and adopted by the UPU in 1882, though not introduced by many countries till much later. Named labels were discontinued by Britain in 1993.

Registration Stamp a special stamp denoting the registration fee and often incorporating a serial number.

Regummed an unused stamp which has lost its original gum (qv) and had new adhesive added to deceive collectors.

Re-issue a stamp which has been withdrawn from use but brought back into service, usually with an overprint to that effect.

Relief Cancel a term used in Australia and New Zealand for a skeleton handstamp (qv).

Relief Printing printing from raised type, often referred to as letterpress, surface printing or typography (qqv).

Remainder a stamp which is no longer valid for postage, sold off cheaply to dealers. In many cases such stamps are defaced or cancelled, or even overprinted.

Repaired Paper paper, usually from the beginning or end of reels used in rotary printing, which has been joined up and is therefore detectale by overlapping, resulting in stamps of double the normanl thickness.

Re-perforation   a form of faking in which imperforate stamps are perforated, or have had their perforations altered to enhance their value. Occasionally (e.g. New Zealand 1860s and 1901) stamps were officially reperforated because the original perforation was imperfect.

Reply Paid Stationery   envelopes, postcards and wrappers bearing special inscriptions, addresses and licence numbers, to enable firms' customers to repy without paying the postage. Businesses using this service pay the postage plus a small handling fee.

Reply Postcard   a double postcard, the return half being intended for a reply from the original addressee. Pioneered by Bavaria and Germany (1872) and used in Britain from 1882 till 1970.

Repp Paper   a ribbed paper with a slightly corrugated appearance.

Reprint   a stamp printed from the original plates after the normal period of validity, to satisfy philatelic demand. Such stamps often differ from the issued originals in the quality or type of paper and colour of ink.

Resetting   a new arrangement of cliches (qv) in a plate, resulting in new varieties.

Resinised Paper see *Goldbeater's Skin.*

Retouch   a minor correction made by hand to the printing plate or cylinder, and showing up on stamps.

Retta   diamond-shaped obliterations used in Egypt and Cyprus.

Returned Letter Stamp   a stamp intended to frank undeliverable mail returned to the sender. Such stamps have been issued by Bavaria, Spain, Wurttemberg and Norway.

Returned Mail   letters and parcels returned to the sender for many reasons, indicated by means of instructional marks and labels (qv). Many countries use special official envelopes to enclose undeliverable letters, or have sealing labels to reclose mail opened to ascertain the name and address of the sender.

Revalidated Stamp   see *Re-issue.*

Revenue Protection   Term used by Royal Mail in connection with the recovery of deficient postage and fines on underpaid mail or infringements of the postal regulations, found on postal markings and labels.

Revenue Stamp see *Fiscal Stamp.*

Reversed Print   a stamp printed in reverse, i.e. on the back of transparent material, such as Goldbeater's Skin (qv).

Rhomboid Roulette   double-pointed roulette producing diamond–shaped cuts, used in Mexican stamps 1868–70.

Ribbed Paper see *Repp Paper.*

Rice Paper   a thin and delicate paper normally used in cooking, but confined to a 1c stamp of El Salvador (1889) and local stamps of Formosa (1895).

Rocket Mail   mail carried by rocket dates from 1928 when experiments were made in Austria. Unofficial and semi-official stamps were issued in the 1930s, but the first official issue was made by Cuba (1939). Some souvenir mail was carried by the Apollo XI moon-shot of 1969 and subsequent spacecraft.

Roman Type   a fount of type distinguished by its seriffed capitals. In Britain it ceased to be used in psotmarks in 1844 but is widely used to this day in overprints.

Rotary Cancellation   a device to speed up hand-cancellation of mail, the obliterating dies being mounted on a revolving drum or wheel, often incorporating a self-inking mechanism.

Rotary Perforation   a method of perforation involving the use of rotating toothed wheels operating on the same lines as line perforation (qv).

Rotogravure   an alternative name for Photogravure.

Rough Perforation   the opposte of clean-cut perforation (qv), often caused by worn or defective pins.

Roulette   French word for a toothed wheel, denoting a form of separation in which the paper is pierced but the holes are not punched out as in perforation.

Royal Mail Postage Label   term used for the Frama labels (qv) used in the UK.

Royal Reprint   a special printing of British 1d stamps in 1864, allegedly at the personal request of Queen Victoria for presentation to her children.

Rugby Shoe   a distinctive type of duplex handstamp (qv) used at Rugby in the 1850s, so-called on account of its shape.

Ruled Paper   paper ruled with lines as a guide to handwriting, used for stamps of Mexico (1887) and Latvia (1919).

Rural Postmarks   distinctive handstamps used by rural postmen in Cyprus.

Safety Paper   specially treated paper to prevent forgery or fraudulent re-use by cleaning off the cancellation.

St Andrew's Cross   a saltire or cross in which the lines intersect diagonally, found on coupons (qv) or labels attached to Austrian stamps and found in British halfpenny booklet panes (1906–11).

Sample Label   an imitation of a stamp, produced by security printers to demonstrate the range and versatility of their products. This has become a popular souvenir of philatelic exhibitions in recent years where stamp printers have stands.

Sample Stamp   a stamp, overprinted or holed in some way to prevent actual use. Such stamps were used (notably by Waterlow & Sons) for demonstration purposes.

Sans-serif Type a fount of type distinguished by the absence of the tiny projections and spurs at the end of the strokes.

Saw-tooth Roulette also known as *percé en scie*, a form of separation distinguished by its zigzag cuts.

Scientific Expedition Stamp a stamp issued for use by a scientific or exploration expedition, e.g. King Edward VII Land (1908), Victoria Land (1911) and the Trans-Antarctic Expedition (1956).

Scots Local Cancellation undated cancellation on British stamps (1854–60) from minor post offices in Scotland, much sought after on account of the range of types and colours used.

Scout Post a service operated by the Boy Scouts, notably the first postal service in Czechoslovakia (1918) and the mail during the Warsaw Rising (1944). In recent years many of the Christmas Charity Posts (qv) in Britain have been operated by Scout groups.

Script Type a fount of type resembling handwriting, used in watermarks and overprints.

Sealing Label a gummed label used for sealing broken or damaged packets, or resealing packets subject to customs examination or opened for return to sender.

Seal a gummed label designed to seal the flaps of envelopes and wrappers. See *Interpostal Seal* and *Christmas Seal*.

Secret Mark a minuscule mark in the design of a stamp, made by the designer, engraver or printer to identify their work or distinguish it from the product of another firm. See also *Hidden Date*.

Security Overprint a device used by Macao on stamps overprinted for airmail (1934). Greek lettering was included to make forgery more difficult. US stamps overprinted "Kans." or "Nebr." were issued in 1929 to minimise losses to the revenue following a spate of post office robberies in these states.

Security Underprint a part of the design printed in a lighter colour below the main impression, often in an intricate pattern.

Seebeck Issues stamps produced by the Hamilton Bank Note Company of New York for various Central American countries (1892–99) and thus named after Nicholas F. Seebeck who struck a deal to reprint the stamps on his own account after they ceased to be valid, in exchange for not charging the countries for producing them in the first place. The reprints (qv) then flooded the market.

Self-Adhesive Label a label with a rubber-based adhesive on the back, protected by peelable backing paper, now widely used for registration and instructional labels.

Self-Adhesive Stamp a type of stamp pioneered by Sierra Leone (1964) and later adopted by Montserrat, Norfolk Island and Tonga in free-form (qv) designs. In recent years rectangular stamps, either imperforate or with die-cut simulated perforations (qv), have been widely used in coils, booklets and ATM panes (qqv) as a convenience to the public.

Self-Service Registration Stamp a stamp combining the features of registration labels (qv) with the fee for special handling, issued by the German Democratic Republic (1967–68).

Selvedge the marginal paper round a sheet of stamps.

Semi-Official Stamp a stamp issued for a private service but having official sanction, such as those issued by airlines and railway companies and the Zemstvos (qv) of Russia.

Semi-Postal American term for charity stamps (qv).

Sensitised Paper paper impregnated with a ferro-prussiate compound sensitive to light, normally used by draughtsmen but also employed for the stamps of Mafeking (1900).

Serial Numbering a method of controlling the issue of labels and stamps. It is commonly found on registration, receipted parcel and recorded delivery labels, as well as on the back of many stamps of Spain and colonies.

Seriffed Type a fount of type characterised by serifs or spurs at the ends of strokes.

Serpentine Roulette also known as *percé en serpentine*, a form of separation in which the cuts form a wavy line.

Serrated Roulette a roulette distinguished by small, semi-circular cuts.

Se-tenant French term meaning "joined together" and applied to stamps of different values or designs printed side by side.

Set-Off an impression picked up by a sheet of stamps from another which has just been printed and on which the ink has not yet dried. It usually appears on the back of stamps, as a mirror print.

Setting arrangement of movable type or cliches (qv) for printing or overprint.

Setting Error a mistake such as transposition, inversion or misalignment of type, or a cliche laid down in the forme (qv) upside down, or in the wrong plate.

Shade a variety or degree of colour.

Sheet the end result of a printing from a plate or cylinder, surrounded by marginal paper.

Sheet Fed a printing press in which the paper is fed in single sheets and not from a continuous roll.

Sheet Marking any mark found on the marginal paper of a sheet.

Sheet Number serial number printed in the corner of the sheet.

Sheet Watermark a large watermark covering the entire sheet of stamps, so that only a portion falls on individual stamps.

Sheetlet a sheet containing fewer stamps than the normal format, often issued for the convenience of users, but increasingly used as a philatelic marketing device, with different stamps se-tenant. In 1994, however, the German Post Office began issuing stamps in sheetlets of 20 with decorative margins in the hope that collectors would be persuaded to collect them entire.

Shifted Transfer duplicated lines on a steel plate, caused when the design is entered from a transfer roller a second time, and resulting in thicker frame-lines or even a doubling of lines.

Ship Letter a letter carried by private ship and subject to special rates of postage. Distinctive postmarks have been used since the 18th century for this purpose.

Shipping Company Stamp a stamp issued by a shipping company to prepay the carriage of letters and packets. Many companies operated international postal services before the advent of the UPU in 1874–75.

Shrinkage the contraction of paper resulting from dampening for intaglio printing, then drying. Uneven shrinkage causes problems for accurate perforation, notably in many Perkins Bacon stamps.

Siderography process of transferring designs from steel dies to plates by means of a transfer press.

Sideways Watermark a watermark which is sideways in relation to the design of a stamp, often found in coil stamps.

Siege Postmark a mark applied to mail either from towns under siege or explaining delay or non-delivery due to the siege.

Siege Stamps and Stationery distinctive stamps and postal stationery used on mail from towns under siege, notably the *Ballon Monté* envelopes of Paris (1870–71) and the stamps from Mafeking (1900), Lorient (1944) and Hela (1945).

Silk Thread Paper type of security paper with coloured silk threads enmeshed in it, used for stamps of Bavaria (1849–68) and Switzerland (1854–62). See also *Dickinson Paper*.

Simulated Perforation see *Imitation Perforation*.

Simple Watermark a watermark appearing on each stamp.

Single Stamp Official term used by the British Post Office for a handstamp with a single-circle, mainly used for counter work. See also *Combined Stamp* and *Double Stamp*.

Sinking Fund Stamp a stamp overprinted C.A. or *Caisse d'Amortissement*, issued by France (1927–31) with a surcharge aimed at reducing the national debt.

Skeleton Handstamp a datestamp with slots round the circumference for the insertion of loose letters to make up the name of a post office. Introduced in Britain in 1840, it has been widely used in many Commonwealth countries since then as a temporary replacement for stamps lost, stolen or destroyed, or pending the supply of a permanent stamp to a new post office.

Sleeper a stamp with a higher value than charged or listed in a catalogue.

Slogan Postmark a postmark, usually applied by machine, in which the usual obliterating lines are replaced by a text, sometimes accompanied by a picture. Handstruck slogans were used in England in 1661–75 but machine slogans were pioneered by the USA in 1893.

Slurred Print otherwise known as a Smudged Print, and denoting an impression which is indistinct or blurred due to a slight shift of the paper during printing.

Socked on the Nose a handstruck cancellation entirely within the area of the stamp.

Soldiers' Stamps stamps issued for the use of troops on active service to indicate exemption from postal charges. The most prolific issues come from Switzerland where distinctive stamps were issued by every regiment, squadron, battery and unit.

Souvenir Card a large card produced by the USPO bearing engraved reproductions of obsolete stamps and intended as a souvenir of international philatelic exhibitions.

Souvenir Sheet sometimes loosely synonymous with Miniature Sheet (qv) but strictly applied to small sheets in which the entire sheet constitutes the stamp, rather than a sheet with a single stamp, perforated or imperforate, in the centre. The term is also applied to small sheets of philatelic interest but no postal validity produced as souvenirs of stamp exhibitions.

Space Filler a stamp in damaged or heavily cancelled condition which fills a space in the collection till a better specimen can be obtained.

Spandrel   the space between the exterior curves of an arch or circle and an enclosing right angle. In stamps this roughly triangular area is often occupied by ornament or figures of value.

Spargummi   German term for economy gum (qv).

Special Delivery Label   a label indicating special handling and acceleration of mail.

Special Delivery Stamp   a stamp prepaying the fee for the special handling of a packet.

Special Event Postmark   a postmark used in connection with a fair, exhibition, or the celebration of a historic anniversary.

Special Fee Stamp   a stamp denoting the fee payable in respect of some special service, such as Advice of Receipt, Late Fee, Certified Mail, Marine Insurance, Personal Delivery and Registration (qqv).

Special Flight Stamp   a stamp produced specifically for a particular airmail journey. Stamps of Holland and Switzerland have been inscribed *Bijzondere Vluchten* and *Pro Aero* respectively.

Specimen Stamp   a stamp overprinted "Specimen", or its equivalent in other languages, to render it postally invalid. Such stamps are often used for record purposes or press publicity.

Spif   acronym from Stamps Perforated with Initials of Firms, coined in Britain but now largely superseded by perfins (q.v.).

Split   a stamp which has been cut up for use as a lesser denomination. See *Bisect* and *Fractional Stamp.*

Sponsored Booklet   a stamp booklet sponsored by a company or organisation, whose advertisements appear exclusively on the interleaves and booklet labels. See also *Prestige Booklet.*

Sponsored Stamp   a stamp whose issue is sponsored by a company or organisation, or produced at the behest of such a company. In this category would come the coil strips supplied to the *Readers' Digest* (qv), Canadian stamps with the McDonald's logo in the sheet margin, and the British 25p stamp in a miniature sheet with the Boot's logo (1994).

Spoon Cancellation   a type of experimental duplex handstamp used in Britain (1853–60) and so-called on account of its shape. See also *Rugby Shoe.*

Squared Circle   the first type of combined stamp (qv) used in England and Wales, introduced in 1879 and widely employed till 1914. The postmarks are distinguished by having a circular centre surrounded by rectangular corners. Similar handstamps were used in Canada, Italy and other countries at the turn of the century.

Stamp   a device for striking or impressing a stamp on paper, hence the piece of paper thus stamped. The term is loosely applied to postage stamps, although fiscal stamps of all kinds also qualify. Postage stamps were handstruck from 1680 onwards, and printed on gummed paper since 1840.

Stamp Card   laminated card resembling a credit card, bearing peelable self-adhesive stamps. Pioneered by North Korea in 1993, although actually manufactured in Sweden.

Stamp Currency   see *Encased Postage Stamp, Fractional Currency* and *Postage Currency.*

Stamp Duty   an inscription pertaining to fiscal usage, but also found on the early postage stamps of the Australian states and New Zealand.

Stamped Paper   paper bearing an impressed or embossed fiscal stamp (qv) denoting a tax on paper or documents.

Stampless Cover   a cover, wrapper or letter sheet which has passed through the post since the advent of adhesive stamps in the country of origin, but which does not bear either an adhesive or imprinted stamp. In this category come covers or cards bearing postmarks, inscribed *Paid* or its equivalent in some other language, e.g. *Taxe Perçue* (French) or *Gebühr Bezahlt* (German).

Star Plate   US plate with a star in the imprint or near the plate number to indicate an experimental spacing of the subjects to obtain better-centred stamps.

Stereotype   a solid metallic plate cast from a mould of movable type. See also *Cliche* and *Woodblock.*

Stitch Watermark   a watermark consisting of a patch of close parallel lines, caused by wire stitches repairing the web of a paper mould, found on many American stamps.

Straight Edge   the imperforate side of a stamp normally perforated on all four sides. This is common on Canadian and US stamps due to the division of panes by guillotine. The term can also be applied to stamps from coils or booklets with opposite sides or outer edges imperforate, although the expression "imperforate at side" is more commonly used in such cases.

Strike Post   a mail service organised privately, or with the sanction of the post office, during a strike of postal workers. Distinctive stamps, postmarks and stationery by the organisers of such posts, as well as explanatory marks indicating delayed mail, are known in this context.

Strip   three or more stamps in a single row.

Submarine Mail   mail conveyed by submarine, usually to evade an enemy blockade. Special stamps for such mail were issued in both world wars as well as the Spanish Civil War (1938).

Sulphuretted   the action of atmospheric pollution on the surface of stamps, causing colours to darken.

Sunday Delivery Stamp   a stamp incorporating an additional fee for delivery of mail on Sunday. Such stamps, raising funds for a sanatorium and rest homes for postal workers, were issued by Bulgaria (1925–29).

Superimposed Adhesive Stamps   adhesive stamps affixed over impressed stamps on postal stationery. This arose in 1868 when stationery of the German states was revalidated by having adhesives of the North German Confederation stuck over the obsolete embossed stamps.

Surcharge   an overprint which alters the face value of a stamp.

Surface Printing   a process, better known as letterpress and sometimes known inaccurately as typography, in which the printing ink lies on the surface of the plate, rather than in the recesses, as in intaglio or photogravure (qqv).

Susse Perforation   a very coarse perforation gauging 7, applied to imperforate French stamps by the firm of Susse Frères of Paris.

Syllabic Alphabets   two alphabets (Kata Kana and Hira Kana) used in Japan for the transliteration of foreign words, employed as code letters identifying the plates of the 1874 series.

Tab   a label attached to the foot of a stamp, from the bottom row of the sheet, pioneered by Israel and used to this day to augment the text or picture on the stamp itself.

Tagged   mainly American term for a stamp overprinted with phosphor bands to assist electronic sorting.

Taille Douce   French term for Intaglio (qv).

Talking Stamps   a set of seven plastic, self-adhesives issued by Bhutan (1973) in the form of miniature gramophone records.

Taxe   French for "charge" inscribed on postage due labels and charge marks used in international mail, often abbreviated to the letter T. *Taxe Perçue* (charge paid) often appears on paid handstamps intended for international mail.

Taxpost   a service of the British Post Office accelerating documents of the Inland Revenue, and denoted by distinctive labels.

Telegraph Cancellation   a datestamp or obliteration applied to stamps on telegram forms. Many 19th century high value postage stamps were, in fact, used telegraphically.

Telegraph Stamp   a stamp, either embossed on forms or adhesive, intended primarily for the telegraph service, but sometimes used postally.

Telegraph Stationery   message forms, receipts, telegrams and telegraphic envelopes.

Temporary Rubber Datestamp   a rubber handstamp issued to minor post offices in many British colonies (notably Jamaica and the Pacific islands).

Testing Label   a label used by postal services to test the efficiency of vending machines. See *Poached Egg.*

Tête-Bêche   French term signifying a pair of stamps upside down in relation to each other.

Textiles as Printing Materials   stamps printed on cloth were pioneered by Hungary (1958) and followed by Bhutan (1969).

Thematic Collecting   the arrangement of stamps according to their theme or subject, instead of in the traditional order by date and country of issue. Known in America as topical collecting.

Thermography   a printing process whereby a raised pattern is created by heating a resinous compound. First used on stamps by Sierra Leone (1965).

Thermoplastics   a technique using plastic substances to create a three-dimensional effect, e.g. Bhutan's sculpture stamps.

Tied   an adhesive stamp on an envelope or card, with a cancellation overlapping the stamp and the surrounding paper.

Tin Can Mail   a service instituted at Niuafo'ou, Tonga in 1882 as a means of getting canisters of letters through the surf to mailboats anchored offshore. The service was revived in 1932 by Walt Quensell who applied up to 23 different cachets to outgoing mail. Both Tonga and Niuafo'ou issued stamps in 1982 to mark the centenary. A similar service, with distinctive cachets, has been used on the island of St Kilda since 1958, reviving a custom practised by the inhabitants from 1734 till the 1930s.

Tinted Paper   paper slightly toned on one side, usually to help the printer avoid printing stamps on the gummed side. This was the case in later printings of the embossed 6d, using a greenish tint, and in stamps of Hanover which had a reddish tint.

To Pay Label   a label indicating that a special handling fee or customs duty is owing on a packet. See also *Postage Due Label.*

Tongs   term (chiefly American) for tweezers (qv).

Too Late   inscription on postmarks explaining an apparent delay in mail which had been posted too late to connect with the last despatch of the day.

Topical Collecting see *Thematic Collecting*.

Toughra   the sign manual of the ruler in Moslem countries, found on stamps of Turkey, Afghanistan and Saudi Arabia.

Tourist Publicity Stamps   stamps featuring scenery and landmarks and highlighting recreational facilities and hotels. Pioneered by Newfoundland (1897) but used by many countries, notably France and Italy which regularly issue such stamps each year.

Trade Card   dual-purpose card, introduced by Guyana in 1994, which could be retained intact as a trade card or peeled off and used as a postage stamp. Cards were printed in English or French and reproduced Disney film posters. See also *Stamp Cards.*

Traffic Lights   nickname for the colour dabs found in sheet margins of multicolour stamps.

Trakback   a service of Royal Mail Parcels involving the barcoding (qv) of parcels.

Transfer   term in lithography for the image laid down on the stone and built up to form the printing plate.

Transfer Roller   term in intaglio for the steel roller which transfers the image from the master die to the plate.

Transit Postmark   a postmark applied to a piece of mail in transit, and therefore distinct from the cancellation at the office of collection and any backstamp (qv) at the office of delivery.

Transorma   a machine for sorting incoming mail for delivery, the name being derived from Transportation and Sorting by Marchand and Andriessen (the inventors). Pioneered by Holland (1927) and used at Brighton (1935–68). Mail addressed to that town in the period of use bore letters and numerals applied at right angles to the address.

Travelling Post Office   a postal facility aboard a train, to accelerate mail handling. The service was pioneered in England in 1838 and has since been a feature of rail networks all over the world, using distinctive postmarks, often recognisable from the names of two or more towns and such keywords or abbreviations as *Zug, Ambulant, Amb., Bahn,* S.T. (Sorting Tender), R.P.O. (Railway Post Office) as well as T.P.O. itself.

Travelling Stamp   alternative term for a Skeleton (qv).

Treasury Essay   a suggested design for postage stamps, submitted as the result of a competition organised by the Treasury, 1839.

Treasury Roulette   a form of experimental separation tested under Treasury auspices in 1853–54.

Treaty Ports   the Chinese ports of Amoy, Canton, Chefoo, Foochow, Hankow, Hoihow, Ningpo, Shanghai, Swatow and Tientsin wherein the foreign powers were permitted by treaty to establish postal agencies. Many of these ports also had local stamps for municipal posts organised by the foreign communities.

Trimmed   pertaining to perforations and signifying thse which have been clipped (in booklets or coils) due to faulty guillotining. It is also applied to the conversion of fiscal stamps to postal use by cutting off a portion of their design (India, Ecuador, Macao).

Tripartite Labels and Stamps   labels and stamps consisting of three detachable parts, often employed in parcel post, one portion being affixed to the parcel, one retained by the despatching office and the third given to the sender as a receipt.

Triptych   a group of three different stamps printed side by side.

Tweezers   term used in Britain for the pronged implement used to pick up stamps without fingering them.

Two-Tier Post   a service of the British Post Office introduced in 1968, dividing all domestic mail into first and second classes. Paid postmarks, as well as small adhesive labels used in government offices, were introduced as a result. In more recent years NVI stamps (qv) have merely borne the class of posting.

Turned Envelope   an envelope turned inside out and re-used, chiefly in the Confederate States during the American Civil War.

Type   (a) a small piece of wood or metal having a letter, numeral or character set in relief at one end, used in movable printing; (b) a major classification of stamps or postmarks according to the salient features of the design or printing method.

Typeset   a design made up entirely of printer's type, rule and ornaments, as distinct from one with a design drawn or engraved for the purpose.

Typewritten Overprints and Surcharges   stamps altered by typewriting include Tonga (1896), Thailand (1902), Long Island (1916), Colombia (1920), Nicaragua (1929) and Pakistan (1947).

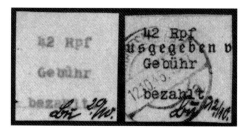

Typewritten Stamp   a stamp wholly or partially created by typewriting. This process was pioneered in the Cayes of Belize (1894), and used in Uganda (1895–96), Ermelo and Carolina, Transvaal (1900), Albania (1913–15), Long Island (1916) and Eckartsberga and Bad Saarow, Germany (1945).

Typography   strictly the arrangement, style and appearance of typeset matter but used philatelically to denote the letterpress process (qv).

Unappropriated Die   term denoting British fiscal stamps which had a space in their design for an overprint signifying the duty for which they were issued. Stamps printed from these dies were used for the military telegraph stamps of 1885 and the postage stamps of British Bechuanaland (1887).

Undeliverable Mail   mail which cannot be delivered because the addressee is dead, gone away, otherwise unknown or cannot be traced. Such mail is then usually returned to the sender bearing distinctive labels or postmarks. See also *Returned Letter Stamps*.

Undenominated Stamp   a stamp which bears no monetary denomination. It may be sold at the going rate applicable to a particular duty during times of rapid inflation (e.g. Hungary, 1946 or Brazil, 1993), or it may be printed in different colours to denote its face value (a common practice in the smaller British colonies), or it may be issued at a time when postal rates are likely to rise (USA and Canada in recent years), or it may be intended for domestic mail (UK, France, South Africa, Switzerland in recent years).

Underprint   a tint or feint pattern underlying the main design of a stamp, usually added as a security measure to render forgery difficult. See also *Back Print, Burelage* and *Moiré*.

Unemployed Intellectuals Stamps   stamps issued by France (1935–40) with a charity premium in aid of dole money for unemployed intellectuals. Hungary issued similar stamps (1940) on behalf of unemployed artists.

Ungummed   a stamp normally issued without any gum on the back, usually in countries with a tropical climate.

Unified Series   term in the UK for the stamps since 1881 used for both postage and revenue purposes.

Unissued   a stamp which has actually been printed for use but whose release has been aborted for some reason (usually a change of political regime).

Universal Postal Union   an international organisation with its headquarters in Berne, Switzerland, established in 1874 for the regulation and standardisation of mail-handling around the world.

Unmounted Mint   a stamp with full original gum and no trace of a hinge mark on the reverse.

Unofficial Stamp   a stamp issued by transportation companies to prepay charges on their parcels and packets. See also *Local Stamp*.

Unused   a stamp which has no cancellation on the face, but which has little or no gum on the back.

Used   a stamp which bears the mark of having been used postally, telegraphically or fiscally.

Used Abroad   a stamp of one country used in another, this usage being identified by the postmark.

Used Fiscally   a postage stamp (or more usually a unified postage and revenue stamp) whose cancellation denotes fiscal usage.

Used on Cover or Entire   a stamp affixed to a cover, and tied thereto by the cancellation.

Used on Piece   a stamp affixed to a piece of the envelope or card, showing the postmark intact.

Used Proof   a proof which has been gummed and affixed to a cover, with a postmark. Proofs which did official postal duty were pressed into service in Lithuania in 1920.

UV Lamp   an ultra-violet lamp used to detect postmarks or pen cancellation which have been removed from stamps, as well as check the fluorescence of modern stamps.

V Label   a serial label, similar to registration labels, but having a prominent letter V (from French *Valeur* = value) instead of the usual R, and often printed in red ink or on pink paper. Such labels denote insured letters and packets.

V Mail   inscription on special forms and envelopes used by American forces in World War II, for a facility similar to the British airgraph service (qv).

Value Converted   an overprint on Mexican stamps (1916–18) signifying conversion to hard currency backed by precious metal.

Value Erased   the removal of the original value shown on a printing plate, in order to create new values by printing in different colours. This practice was used in Corrientes, Argentina (1860–80).

Value Tablet   the space on a stamp carrying the monetary value.

Variety   a stamp differing in some detail from the normal issue.

Varnish Lines   bars of varnish applied diagonally to the face of Austrian stamps (1901–07) to prevent cleaning and re-use.

Vending Machine Stamps   stamps produced specifically for use in coin-operated machines, sometimes with a different watermark or perforation from sheet stamps, or even in a different design and smaller format.

Vervelle name given to a distinctive shade of the French 1 franc stamp of 1851, after the philatelist who discovered a sheet of this variety in the personal papers of Anatole Hulot, the superintendent of the government printing works.

Vignette a picture which shades off gradually into the surrounding background, but in philately used generally to describe the pictorial motif occupying the central part of a design.

Wallpaper Cover envelopes homemade from wallpaper in the southern states during the American Civil War.

War Stamp a stamp issued in time of war, either directly bearing on the war itself, or having a motif publicising the war effort. See *Bantams* and *Propaganda Stamp.*

War Tax Stamp a stamp either bearing a premium on mail posted during wartime, or for compulsory usage to raise funds for the conduct of a war, pioneered by Spain (1874) during the Carlist Wars and widely used during World War I.

Watermark a design, device or pattern in paper, usually visible when held up to the light.

Watermark Error any error or defect in the watermark, ranging from inversion or misplacement to missing bits, or the substitution of the incorrect motif. The use of the wrong watermark is also a major example.

Web Paper paper in continuous rolls used in a rotary press.

Wet Printing process in which the paper is dampened prior to use (notably in intaglio). Uneven shrinkage of the paper when drying often results in stamps differing slightly in dimensions.

Winchester Paper form of security paper with an underprinted pattern, used for the airmail stamps of Venezuela (1932).

Wing Margin an extension to the margin of a stamp on one side, caused in British stamps produced by De La Rue when the interpane gutters (qv) were perforated down the middle instead of at the sides, close to the stamps.

Wire Mark irregular, wavy line appearing at the foot of some American sheets, due to the wire at the foot of the paper web during the paper-making process.

Woodblock inaccurate nickname for the triangular stamps of the Cape of Good Hope 1861 produced

locally in letterpress instead of intaglio like the London printings.

Woodcut stamps printed from an incised wooden block, notably some Indian states and Polish POW issues of the Second World War.

Worn Plate a printing plate which, due to constant usage, shows signs of wear. Stamps from worn letterpress plates will have coarse, blurred lines, the finer details being filled with colour, while those from worn intaglio plates generally have a much lighter appearance than stamps from new plates.

Wove Paper the normal type of paper used for printing stamps, with a fine network of interlocking fibres, as opposed to Laid Paper (qv).

Wrapper strictly any sheet of paper enclosing a letter or packet, hence an envelope; but more specifically applied to strips of paper for sending newspapers through the post.

Wreck Cover a piece of mail salvaged from the wreck of a ship or aircraft, often showing marks of fire or immersion in the sea, with explanatory cachets and labels attached prior to delivery.

Xeroxed Stamp a stamp produced by a photocopying machine. This practice has been widely resorted to in the Ukraine since 1991, latterly using colour instead of black ink to prevent forgery, or distinctive paper, including the backs of unissued paper money.

X Label a label bearing a saltire or St Andrews Cross (qv), attached to stamps issued by Austria (1850) to fill up blank spaces on the sheet and prevent forgers using the paper. A similar practice applies to British stamp booklets (1904). Labels designated PP 47 were introduced in 1907 and bore a prominent cross in red, to indicate parcels sent out more than once for delivery and therefore already entered on the X List (qv).

X List a list kept at every British post office (1886–1915) on which was entered the details of all parcels which were conveyed at any point of their journey by rail, the reason being that a payment had to be made to the railway companies in such cases. A reference to the X List occurs on many types of parcel label from 1888 onwards.

Xylography the use of wood engraving in the production of stamps. Some stamps of Victoria (1854–59) were printed directly from wood blocks, while others were printed from stereotypes (qv) taken from woodblock dies.

Yachts collectors' term for the German colonial keytype stamps featuring the Imperial Yacht *Hohenzollern* 1900–16.

Zemstvo Posts local posts organised in each *zemstvo* (an administrative area of Russia) as feeder services to the imperial posts from 1864 till 1917. Numerous stamps were issued by these services, often heraldic or pictorial in design.

Zeppelin Posts   mail transmitted by German dirigible balloons between 1909 and 1937 and ranging from the demonstration flights of the *Schwaben* to the great trans-continental and polar flights of the *Hindenburg* and *Graf Zeppelin*. Numerous cards, envelopes, cachets, postmarks and stamps were issued, not only by Germany, but also by the countries served by these flights.

Zigzag Roulette   also known as *perce en pointes*, a form of separation in which short cuts were set at a sharp angle, similar to, but smaller and finer than, saw-tooth roulette (qv).

Zincography   process of engraving or etching designs on zinc plates, sometimes termed photozincography.

Zip Code   a postcode (qv) used in the USA, the name being derived from Zone Improvement Plan. It was introduced in 1963 five digits being assigned to every address (the first two identifying the state and the last three the town). More recently an additional four digits have been adopted to make mail sorting more precise. The code numbers not only appear on most postmarks but publicity has been generated by distinctive stamps and a cartoon character called Mr Zip, shown on sheet margins and slogan postmarks.

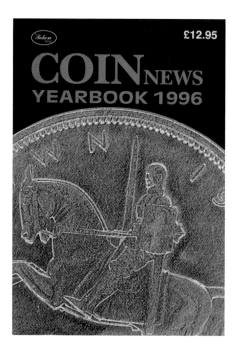

GLOSSARY OF PHILATELIC TERMS

The following list of keywords and terms used in stamp handbooks, catalogues, dealers' price lists and auction catalogues should enable English-speaking philatelists to use these reference works. The equivalent expression in the four major European languages is provided opposite the English term. Note that nouns are always capitalised in German.

ENGLISH	FRENCH	GERMAN	ITALIAN	SPANISH
abbreviation	abbreviation	Abkurzung	abbreviazione	abreviacion
above	en haut	oben	sopra	arriba
affixed	affiche	angeklebt	affisso	puesto
air letter	aerogramme	Luftpostbrief	lettera per posta aerea	carta aerea
airmail	poste aerienne	Flugpost Luftpost	posta aerea	correo aereo
albino	albinos	Albino	albino	albino
auction	vente	Auktion	asta	almoneda
back	revers	Ruckseite	rovescio	reves
background	fond	Grund	fondo	fondo
barred	barre	verriegelte	barrato	barreado
bisect	coupe en deux	halbiert	tagliato in due	cortado por la mitad
black	noir	schwarz	nero	negro
blank	en blanc	leer	in bianco	en blanco
block	bloc	Block	blocco	bloque
blue	bleu	blau	blu, azzuro	azul
blued	bleuté	geblaeut	tinto di azzuro	azulado
bluish	bleuatre	blaulich	bluastro	
booklet of stamps	carnet de timbres	Markenheftchen	quadernetto di francobolli	cuadernillo de sellos
border	cadre	Rand	bordo	borde
bottom	fond	Boden	basso	fondo
brown	brun	braun	bruno	castano
buff	chamois	samisch	camoscio	anteado
cancellation	oblitération	Entwertung	annullo	matasello
cancelled	annulé	ausser Kurs gesetzt	annullato	annulado
cancelled to order	oblitération de complaisance	Gefalligkeits -stempel	annullamento di favore	matasello de complacencia
cancelled	oblitéré	gestempelt	usato	cancelado
catalogue	catalogue	Katalog	catalogo	catalogo
censored	censure	Zensuriert	censurato	censurado

ENGLISH	FRENCH	GERMAN	ITALIAN	SPANISH
centred	centre	zentriert	centrato	centrado
charity	semi-postale	halbamtlich	beneficenza	beneficencia
circle	cercle	Kreis	cerchia	circulo
closed	ferme	geschlossen	chiuso	cerrado
coil	rouleau	Markenrolle	rotolo	rollo
colour	couleur	Farbe	colore	color
commemorative	emission commemoratif	Gedenkausgabe	emissione commemorativa	emision conmemorativo
copperplate	taille douce	Kupferstich	calcografia	calcografia
copy	copie	Abzug	copia	copia
corrected	rectifié	berichtigt	corretto	corregido
counterfeit	faux	falsch(ung)	falso	falso
cover	lettre	Brief	lettera	carta
cracked	craquelé	bruechig	rotto	agrietado
cross	croix	Kreuz	croce	cruz
cut square	fragment d'enveloppe	Kuvertauschnitt	ritaglio di busta	recorte de sobre entero
damaged	abimé	beschädigt	difettoso	defectuoso
dark	fonce	dunkel	cupo	oscuro
date	date	Datum	data	fecha
design	dessin	Entwurf	disegno	dibujo
die	coin	Pragestempel	stampo	troquel
double	double	doppel	doppia	doble
downwards	en bas	abwarts	all'ingiu	hacia abajo
dropped	abaissé	abwerft	abbassato	echado
embossed	imprimé en relief	Pragedruck	stampato a rilievo	estampada en relieve
engraved	grave	gestochen	stampato	grabado
engraving	gravure	Stich	calcografico	calcografia
entire	entier	Ganzsache	intiero	entero
envelope	enveloppe	Briefumschlag	busta	sobre
error	erreur	Fehldruck	errore	error
essay	essai	Probedruck	saggio	ensayo
express	expres	Eilboten	espresso	expreso
faded	fletri	abgefaerbt	sbiadito	destento
field post	poste de campagne	Feldpost	posta da campo	correo de campana
first day	premier jour	Ersttag	primo giorno	primer dia
foreign	étranger	Ausland	estero	extranjero
forerunner	precurseur	Vorlaufer	prescursore	precursor
forgery	falsification	Falschung	falsificazione	falsificacion
format	format	Format	form	tamano
franking	affranchissement	Frankatur	franquigia	franquicio
genuine	authentique	echt	autentico	autentico
green	vert	grun	verde	verde
grey	gris	grau	grigio	gris
gum	gomme	Gummi	gomma	goma
gutter	interpanneau	Zwischensteg	spazio in mezzo due bolli	pasillo entre dos sellos
handstamp	cachet à la main	Handstempel	timbro a mano	matasello de mano

ENGLISH	FRENCH	GERMAN	ITALIAN	SPANISH
head	tête	Kopf	testa	cabeza
hinge	charnière	Falz	linguella	fijasello
horizontal	horizontal	waagerecht	coricato	horizontal
illustration	illustration	Abbildung	illustruzione	ilustracion
imperf	non-dentelé	ungezahnt	non dentellato	sin dentar
impression	impression	Abdruck	impressione	impresion
inverted	renverse	kopfstehend	capovolta	invertido
inscription	inscription	Inschrift	inscrizione	inscripcion
issue	émission	Ausgabe	emissione	emision
label	etiquette	Etikett	etichetta	etiqueta
laid	vergé	gestreift	vergato	listado
left	gauche	links	sinistro	izquierdo
lettercard	carte-lettre	Kartenbrief	carta-lettera	carta tarjeta
letterpress	typographie	Buchdruck	tipografia	tipografia
light	clair	hell	chiaro	claro
lithography	lithographie	Steindruck	litografia	litografia
margin	bord de feuille	Rand	margine	margen
mint	neuf	postfrisch	nuovo	nuevo
mixed franking	affranchissement mixte	Mischfrankatur	affrancata mista	franquicia mixta
money order	mandat	Postanweisung	vaglia postale	giro postal
narrow	étroit	schmal	stretta	estrecho
not issued	non emis	unverausgabt	non emesso	no emitido
numeral	chiffre	Ziffer	cifra	cifra
off centre	mal centre	dezentriert	mal centrato	descienrado
official	officiel	amtlich	ufficiale	oficial
offset	decalé	Abklatsch	offset	offset
on back	au verso	Ruckseite	a tergo	al dorso
open	ouvert	offen	aperto	abierto
orange	orange	orange	arancio	laranja
overprint	surcharge	Auf/Uberdruck	soprastampa	sobrecargo
paid	payé	bezahlt	pagato	pagado
pair	paire	Paar	paio	pareja
paper	papier	Papier	carta	papel
parcel	colis	Postpaket	pacco (pacchi)	paquete
pen-cancelled	trait de plume	Federstrich	annullato a penna	obliterado de pluma
perforated	dentelé	gezahnt	dentellato	dentado
perforation gauge	odontometre	Zahnungsmesser	odontometro	odontometro
photogravure	heliogravure	Raster-tiefdruck	foto-calcografia	hueco-grabado
piece	fragment	Stuck	frammento	fragmento
postage due	timbre-taxe	Portomarke	segnatasse	sello de tasa
postage stamp	timbre-poste	Briefmarke	francobollo	sello de correos
postcard	carte postale	Postkarte	carta postale	tarjeta
postmark	marque postale	Abstempelung	timbro postale	matasello
post office	bureau de poste	Postamt	ufficio postale	oficina postal
precancel	pre-oblitéré	Vorausentwertung	preannullato	preobliteracion

ENGLISH	FRENCH	GERMAN	ITALIAN	SPANISH
price	prix	Preis	prezzo	precio
printing (number)	tirage	Auflage	tiratura	tirada
printing	impression	Druck	stampa	impresion
proof	épreuve	Probedruck	prova	prueba
purple	pourpre	purpur	porpura	purpura
red	rouge	rot	rosso	rojo
re-entry	rentre	nachgraviert	reinciso	regrabado
re-engraved	regravé	nachgraviert	reinciso	regrabado
registered	raccomande	einschreiben	raccomandata	certificada
regummed	regommé	nachgummiert	rigommato	regomado
reprint	reimpression	Nachdruck Neudruck	reimpressione ristampa	reimpresion
revenue stamp	timbre-fiscal	Stempelmarke Steuermarke	francobollo fiscale	sello fiscal
reverse	revers	Ruckseite	rovescio	reves
right	droit	rechts	destra	derecho
rouletted	percé	durchstochen	forto	cortado en linea
sale	vente	Verkauf	vendita	venta
set	serie	Satz	serie	serie
sheet	feuille	Bogen	foglio	hoja
side by side	se-tenant	Zusammendruck	a lato di	a lo largo
size	taille	Grosse	taglio	tamano
small	petit	klein	piccolo	pequeno
souvenir sheet	bloc-souvenir	Gedenkbock	blocco	hoja-bloque
specimen	specimen	Muster	saggio	muestra
sticker	etiquette	Etikett	etichetta	etiqueta
strip	bande	Streifen	striscia	tira
surcharge	surcharge	Uberdruck	soprastampa	sobrecargo
tax	taxe	Gebuhr	tassa	impuesto
tête-bêche	tête-bêche	Kehrdruck	alla rovescia	al reves
thick	epais	dick	spesso	grueso
thin	mince	dunn	sottile	delgado
thinned	aminci	verdunnte	assottigliato	adelgado
trial	épreuve essai	Druckprobe	prova di stampa	prueba
type	type	Type	tipo	tipo
typographed	typographie	Buchdruck	tipografia	tipografia
unmounted	sans charniere	falzlos	illinguellato	sin charnela
used	oblitéré	gebraucht	usato	usado
value	valeur	Wert	valore	valor
variety	varieté	Abart	varieta	variedad
vertical	vertical	senkrecht	verticale	vertical
watermark	filigrane	Wasserzeichen	filigrana	filigrana
white	blanc	weiss	bianco	blanco
wide	espace	weit	largo	ancho
without	sans	ohne	senza	sin
yellow	jaune	gelb	giallo	amarillo

. . . If you are interested in gallantry, then you should be reading

MEDAL NEWS

The **magazine devoted to all aspects of Military History, Medals and Gallantry**

MEDAL NEWS is a must for all collectors and medal enthusiasts, providing informative articles, auction reports, news and views as well as a FREE Medal Tracker service to help you reunite broken groups and further your collectiing interest. **PLUS** the Classified Adverts are FREE to all subscribers of **MEDAL NEWS.**

Available on subscription only
UK £25, Overseas £28, Airmail £40
(10 issues per year)

Payment also accepted by Dollar cheques or Access/Visa card.

O.A.T. **AERO CORREO**

AEREO **RECARGO**

V.R.I.

PERÇUE

O. W. OFFICIAL

PD

KEY WORDS AND ABBREVIATIONS IN STAMP, LABEL AND POSTMARK INSCRIPTIONS

A (*Anotacion*, Spanish for "registration"), registered letter stamps of Colombia, 1865 and 1870.

A overprint on air stamps of Colombia, 1950–53 to denote Avianca, the state airline.

Aangebragt per Land-Mail (Dutch "brought by land mail"), postage due labels of the Dutch East Indies, 1845-6.

Acores Azores.

Admiralty Official overprint on British stamps for use by the Admiralty 1903-4.

Advertised mark on undeliverable letters indicating that they had been advertised before being returned to sender.

A.E.F. (*Afrique Equatoriale Française*), stamps of French Equatorial Africa, 1936.

Aerea overprint on air stamps of Ecuador

Aereo overprint or inscription on stamps of Spanish-speaking countries denoting airmail.

Aereo Exterior 1931 overprint on Guatemala stamps of 1929 for use on overseas airmail.

Aereo SEDTA (*Sociedad Ecuatoriana de Trasportes Aereos*), postal tax stamps of Ecuador, 1938.

Aero Correo overprint on air stamps of Honduras.

Aero O Y on air stamps of Finland.

Aerphost Gaelic "airmail", on Irish airmail labels.

Aer-Phost Irish airmail stamps, 1949.

Affranchts (*Affranchissements*) overprint on French stamps to denote pre-cancellation.

Afft Oc overprint with a cross and new value, Tunisian charity stamps, 1923.

Africa Occidental Espanola Spanish West Africa.

Africa Orientale Italiana Italian East Africa.

Afrique Equatoriale Francaise French Equatorial Africa.

Afrique Occidentale Francaise French West Africa.

AH PD overprint on Azores for use in Angra, Horta and Ponta Delgada 1896.

Aidez les Tuberculeux (French for "help the tuberculous") on charity stamps of Tunisia.

Air on air stamps of Canada.

Airmail overprint on air stamps of Canal Zone and Phillipines.

Airpost airmail stamps of Newfoundland.

Ajanlas, Ajl. (Magyar for "registered") overprint on undenominated stamps of Hungary, 1946.

ALALC (*Asociacion Latino Americana de Libre Comercio*) "Latin-American Free Trade Association", on stamps of Uruguay, 1970.

Alcance y U.H. late fee stamps, Uruguay.

Alfabetizacion literacy campaign stamps of Ecuador and Mexico.

Allemagne (French for "German") overprint on Belgian stamps for use in parts of Germany administered by Belgium after the First World War.

A.M. overprint on Mexican stamps for Aguascalientes during the Civil War 1914.

A.M. (abbreviation for *Axia Metallike*, Greek for "value in coin") overprint or inscription on Greek stamps 1900–02.

Ambulance Laquintinie Cameroun charity stamps, 1941 to raise money for ambulances for the Free French forces.

A.M.G. F.T.T. Allied Military Government, Free Territory of Trieste, overprint on Italian stamps for Trieste, 1947–54.

A.M.G.-V.G. Allied Military Government, Venezia Giulia.

AM Post Deutschland Allied Military Post, Germany, 1945–46.

Amsterdao compulsory tax stamps of Portugal 1928 to raise funds to send the national team to the Olympic Games at Amsterdam.

Amtlich Eroffnet Durch die K.W. Postdirection (German for "officially opened by the Royal Wurttemberg Postal Authority") on returned letter stamps of Wurttemberg.

Amtlicher Verkehr (German for "official business"), official stamps of Wurttemberg.

Anciens Combattants overprint on charity stamps of Tunisia raising money for ex-servicemen.

Annule (French for "annulled") overprinted on stamps which have been invalidated or demonetised.

Anotacion on registered letter stamps of Colombia.

A.O. *(Autre Objets)* French postal labels affixed to small packets to denote mail other than letters.

A.O. *(Afrique Orientale)* overprint on Belgian Congo to denote use in occupied German East Africa, 1918.

AOF *(Afrique Occidentale Française)* French West Africa, 1945.

A.O.I. *(Africa Orientale Italiana)* postage due labels of Italian East Africa.

A Payer te Betalen (French and Flemish for "to pay") postage due labels of Belgium.

A Percevoir (French for "to pay") postage due labels of Canada, France and French colonies.

A Percevoir below numerals of value in a typeset frame, with no other inscription—Guatemala, 1876–79.

A.P.O. Army Post Office.

Aportacion Voluntaria (Spanish for "voluntary contribution") charity stamps and labels of the Spanish Civil War, 1936–39.

Apres le depart (French for "after departure") instructional mark on letters posted after the last mail collection of the day, either to explain the delay or to indicate that a late fee was recoverable from the addressee.

A.R. Sometimes said to denote "Acknowledgment of Receipt" but more correctly "Advice of Receipt": inscribed on postmarks and postal stationery connected with this international service. Also inscribed on stamps provided for this purpose by Colombia, Chile, El Salvador and Montenegro.

Arbe Overprint on Fiume for use in the Dalmatian island of Rab, 1920.

Archipel des Comores Comoro Archipelago.

A Receber (Portuguese for "to pay") postage due labels of Portugal and colonies.

Armenwet (Dutch for "poor laws") overprint on stamps of the Netherlands, 1913–18 for use on official mail in connection with the poor law administration.

Army Official overprint on British stamps for military official mail 1896–1904.

Arriba España (Spanish for "Up with Spain") inscribed or overprinted on many issues of the Spanish Civil War, 1936–39.

Arvizkarosultaknak Kulon (Magyar for "on behalf of flood victims") on tabs forming extensions to the definitive series of Hungary converting them to charity stamps 1913.

Asegurado (Spanish for "secured") on insured mail labels of Latin American countries.

Asistenta Sociala (Roumanian for "social assistence") on compulsory tax stamps of Roumania.

ASP (Afro-Shirazi Party) Zanzibar, 1967.

Assicurato (Italian for "secured") on insured mail labels of Italy and San Marino.

Assistencia overprint on stamps of Portugal and colonies for poor relief charity.

Assistencia Publica compulsory tax stamps of Portuguese India, 1960.

A & T overprint on French colonial general issue for Annam and Tonquin, 1888 (now Vietnam).

At Betale (Norwegian for "to pay") Norwegian postage due labels, 1889–1923.

ATM (Automatenmarken) German term of automatic machine vending labels.

ATM (Automatic Teller Machine) American term denoting self-adhesive stamps sold in small sheets or blocks from special vending machines.

Aunus overprint on Finnish stamps for use during the occupation of Olonetz, Russia, 1919.

Ausser Kurs gesetzt (German for "taken out of use") overprint to denote Swiss stamps no longer valid for postage.

Aviacion on airmail labels of Uruguay.

Aviao (Portuguese for "airmail") overprint with jumbled Greek letters on Macao air stamps, 1936.

Avion Nessre Tafari Ethiopian airmail stamps, 1931.

Avionska Posta Yugoslav air stamps, 1949.

Aviso de Recepcion (Spanish for "advice of receipt") on stamps of El Salvador, 1897.

Avisporto maerke (Danish for "newspaper postage stamp") Danish newspaper stamps, 1907–15.

Ayudo de Ecuador ("aid for Ecuador") overprint on charity stamps of Paraguay raising money for earthquake victims.

A.Z. laureated overprint on Albanian stamps of 1927 denoting Ahmed Zogu, president of the republic, later King Zog I.

Azad Hind (Hindi for "Free India") inscribed on stamps printed in Nazi Germany for use in India after the British were driven out. The stamps were, of course, never issued.

B. overprint on stamps of the Straits Settlements for use at the British post office in Bangkok, 1884–85.

B (in oval) Belgian railway parcel stamps.

BA (British Administration) overprint on British stamps for use in Eritrea, Somalia and Tripolitania, 1948–50.

Bajar Porto (Indonesian for "postage due") on Indonesian postage due labels since 1950.

Banat Bacska overprint on Hungarian stamps, 1919 for use in part of Transylvania between Serb and Roumanian occupation.

Baranya overprint on Hungarian stamps, 1919 during Serb occupation.

BATYM Batum, 1919, under British occupation.

Bayern Bavaria.

B.C.A. British Central Africa (later Nyasaland and now Malawi).

B.C.M. British Consular Mail, Madagascar.

B.C.O.F. (British Commonwealth Occupation Force) overprint on Australia stamps for use in Japan, 1946.

B. Depto. Zelaya Overprint on stamps of Nicaragua, 1904–11 for use at Bluefields in the province *(departamento)* of Zelaya.

Belgie, Belgique Belgium.

Belgien Belgium under German occupation, 1914–18.

Belgisch Congo Belgian Congo.

Benaders (Farsi for "seaports") overprint on Persian stamps sold at ports on the Persian gulf, 1922.

Benadir (Swahili for "seaport") Italian Somaliland.

Bentjana Alam (Indonesian for "national disaster") overprint on charity stamps of 1953.

Besa (sacred oath) overprinted on Albanian stamps, 1914.

Besetzes Gebiet Nordfrankreich (German for "occupied district of northern France") framed overprint across pairs of French stamps. Dunkirk, July 1940.

B.G. (abbreviation for Bollo Gazzette, Italian for "newspaper stamp") Modena.

Bijzondere Vluchten (Dutch for "special flights") inscribed on airmail stamps of the Netherlands, 1938–56.

B.I.O.T. (British Indian Ocean Territory) overprint on stamps of the Seychelles, 1968.

BIT (Bureau Internationale du Travail) inscribed or overprinted on Swiss stamps for use by the International Labour Office; also inscribed or overprinted on stamps of Brazil, Czechoslovakia, Uruguay and other countries to denote ILO Congresses.

BLCI (inscribed in the four corners), Bhopal, 1884–96 and 1902.

B.L.P. (Buste Lettere Postali, Italian for "postal letter envelopes") overprint on Italian stamps, 1921 denoting a discount to war veterans" organisations which affixed them to advertising envelopes which they then sold to the public at a profit.

B.M.A. (British Military Administration) overprint on stamps of Sarawak, 1945 for use in Brunei, Labuan and North Borneo as well as that state.

B.M.A. with Eritrea, Somalia or Tripolitania, overprinted on British stamps for use in these Italian colonies during the Second World War.

B.N.F. *(Base Navale Française)* overprint on stamps of the French post offices in the Levant for use at the naval base in Castellorizo off the Turkish coast, 1920.

Board of Education overprint on British stamps for the use of school inspectors 1902–04.

Boehmen und Maehren Nazi protectorate of Bohemia and Moravia, 1939–44.

Bogache, Bogchah unit of currency inscribed on stamps of the Yemen.

Boka Kotorska overprint on Yugoslav stamps for use in the Bight of Kotor (Boche de Cattaro) under German occupation 1944.

Bollo della Posta di Sicilia (Italian for "stamp of the posts of Sicily) Sicily, 1859.

Bollo della Posta Napoletana ("stamp of the Neapolitan posts") Naples, 1858.

Bollo Postale ("postal stamp") special delivery stamps of San Marino.

Bollo Straordinario per le Poste ("extraordinary stamp for the posts") Tuscany newspaper stamps, 1854.

Bosna Bosnia

Bosnien Bosnia

Bouvet Oya overprint on Norwegian stamps, 1934 for use on mail from the Bouvet Islands during an Antarctic expedition.

B.P.C. *(Bureau de Poste de Campagne*, French for "field post office") Belgian military post.

Brandkastzegels (Dutch for "fire safe stamps") inscribed on special marine insurance stamps affixed to packets carried in fire–proof safes aboard ships.

Braunschweig Brunswick.

Brezdomcem Den Obdachlosen (Slovene for "homeless relief fund") overprint on Italian express letter stamps for use in Slovenia 1944.

Briefpost (German for "letter post") inscribed on general issues of the French zone of occupation, 1945–46.

British Consular Mail inscribed on stamps issued by the British consulate in Madagascar, 1884–86.

Buiten Bezit (Dutch for "outer possessions") overprint on Netherlands Indies stamps for use in the outer islands, 1908.

Bundesrepublik Deutschland (German for "Federal Republic of Germany") inscribed on stamps of West Germany, 1949.

C (for Spanish *Campana*, countryside) overprint on stamps of Paraguay, 1922–42 for domestic use.

Cabo overprint on stamps of Nicaragua for use in the province of Cabo Gracia a Dios (Cape Thanks to God), 1904–9.

Cabo Jubi Cape Juby.

Cabo Verde Cape Verde Islands.

Caches (French for "cash", Chinese currency) overprint on postage due labels of the French colonies general issue for use in French Settlements in India.

Caisse d"Amortissement (French for "sinking fund") overprint or inscription on stamps of 1927–31 issued with a surcharge to raise money for the reduction of the national debt.

Campana Contra el Paludismo (Spanish for "campaign against malaria") inscribed on compulsory tax stamps of Mexico, 1939.

Canarias Canary Islands, 1936–37.

Cancelled overprint on stamps of certain British colonies to denote invalidation before sale to collectors at a greatly reduced price.

Cancelled V-R-I overprint on South African Republic 1901 for use at Wolmaransstad, Transvaal.

Cantonal Taxe (cantonal postage) Zurich, 1843–46.

CARICOM (acronym for Caribbean Community) on stamps of the West Indies, 1994.

CARIFTA (acronym for Caribbean Free Trade Area) on stamps of Antigua, Barbados, Guyana and Trinidad, 1969.

Cartilla Postal Spanish franchise stamps provided for the use of Don Diego Castell in mailing copies of his book on the postal history of Spain, 1869.

CBRS (Charles Brooke, Rajah of Sarawak) appearing in the corners of Sarawak stamps, 1871.

CCCP USSR.

C.CH. overprint on French colonial stamps for Cochin China, 1892.

C.C.T.A. (*Commission de Co–operation Technical d'Afrique*) inscription on the stamps marking the tenth anniversary of the Commission for Technical Co-operation in Africa south of the Sahara, issued by many African countries of the French Community in 1960.

C. Dpto Zelaya overprint on Nicaragua for use in Cabo Gracias a Dios.

Cechy a Morava (Czech for "Bohemia and Moravia") overprint or inscription during the Nazi protectorate, 1939–44.

C.E.F. overprint on Indian stamps for use by the China Expeditionary Force during the Boxer Rebellion, 1900.

C.E.F. overprint on German colonial stamps of Kamerun to denote Cameroons Expeditionary Force, 1915.

Cent. overprint in Frakturschrift in German stamps, for use in territory occupied by the Western Command (northern France) 1916.

Centesimi (Italian unit of currency) overprint on Austrian field post stamps for use in parts of Italy occupied by Austrian forces, 1918.

Centesimi di Corona overprint on Italian stamps for use in Dalmatia, 1921–22.

Centimes diagonal overprint on German stamps for use in Turkey 1908–14.

CEPT (*Conference Europeen des Postes et Telecommunications*) inscription, often accompanied by the interlocking posthorn logo, on "Europa" stamps issued annually since 1960.

Cerrado (Spanish for "sealed") on resealing labels of Mexico.

Certificada (Spanish for "registered") on Bolivian stamps, 1879–85.

Certificado on registered letter stamps of El Salvador and Venezuela.

Ceska Republika Czech Republic.

Ceskoslovenske Armady Sibirske (Czech for "Czechoslovak Siberian Army") on stamps of the Czechoslovak Legion 1919.

Ceskoslovenske Vojsko na Rusi (Czech for "Czechoslovak Forces in Russia") on stamps of the Czechoslovak Legion operating in Siberia, 1919–20.

Ceskoslovensko, Cesko-Slovensko Czechoslovakia.

CFA (*Communaute Francaise d'Afrique*, "French African Community") denoting colonial currency on the stamps used in Reunion.

C.G.H.S. (*Commission de Gouvernement Haute Silesie*) overprint on German official stamps fur use in Upper Silesia during the plebiscite period, 1920–21.

Ch. Taxe overprint on stamps of the French Levant for use as postage due labels of Syria, 1920.

Chemins de Fer (French for "railways") Belgian railway stamps.

Chiffre Taxe postage due labels of France and colonies, as well as Turkey, 1914.

C.I.C.I. (abbreviation for Congress of the International Colonial Institute) overprint on Portugal for use as a franking stamp 1933.

CIHS (*Commission Interalliée Haute Silesie*) overprint on German stamps used by the Inter-allied Commission superintending the plebiscite in Upper Silesia, 1920.

Cinquantenaire 24 Septembre 1853–1903 overprint on French colonies postage due labels for use in New Caledonia to celebrate the centenary of the colony.

CIS (*Commission Interalliée Slesvig*) on stamps of the Inter-allied Commission superintending the plebiscite of 1920 in Schleswig.

C.M.T. overprint on Austrian stamps for use in the western Ukraine under Roumanian occupation, 1919–20.

Co. Ci. (abbreviation for *Commissarioto Civile*, "civil commissariat") overprint on Yugoslav stamps for use in the province of Ljubljana (Laibach) under Italian occupation, 1941.

Colis Postal, Postaux French for "postal parcel(s)" inscribed or overprinted on stamps of France, French colonies and Haiti.

Colis Postal Postcollo French and Flemish inscription on Belgian parcel stamps.

Comissao Portuguesa de Prisioneiros de Guerra overprint on Portuguese franking stamps for the Portuguese Commission for Prisoners of War.

Commissariato Genle (Italian for "general commission") Jubaland.

Commission d"Administration et de Plebiscite overprint on German stamps for use in Allenstein during the plebiscite period, 1920.

Commission de Controle Provisoire (Provisional Control Commission) overprint on stamps issued under Albanian military authority, 1917 and 1949.

Commission de Gouvernement Haute Silesie on stamps of the Upper Silesia Government Commission during the plebiscite of 1920.

Commission fur Retourbriefe (German for "returned letter commission") on returned letter stamps of Bavaria and Wurttemberg.

Companhia de Mocambique Mozambique Company, 1918–41.

Companhia do Nyassa Portuguese Nyassa Company.

Complementario on postage due labels of Mexico.

Comunicaciones inscription on otherwise anonymous stamps of Spain, 1872–99.

Confed. Granadina (Granadine Confederation) Colombia 1859–60.

Confoederatio Helvetica (Latin for "Swiss Confederation") on Swiss stamps of 1941.

Congreso de los Diputados on Spanish stamps of 1896–98 intended for the use of members of parliament.

Construccion overprint on compulsory tax stamps of Guatemala for a public building programme.

Continente inscribed on Portuguese stamps for use on the mainland and not in the offshore islands of Azores and Madeira.

Contrasena Estampilla de Correos (Spanish for "countersigned postage stamp") on stamps of Venezuela, 1873–76.

Contre le Faim (French for "against hunger") overprint on Rwanda.

Coo Cos, Aegean Islands.

Coree Korea.

Corps Expeditionnaire Franco-Anglais (Franco-British Expeditionary Corps) overprint on stamps of Gabon for use in Cameroun, 1915.

Correio (Portuguese for "posts") on stamps of Portugal and colonies.

Correio Aereo on Portuguese airmail stamps of 1936-41.

Correo (Spanish for "posts) on stamps of Spain and Latin America.

Correo Aereo on air stamps of Spain and Latin America since 1920.

Correo Aereo D.S. overprint on Bolivia for domestic airmail.

Correo Aereo Habilitado ("valid for airmail") overprint on Paraguay.

Correo Aereo Interior overprint on Nicaragua for domestic airmail.

Correo Aereo Interno overprint on the Dominican Republic for domestic airmail.

Correo Aereo Nacional overprint on Cuba for domestic airmail.

Correo Oficial on official stamps of Spain and Latin America.

Correo Oficial Aereo overprint on Honduras for official airmail.

Correos Aereo on air stamps of Colombia.

Correos Aereos on air stamps of Mexico.

Correos de Oficial overprint on El Salvador for official use.

Correos Departamentales overprint on Colombia for official use.

Correos Devolucion de Correspondencia Sobrante (Spanish for "return of undeliverable correspondence") on Spanish returned letter stamps.

Correos Fonopostal on stamps issued by Argentina in 1939 to prepay the postage on special flexible gramophone records whereby the sender could transmit an oral message by post.

Correos Franco on stamps of Spain from 1850 onwards.

Correos Interior Franco Philippine Islands.

Correos Nacionales (national posts) overprint on fiscal stamps of Guatemala to convert them to postal use.

Correos y Telegrafos (Spanish for "posts and telegraphs") on stamps of Argentina from 1890 onwards.

Correo Urbano de Bogota Bogota municipal mail, Colombia.

Correo Urgente on express mail stamps of Colombia.

Correo Urgente Urbana on municipal special delivery stamps of Colombia.

Correspondence Militaire on military mail stamps of New Caledonia.

Correspondencia a Debe (Spanish for "underpaid mail") on postage due labels of Panama.

Correspondencia Oficial on official stamps of Chile, dominican Republic and Mexico.

Correspondencia Urgente (Spanish for "urgent mail") on Spanish express delivery stamps since 1905.

Costa Atlantica B or **C** overprint on Nicaraguan stamps for use at Bluefields or Cape Gracias a Dios on the Atlantic coast, 1907 due to fluctuations in the value of currency locally.

Cote d"Ivoire Ivory Coast.

Cote du Niger French Niger Coast

Cote Francaise des Somalis French Somali Coast.

Cour Internationale de Justice overprint on Dutch stamps for use at the International Court of Justice in The Hague.

Cour Permanente de Justice Internationale Permanent Court of International Justice, The Hague.

Courrier de la Societe des Nations League of Nations.

Courrier du Bureau International d"Education International Education Office.

Courrier du Bureau International du Travail International Labour Office.

CP abbreviation for *Colis Postal* (qv) overprinted in 1904 on stamps of the Ivory Coast intended for parcels.

C.R. (Cakobau Rex) on stamps of Fiji, 1871.

Croce Rossa on charity stamps of Italy and San Marino for the Red Cross.

Croissant Rouge Turc on charity stamps of Turkey for the Red Crescent.

Croix Rouge (French for "Red Cross") on charity stamps of Ethiopia 1945 and many French stamps.

Cruz Roja (Spanish for "Red Cross") on compulsory tax stamps of Honduras (1941) and Colombia (1966).

Cruz Vermelha (Portuguese for "Red Cross") on Brazilian charity stamps of 1935.

Crveni Krst on Yugoslav Red Cross stamps.

CS or **CSA** Confederate States of America.

Csomag or **Cs.** (Magyar for "parcel") overprinted on undenominated Hungarian stamps, 1945.

D albino on a black circular ground, overprint on Dutch East Indies denoting Dienst (service) for official mail.

D in three corners of triangular stamps, on personal delivery postage due stamps of Czechoslovakia 1937.

Dai Nippon (Japanese for "Greater Japan") overprint on stamps of Malaya and the Straits Settlements during the Japanese occupation in the Second World War.

Dai Nippon Yubin Perak and Selangor under Japanese occupation.

Danmark Denmark.

Dansk Vestindien Danish West Indies.

Datia Duttia.

DBP Cyrillic abbreviation for *Dalny Vostochnaya Respublika,* overprinted on Russian stamps for the Far Eastern Republic.

D. de A. Antioquia.

DDR abbreviation for *Deutsche Demokratische Republik,* German Democratic Republic.

Decreto de 27 Jani"o 1870 overprint on Escuelas (schools) stamps of Venezuela.

Dedeagh Dedeagatz.

Defensa Nacional (Spanish for "national defence") overprint on compulsory tax stamps of Ecuador.

Deficiente on postage due labels of Nicaragua and Paraguay.

Deficit on postage due labels of Peru.

Delegacoes Red Cross franking stamps of Portugal, 1926.

De A *(Departamento de Antioquia)* Antioquia, 1890.

De Oficio official stamps of El Salvador and Peru.

Den Waisen Sirotam (German and Slovene for "orphans") overprint on Italian air stamps as compulsory tax stamps of Slovenia 1944.

Desmit Rbl. ("ten roubles" surcharge) Latvia 1921.

Deutsche Bundespost German Federal Post, on stamps of Germany since 1949.

Deutsche Demokratische Republik German Democratic Republic.

Deutsche Feldpost German Field Post.

Deutsche Militaer-Verwaltung Montenegro overprint on Yugoslav stamps during the German occupation of Montenegro, 1943.

Deutsche Neu-Guinea German New Guinea.

Deutsch-Ostafrika German East Africa.

Deutsche Post Germany under allied occupation, 1946–48; East Germany, 1990 pending re-unification with the Federal republic.

Deutsche Post Osten German Post in the East (i.e. Poland), 1939.

Deutsche Reichspost on stamps of the German Empire 1872–89.

Deutsches Reich (German Empire) Germany, 1872–1944.

Deutschosterreich (German Austria) overprint on Austrian stamps, 1919–20.

Deutsch Sudwesafrika German South West Africa.

Devastacion de la Ciudad (Spanish for "devastation of the city") on compulsory tax stamps of the Dominican Republic, 1930, following the destruction of the capital by hurricane.

D.F.U. Frim. Udst. overprint on Danish stamps signifying "stamp exhibition of Denmark's Philatelists Union", 1938.

Dienst (Dutch for "service") overprint on Dutch East Indies for official mail.

Dienstmarke (German for "service stamp") inscription or overprint on stamps of Bavaria, Danzig, Germany, Liechtenstein, Prussia and Saar for official mail.

Dienstsache (German for "service matter") on official stamps of Liechtenstein.

Diligencia (Spanish for "mailcoach") Uruguay 1856.

Dinero (Spanish unit of currency) Peru 1858–62.

Dios Patria Libertad (Spanish for "God, Fatherland and Liberty") on stamps of the Dominican Republic, 1879.

Dios Patria Rey (Spanish for "God, Fatherland and King") on Carlist stamps of Spain, 1874–75.

Diwi Rubli ("two roubles") surcharge on stamps of Latvia.

D.J. overprint on French Somali Coast stamps of 1893 for use in Djibouti.

D.L.O. Dead Letter Office (handling undeliverable mail).

DM (abbreviation for *Dienstmarke,* service stamp) overprint on stamps of Danzig for official use.

DMSZ (abbreviation for *Dienstmarke* and *Sluzba Zamek,* the German and Czech for "official stamp") inscribed in the corners of official stamps of Bohemia and Moravia.

Doplata postage due labels of Poland.

Doplatit or Doplatne postage due labels of Czechoslovakia.

Drijvende Brandkast (Dutch for "floating safe") on marine insurance stamps of the Netherlands and Dutch East Indies, 1921.

Drzava (Serbo-Croat for "state") on stamps of Bosnia (1918) and Yugoslavia 91919).

Due Grana (value) without a country name — Neapolitan Provinces, 1861.

Duitsch Oost Afrika Belgische Bezetting (Flemish for

"German East Africa Belgian Occupation") overprint on Belgian Congo for the occupation of Ruanda-Urundi, 1916.

Duitschland (Flemish for "Germany") overprint on Belgian stamps for use in parts of Germany under Belgian administration after the First World War.

E (*Eisenbahn*, German for "railways") overprint or perforation on Bavarian stamps for use on official railway mail.

E.A.F. overprint on British stamps for use by East African Forces occupying Italian East Africa.

E.C. (*Ejercito Constitutionalista,* Constitutionalist Army) overprint on Mexican stamps of Guyamas 1915.

E.C. de M. (*Ejercito Constitutionalista de Mexico,* Constitutionalist Army of Mexico) overprint on Mexican stamps used at San Luis Potosi 1914.

E.C.M. (*Ejercito Constitutionalista Mexicano,* Constitutionalist Army of Mexico) overprint on Civil War stamps of Matehuala 1914

ECAFE acronym for Economic Commission for Asia and the Far East, on stamps of the Philippines, 1947.

Edificios Postales (Spanish for "postal buildings") overprint on compulsory tax stamps of El Salvador, 1931.

Educacion Nacional on charity stamps of Peru, 1950 raising money for state education.

EEF (Egyptian Expeditionary Force) on the first stamps of Palestine, 1918.

Eesti Estonia.

Eesti Ohopost on airmail stamps of Estonia.

EE.UU. *Estados Unidos* (Spanish for "United States") on stamps of Colombia, Mexico and Venezuela.

E.F.O. (*Etablissements Françaises d'Oceanie*) French Oceanic Settlements.

EFTA European Free Trade Area on stamps of the UK and other countries in western Europe, 1967.

Efterporto on postage due labels of the Danish West Indies.

Egeo Aegean Islands under Italian administration, 1912.

Eilboten German express mail labels.

Eilmarke German express or special delivery stamps.

Einschreiben (German for "registered") on registration labels.

Eire (Gaelic for "Ireland") Irish Free State or republic of Ireland.

Eisenbahn (German for "Railways") on railway stamps of Germany.

Ejercito Constitutionalista Transitoria (Spanish for "Transitory Constitutionl Army") Sonora, Mexico, 1913.

Ejercito Renovador (Spanish for "Renovator Army") Sinaloa, Mexico, 1923.

Elsass-Lothringen Alsace-Lorraine under German occupation, 1940.

Elua Keneta Hawaii.

Emp. Ottoman Turkey.

Encomendas Postais (Portuguese for "parcel post") on parcel stamps of Portugal.

Encomienda or Encomiendas on parcel stamps of Uruguay, 1929.

Entrega Especial (Spanish for "special delivery") on stamps of Cuba, Spain and Latin American countries.

Entrega Inmediata (Spanish for "immediate delivery) on special delivery stamps of Cuba, Mexico and Spain.

E.R.I. (*Edwardus Rex Imperator*) overprint on stamps of the South African Republic (Transvaal) at the end of the Boer War to denote British occupation.

Erste K.K. pr. Donau Dampfschiffahrt Gesellschaft (First Royal and Imperial Danube Steamship Company) on stamps of the Danube Steam Navigation Company, 1866–71.

ES (abbreviation for *Estado de Sonora*, "state of Sonora") overprint on Mexican stamps for use in Sonora during the Civil War of 1914.

E.S. (abbreviation for *Estado Soberano,* Spanish for "sovereign state") on stamps of Antioquia and Panama

Escuelas (Spanish for "schools") on many stamps of Venezuela, intended primarily to denote a tax raising money for state education, but used indiscriminately for postage.

Espana Spain.

Espana Franqueo (franked) on Carlist stamps of Spain, 1873.

Espresso (Italian for "express") on stamps of Italy and colonies, San Marino and the Vatican.

Estado S. (Spanish for "sovereign state") on stamps of Tolima.

Estado Soberano (Spanish for "sovereign state") on stamps of Bolivar and Santander.

Estados Unidos de Nueva Granada (United States of New Granada) Colombia.

Est Africain Allemand Occupation Belge (French for "Belgian occupation of German East Africa") overprint on stamps of the Belgian Congo for use in Ruanda-Urundi.

Estampillas de Correo Contrasena (Spanish for "provisional postage stamp" overprint on stamps of Venezuela.

Estensi Modena.

Estero (Italian for "overseas") overprint on Italian stamps for use in post offices and agencies in South America, Africa, Turkey and the Levant.

Estland Estonia under German occupation, 1942.

Etablissements de l'Oceanie French Oceanic Settlements, Polynesia.

Etablissements Francaises dans l''Inde French Settlements in India.

Etat du Inchi ya Katanga Katanga.

Etat Francais French State, 1943.

Etat Ind. du Congo Congo Free State, 1886–98.

Etiopia Ethiopia under Italian occupation, 1936.

EU abbreviation for *Estados Unidos* (United States) on stamps of Brazil and Colombia.

Exposicion General Espanola (Spanish General Exhibition), Spain 1929.

Expres (French for "express") on express stamps of Canada, Egypt, France and USSR.

Expreso (Spanish for "express") on express stamps of the Dominican Republic, Ecuador, Guatemala, Panama, Peru and Venezuela.

Express Delivery on express stamps of Mauritius and New Zealand.

Exterior parcel stamps of Ecuador and Uruguay.

Extra Rapido express airmail stamps of Colombia.

F overprint on French stamps of 1939 for use by Spanish refugees (fugitives) from the Civil War.

Factaj on parcel stamps of Roumania, 1928.

Faltpost (Swedish for "field post") on military reply franks 1929–42.

F.A.M. Foreign Air Mail, on handstamps and labels on US airmails.

FAO Food and Agricultural Organization, on many stamps since 1954.

Fardos Postales on parcel stamps of El Salvador, 1895.

Fco Bollo (abbreviation for "postage stamp") on Italian stamps of 1865.

Federacion Venezolano Venezuela.

Feldpost 2kg overprint on German stamps to denote the transmission of servicemen"s parcels up to that weight during the Second World War.

Ferrocarril Oriental overprint on Guatemalan stamps of 1929 to mark the opening of the Eastern Railway.

Festas da Cidade (Portuguese for "city festival") on compulsory tax stamps of Portugal, 1913.

Festung Lorient overprint on French stamps for use by the German fortress at Lorient, cut off by the Allied advance after D-Day.

Filipinas Philippine Islands.

Flugfrimerki (Icelandic for "airmail stamps").

Flugpost (German for "airmail") on stamps of Austria, Danzig and Germany.

Flugpostmarke (German for "airmail stamp") on stamps of Germany.

F.M. abbreviation for *Franchise Militaire,* overprinted or inscribed on French stamps for use by service personnel.

F.N.F.L. *(Forces Navales Francaises Libres*, Free French Naval Forces) overprint on stamps of St Pierre et Miquelon, 1941–42.

FNR abbreviation for *Federativna Narodna Republika* (Federated People"s Republic) on stamps of Yugoslavia.

Fomento Aero Comunicaciones compulsory tax airmail stamps of Ecuador, 1945.

Fondul Aviatici (aviation fund) on compulsory tax stamps of Roumania, 1937.

Forces Francaises Libres Levant (Free French Forces, Levant) overprint on stamps of Lebanon and Syria by the Free French, 1942.

F.P.O. abbreviation for Field Post Office found on many military postmarks, often with an identifying number.

Fr., Franc. or **Française** France.

Franca (Spanish for "free") on provisional stamps of Chiclayo and Ancachs, Peru during the Pacific War, 1884.

Franco (Free) on early stamps of Philippines, Switzerland denoting prepayment or free postage.

Franco Bollo (Italian for "postage stamp") Sardinia, 1851–61, Italy 1862–63, Roman States 1852–68 and Sicily 1859–61.

Francobollo di Stato Italian stamps for official correspondence.

Franco Bollo Postale Roman States.

Francobollo Toscano Tuscany.

Franco Correos Spain.

Franco Marke Bremen 1856–60.

Franco Scrisorei Moldavia-Walachia 1862.

Frankeerzegel Surinam and Curacao.

Franqueo Peru.

Franqueo Deficiente postage due labels of Ecuador, El Salvador, Nicaragua and Paraguay.

Franqueo Impresos newspaper stamps of Spain 1872–73.

Franqueo Oficial Official stamps of Latin American countries.

Franquicia Postal franking stamps of Spain 1881.

Frei Durch Ablosung (German for "free under special exemption") on German accountancy stamps of Prussia 1903 and Baden 1905 to check on the volume of official mail transmitted in these states.

Freimarke (German for "free stamp" , i.e. postage stamp) Prussia 1859–60, Thurn and Taxis 1852–67 and Wurttemberg 1851–73.

Freistaat Bayern (Bavarian Free State) Bavaria 1919–20.

Freie Stadt (German for "free city") Danzig 1921–39.

Frimaerke KGL Post (Danish for "royal mail stamp") Denmark 1851.

Frimarke Lokalbref (Swedish for "local letter stamp") Stockholm, Sweden.

Frimerki Iceland.

F.R.M. K.G.L. Denmark 1854.

Fuerstentum (German for "principality") Liechtenstein.

Fur Berliner Wahrungsgeschadigte (German for "for the harm done to the Berlin economy") on charity stamps used in West Germany during the Berlin blockade by the USSR 1949–50.

Fur Kriegsbeschadigte (German for "for war wounded") charity overprints of Bavaria and Germany 1919.

G. overprint on Cape of Good Hope for use in Griqualand West.

GAB overprint on French Colonies general issues for Gabon.

Gbno. Const. (*Gobierno Constitutionalista,* Spanish for "Constitutionalist Government") Salamanca, Mexico 1914.

G.C. (*Grande Consommation,* French for "large consumption") inscription in the sheet margins of French stamps of 1917 denoting paper of a poorer quality as a wartime economy.

GC (*Gobierno Constitutionalista*) overprint on Mexican stamps used at Acambaro 1914

GCM (*Gobierno Constitucionalista Mexicano,* Mexican Constitutionalist Government) overprint by the Constitutionalist forces led by Carranza and Obregon, on Mexican stamps during the Civil War 1914.

GCM (*Gobierno Conventionista Mexicano*) overprint on Mexican stamps by the Conventionist forces led by Villa and Zapata 1914.

G & D on French colonies stamps, for Guadeloupe and Dependencies 1903–04.

Gd. Liban Great Lebanon 1924–25.

Gdansk Polish post office in Danzig 1925–37.

GD-OT overprint on Bohemia and Moravia for newspaper stamps.

G.E.A. (German East Africa) overprint on East Africa and Uganda stamps for use in Tanganyika 1917–21.

Gebuhr bezahlt (German for "postage paid") on provisional local issues of 1923 and 1945–46 of Germany.

Gebyr overprint on Danish stamps of 1923 denoting special posting fees.

Gebyrmaerke Danish late fee stamps 1926–34.

Gen. Gouv. Warschau (German for "general government, Warsaw") overprint on German stamps for use in occupied Poland 1916–17.

General Gouvernement Poland under German occupation 1940–45.

Gerusalemme overprint on Italian stamps for use in Jerusalem 1909–11.

G.F.B. (*Gaue Faka Buleaga,* Polynesian for "on government service") overprint on stamps of Tonga 1893.

Giornali (Italian for "newspapers") newspaper stamps of Sardinia 1861 and Italy 1862.

G.N.R. (*Guardia Nazionale Repubblicana,* Republican National Guard) overprint on Italian stamps for use in the Fascist stronghold of Brescia 1943–44.

Gobierno (Spanish for "government") official stamps of Peru 1890–1914.

Gobierno Const. overprint on Mexican stamps used at Leon and Tuxtla in 1914.

Gobierno Constitucionalista various overprints, in capitals or lower-case lettering, in one, two or three

lines, on Mexican stamps used at Aguascalientes, Baja California, Chihuahua, Ciudad Gonzales, Ciudad Juarez, Coahuila, Durango, Mazatlan, Mexico City, Monterrey, Queretaro, Salvatierra, Sinaloa, Sombrerete, Tequisquiapan, Torreon and Zacatecas during the advance of the Constitutionalist forces in the Civil War 1914.

Golfe de Benin Benin 1893.

Gorny Slask Polish for Upper Silesia.

Governo Militare Alleato (Allied Military Government) on stamps of Italy under Allied occupation 1943.

Govt. Parcels overprint on British stamps 1883–1904 for use on parcels from government departments.

G.P.E. overprint on French colonies for use in Guadeloupe 1884.

G.P.M or **G.P. de M.** (*Gobierno Provisorio de Mexico,* Provisional Government of Mexico) overprint on Mexican stamps 1916 denoting values in silver currency.

Grand Liban Great Lebanon 1924–25.

G.R.I. (*Georgius Rex Imperator,* George King and Emperor) overprint on German colonial stamps during the British occupation of the Marshall Islands, New Guinea and Samoa 1914. Typewritten overprint on Turkish fiscal stamps used at Long Island 1916.

Grossdeutsches Reich (Greater German Reich) inscription on stamps of Nazi Germany 1944–45.

G.R. Post Mafia Overprint on stamps of German East Africa and the Indian Expeditionary Force for use at Mafia Island 1915–16.

Guine overprint on stamps of Cape Verde Islands for use in Portuguese Guinea 1881–85.

Guinea Ecuatorial Equatorial Guinea.

Gultig 9. Armee (German for "valid, 9th Army") overprint on German stamps for use by troops occupying Roumania 1918.

Guy. Franc. overprint on French colonies for use in French Guiana 1886–88.

G.W. overprint on Cape of Good Hope stamps for use in Griqualand West 1877.

Habilitado (para) Correos (Spanish for "valid for postage") overprint on revenue or telegraph stamps of the Philippines 1881–97.

Haga Patria (Spanish for "do for the fatherland") on compulsory tax stamps of Mexico 1929.

Hatay Devleti (Turkish for "Hatay Post") overprint on Turkish stamps for use in Hatay (Alexandretta) 1931–38.

Haute Silesie Upper Silesia.

Haute Volta Upper Volta.

Haut Senegal et Niger Upper Senegal and Niger.

Hazateres overprint on Hungary 1938 to denote the "returned territory" taken from Czechoslovakia as a result of the Munich agreement.

H.E.H. the Nizam's Government Hyderabad 1927.

Hellas Greece.

Helvetia Switzerland

Herzogth or **Herzogthum** (German for "duchy") Schleswig and Holstein 1864–66.

HH Nawab Shah Jahan Begam Bhopal.

H.I. & U.S. Postage (Hawaiian Islands and United States) on Hawaiian "Misisonary" stamps 1851–52.

Hirlapjegy newspaper stamps of Hungary 1900.

Hivatlos postage due labels of Hungary.

Hochwasser (German for "high water", i.e. flood) overprint on Austria to raise funds for flood victims.

Hollandshjalp (Icelandic for "aid to Holland") overprint on a charity stamp issued by Iceland in 1953 to aid victims of Dutch flood disasters.

Hopflug Itala (Icelandic for "Italian mass flight") overprint on air stamps of 1933 to commemorate the mass-formation flight led by Italo Balbo from Italy to Chicago via Iceland.

Hrv., Hrvatska Croatia.

Hrzgl Frm (*Herzogliche Frimarke*, Ducal postage stamp) Holstein 1864.

Idrovolante Napoli-Palermo-Napoli overprint on Italian stamps for use on mail carried by seaplane from Naples to Palermo and back 1917.

I.E.F. (Indian Expeditionary Force) overprint on Indian stamps for use by military forces in Europe and East Africa in the First World War.

I.E.F. "D" overprint on Turkish stamps for use in Mesopotamia (Iraq) under British occupation 1919.

Ierusalem overprint on Russian stamps for use at the Russian post office in Jerusalem 1909–10.

I Gildi '02-'03 (Icelandic for "revalidated") overprint on Icelandic stamps intended for official mail 1902–03.

Ile de la Reunion Reunion Island.

Ile Rouad Rouad (or Arwad) Island.

Iles Comores Comoro Islands.

Iles Wallis et Futuna Wallis and Futuna Islands.

Imperio Colonial Portugues postage due labels for use in the Portuguese colonies in Africa 1945.

Imperio Mexicano (Mexican Empire) on stamps portraying the Emperor Maximilian 1866.

Imper. reg. posta austr. (Latin abbreviation signfiying "Imperial and Royal Austrian Post") on stamps of the Austrian post offices in Turkey 1883.

Impresos (Spanish for "newspapers") Cuba 1888 and Philippine Islands 1886–96.

Imprime (French for "printed matter") overprint on Turkish stamps for newspapers and periodicals 1891–92.

Imprimes overprint on Persian stamps for newspapers 1891–1908.

Impto. or **Impuesto de Guerra** (Spanish for "war tax") on compulsory tax stamps of Spain 1874–98.

Impuesto de Encomiendas (Spanish for "parcel tax") on parcel stamps of Uruguay.

Inchi ya ("State of") Katanga.

Inde Francaise French India.

India Portugueza Portuguese India.

Industrielle Kriegswirtschaft (German for "war board of trade") overprint on Swiss stamps for official mail 1918.

Infancia (Spanish for "childhood") on child welfare compulsory tax stamps of Mexico 1929.

Inkeri Ingria (North Ingermanland).

Inland sole inscription on 3c stamps of Liberia 1881.

Inselpost (German for "island post") overprint on Germany military stamps for use in Crete, Rhodes and Leros 1944–45.

Instrucao (Portuguese for "education") overprint on Portuguese India for use as compulsory tax stamps in Timor.

Instruccion (Spanish for "education") on stamps of Venezuela 1893–5, originally intended for fiscal use but extensively used on mail.

Interinsular Postage Bahamas 1859.

Interior parcel stamps of Uruguay 1922–26.

Inter Island Hawaii 1859–64.

Ionikon Ionian Islands.

I.O.V.R. compulsory tax stamps of Roumania 1947–48.

I Polska Wystawa Marek (first Polish philatelic exhibition) overprint on Polish stamps 1919.

I.R. overprint on US stamps 1895–98 for fiscal use by the Internal Revenue department.

Irian Barat West Irian (formerly Dutch New Guinea).

I.R. Official overprint on British stamps 1882–1904 for official mail of the Board of Inland Revenue.

Island Iceland.

Isla de Pascua Easter Island.

Islas Galapagos Galapagos Islands.

Isole Cephalonia e Itaca overprint on Greek stamps for the Ionian Islands (Cephalonia and Ithaca) under Italian occupation.

Isole Italiane dell" Egeo Aegean Islands under Italian administration.

Isole Jonie Ionian Islands under Italian occupation 1941.

Istra Slovensko Primorje (Serbo-Croat for "Slovene coast of Istria") Istria under Yugoslav administration.

Istria Littorale Sloven (Italian) Slovene coast of Istria under Italian administration.

Ita-Karjala East Karelia under Finnish occupation.

I.T.U. International Telecommunications Union.

Jamahiriya (Arabic for "republic") on stamps of Libya since 1977.

Jamhuri (Swahili for "republic") overprint on Zanzibar 1964.

JBRS initials of Sir James Brooke, Rajah of Sarawak, inscribed in the corners of Sarawak stamps 1869.

Jeend Jind.

J.N.F. Jewish National Fund labels, temporarily used for postage in 1948 and forerunners of the stamps of Israel.

Jornaes (Portuguese for "journals") newspaper stamps of Portugal and colonies.

Journaux Dagbladen (French and Flemish for "newspapers") newspaper stamps of Belgium.

J.R.G. (*Junta Revolucionario de Gobierno*, Revolutionary Junta of Government) overprint on air stamps of Venezuela 1947.

Judenpost (German for "Jewish Post") Lodz (Litzmannstadt) ghetto stamps 1944.

Juegos Olimpicos (Spanish for "Olympic Games") on charity stamps of Costa Rica 1924.

Jugoslavija Yugoslavia.

Kais. Koenigl. Oesterr. Post (Imperial and Royal Austrian post) Austria.

Kalayaan Nang Pilipinas Philippines under Japanese administration 1943.

Kamerun Cameroun (Cameroons) under German administration.

Kans. overprint on US stamps for use in Kansas 1929 as a check on the misuse of stamps stolen in post office burglaries.

Karjala Karelia 1922.

Karki Calchi.

Karlfonds (Charles Fund) charity stamps of Bosnia and Herzegovina 1918.

Karnten Abstimmung Carinthia plebiscite 1920.

Karolinen Caroline Islands.

Kemahkotaan (Malay for "coronation") overprint on Johore 1896.

Kentta–Posti or Kenttapostia (Finnish for "military post") Finland military stamps 1941–63

K.G.C.A. initials of the Carinthian (Karnten) Government Commission, zone A, overprinted on Yugoslav stamps for use in Carinthia during the plebiscite 1920.

Kgl Post Frm (*Kongeligt Post Frimaerke*, Royal Post stamp) Danish West Indies 1855–73.

Kibris Cumhuriyeti (Turkish for "Cyprus Republic").

Kibris Turk Federe Devlete Postalari Posts of the Turkish Federated State of Cyprus.

KKK (abbreviation for *Kataastaasan Kagalanggalang Katipunan*), Tagalog for the independence movement in the Philippine Islands which issued its own stamps in the 1890s during the guerrilla campaign against Spanish rule.

K.K.L. (*Keren Kayemeth l'Israel*, Hebrew for "Jewish National Fund") charity labels raising money for the purchase of land in Palestine, used as stamps in the interim period between the breakdown of the British mandate and the proclamation of the state of Israel 1948.

K.K. Oesterr Post (Royal and Imperial Austrian Post) on stamps of Liechtenstein under Austrian postal administration 1912–18.

K.K. Post-stempel (Royal and Imperial postage stamp) newspaper stamps of Austria and Lombardo-Venezia 1851–63.

Klaipeda Memel under Lithuanian administration 1923.

Kongeligt Post Frimaerke (Royal Post stamp) Denmark 1851.

Kontoret for Behandling af Ubesorgede Postsager (Danish for "Office for the treatment of undeliverable mail") on Danish labels affixed to returned mail.

Korca or **Korce** Koritsa, Albania 1917.

Koztarsasag (Magyar for "republic") overprint on Hungarian stamps 1919.

K.P. abbreviation for *Kagamitang Pampamahalaan*, Tagalog for "official mail", overprint on Philippine stamps under Japanese occupation.

KPb Cyrillic abbreviation for *Carbovanetz*, unit of currency in Ukraine, overprint or inscription on many provisional issues since 1991.

K.P.K. (*Kobenhavns Philatelisten Klub*) overprint, with date, on Danish stamps to celebrate the 50th anniversary of the Copenhagem Philatelic Club 1937.

Kr. followed by numerals overprint on Swedish stamps for parcel post.

Kraljevstvo Srba Hrvata i Slovenaca (Serbo-Croat for "kingdom of Serbs, Croats and Slovenes") overprint on stamps of Bosnia and Hungary for Yugoslavia 1919–20.

Kreis (German for "circle" or "district") Wenden 1878–80.

KSA abbreviation for the Kingdom of Saudi Arabia.

K.u.K. (abbreviation for *Kaiserliche und Koenigliche*) Austria or Bosnia and Herzegovina.

K.u.K. Feldpost (Imperial and Royal Field Post) overprint on Italian or Roumanian stamps during Austro–Hungarian military occupation 1918.

K. u. K. Militarpost (Imperial and Royal Military Post) on stamps of Bosnia and Herzegovina 1912–18.

Kurland Courland under German occupation 1945.

Kuzey Kibris Turk Cumhuriyeti Northern Cyprus Turkish Republic.

Kwidzyn Marienwerder

K Wurtt. Post Wurttemberg.

L. (abbreviation for Lansa, the state airline) on airmail stamps of Colombia 1950.

LAB initials of the airline *Lloyd Aero Boliviano*, on air stamps of Bolivia.

La Canea Italian post office in Crete 1901–06.

La Georgie Georgia 1919.

Laibach Ljubljana (Slovenia) under German occupation.

Land-Post Porto-Marke rural postage due labels of Baden 1862.

Landstormen overprint on Swedish stamps of 1916 raising money to clothe army reservists.

Lansa Name of airline, on Colombian air stamps 1950.

L.A.R. Libyan Arab Republic.

Lattaquie Latakia.

Lawinenopfer (German for "avalanche aid") overprint on Austrian charity stamps.

Latvija Latvia.

Legi Posta (Magyar for "airmail") airmail stamps of Hungary.

Letadlem Czechoslovak for "airmail".

Letecky Posta Czechoslovak for "airmail".

Ley 8310, 16708 (Law number 8310, 16708 etc) overprint on Peruvian stamps for use as compulsory tax stamps, quoting the government decree authorising the issue.

L.F.F. Liberian Field Force 1916.

L.H.I. manuscript overprint on Australian stamps used in Lord Howe Island 1930.

Libau overprint on German stamps for use in Liepaja, Latvia 1919.

Lietuva Lithuania.

Lietuvos Pastas (Lithuanian Post).

Lignes Aeriennes F.A.F.L. Free French military airmail, Syria.

Lindbergh Enero 1928 overprint on Costa Rican airmail stamp honouring Charles Lindbergh's goodwill tour of Central America.

Linea Aerea Nacional (National Airline) airmail stamps of Chile 1931.

Lineas Aereas del Estado (State Airlines) airmail stamps of Argentina.

Lisboa (Lisbon) on Red Cross franchise stamps of Portugal 1926 and 1936.

Litwa Srodkowa Central Lithuania under Polish occupation 1920–21.

Ljubljanska Pokrajina Provinz Laibach (Serbo-Croat and German) overprint on Italian stamps for use in the province of Ljubljana (Laibach), Slovenia under German occupation.

L. Marques Lourenco Marques.

L. McL. (*Lady McLeod*) steamship stamp of Trinidad 1847.

Local-Taxe Zurich 1843–46.

Loja Franca security overprint on stamps of Ecuador for use in the province of Loja, and thus distinguishing legitimate stamps from those which had been looted after postal stores in Guayaquil were destroyed by fire in July 1902.

Lokalbref (Swedish for "local letter") on stamps intended for the Stockholm municipal postage rate.

Los Rios security overprint on Ecuador 1902; see Loja above.

Losen postage due labels of Sweden 1874–82.

Lothringen Lorraine under German occupation 1940.

Lotnicza (Polish for "airmail") on Polish air stamps and labels.

L.P. overprint on Russian stamps for use in Latvia 1919.

L. & S. Post overprint on Newfoundland airmail stamps converting them to land and sea post 1933.

LTSR Lithuanian stamps overprinted in 1940 when the republic was absorbed by the USSR.

Lucha contra el Cancer overprint or inscription on stamps of Panama.

Luchtpost on airmail stamps of the Netherlands and colonies.

Luchtpostdienst (airmail service) on air stamps of the Belgian Congo 1930.

Luchtpostzegel (airmail stamp) Netherlands 1933.

Luftfeldpost (airmail field post) Germany 1942.

Luftpost air stamps and labels of Germany and Sweden.

Lugpos (Afrikaans) on air stamps and labels of South Africa.

M on stamps of the Allied military government of Germany 1945.

M Belgian military parcel stamps 1939 and 1967.

M.A. overprint on Argentina for official mail of the Ministry of Agriculture 1913–38.

Magyar Kir. Hirlap Belyeg (Royal Hungarian Newspaper Stamp) newspaper tax stamps of Hungary.

Magyar Kir(alyi) Posta Hungarian Royal Post.

Magyar Nemzeti Kormany Szeged 1919 Hungarian People's Government, Szegedin 1919.

Magyar Nepkoztarsasag Hungarian People's Republic.

Magyarorszag Hungarian State.

Magyar Tanacskoztarsasag Hungarian Soviet Republic 1919.

M.A.L. abbreviation for Military Authority Lire, the currency used in Italian colonies under British military occupation.

Manchukuo Manchuria.

Marianas Espanolas overprint on Philippines stamps for the Spanish administration of the Mariana Islands 1899.

Marianen German administration of the Mariana Islands 1899–1916.

Maroc Morocco under French administration.

Marokko German post offices in Morocco.

Marruecos Spanish administration of Morocco.

Marschall-Inseln or **Marshall-Inseln** Marshall Islands under German administration.

M.B.D. overprint on stamps of Nandgaon, India to denote official use 1893–94.

Mbr. or **Mbretnia Shqiptare** Kingdom of Albania 1928–43.

Mledhja Kushtetuese overprint or inscription on air stamps of Albania under Italian administration 1939.

Mecklenb. Schwerin Mecklenburg Schwerin.

Mecklenb. Strelitz Mecklenburg Strelitz.

Mecklbg-Vorpomm Mecklenburg-Vorpommern 1945.

Media Onza (Spanish for "half ounce") on official stamps of Spain 1854–63.

M.E.F. overprint on British stamps for use by the Middle East Forces during the Second World War.

Mejico Mexico.

Memelgebiet Memel territory.

Mensajerias (Spanish for "messages") on special delivery stamps of Uruguay 1921–59.

Metelin Russian post office at Mytilene, Lesbos 1910.

M.G. overprint on Argentine stamps for use by the Ministry of War (*Ministerio de Guerra*) 1913–38.

M.H. overprint on Argentine stamps for the Ministry of Finance (*Ministerio de Hacienda*).

M.I. overprint on Argentine stamps for use by the Ministry of the Interior.

Militarpost (German for "military post") Bosnia and Herzegovina.

Mily Admn overprint on Burmese stamps to signify British Military Administration 1945.

Mit Luftpost (German for "with airmail") on airmail labels.

M.J.I. overprint on Argentine stamps for use by the Ministry of Justice and Public Instruction *(Ministerio de Justicia y Instruccion Publica)*.

M.M. overprint on Argentine stamps for use by the Ministry of Marine.

Modonesi Modena.

Monster overprint on Dutch stamps to signify "specimen".

M.O.P. overprint on Argentine stamps for use by the Ministry of Public Works *(Ministerio de Obras Publicas)*.

Moyen Congo Middle Congo.

M.Q.E. Martinique 1887.

M.R.C. overprint on Argentine stamps for the Ministry of Foreign Affairs and Religion *(Ministerio de Relaciones Exteriores y Culto)*.

Muestra (Spanish for "sample") overprint denoting specimen stamps.

Multa (Spanish for "mulct"or "fine") inscribed on postage due labels of several Latin American countries.

Multada (Spanish for "fined") on postage due labels of Chile 1894–96.

Multas overprint on stamps of Ecuador 1929 to convert them to postage due labels.

Muster (German for "sample") overprint denoting specimen stamps.

Mutilados da Guerra (Portuguese for "war maimed") on compulsory tax stamps of Mozambique 1920.

M.V.i.R. (abbreviation for *Militarverwaltung in Rumanien*, military administration in Roumania) overprint on German and Roumanian stamps during the German occupation of 1917–18.

M.V.S.N. (abbreviation for *Milizia Volontaria di Sicurezza Nazionale*, Voluntary Militia for National Defence) on Italian stamps 1926–28.

Nachmarke (German for "new value") overprint on Austrian stamps used as postage due labels 1921.

Nach Porto postage due labels of Liechtenstein under Swiss postal administration.

Nandgam Nandgaon.

Na Oswiate (Polish for "public instruction") on Polish charity stamps 1927.

Napoletana Naples.

Na Skarb (Polish for "national funds") on charity stamps 1924.

Na Slask (Polish for "for Silesia") on charity stamps of Central Lithuania 1921.

Nationaler Verwaltungsausschuss (German for "national administration committee") overprint on Montenegrin stamps under German occupation 1943.

Nationalsozial. Deutsche Arbeiterpartei (National Socialist German Workers Party) official stamps for the use of the Nazi Party in Germany.

Nations Unies Office Europeen United Nations European Office in Geneva.

NCE New Caledonia.

N.D. Hrvatska Croatia 1943–44.

Nebr. overprint on US stamps for use in Nebraska 1929, to control the use of stamps fraudulently used as a result of post office burglaries. See also **Kans.**

Ned. Antillen Netherlands Antilles.

Nedelja Crvenog Krsta (Serbo-Croat "Red Cross Fund") on compulsory tax stamps of Yugoslavia.

Nederland Netherlands

Nederlandsch–Indie Dutch East Indies.

Ned. Indie or **Nederl. Indie** Dutch East Indies.

Negous Teferi overprint on stamps of Abyssinia (Ethiopia) 1928 to mark the coronation of the Emperor Haile Selassie I.

Nemzeti Magyar Kormany Szeged overprint on Hungarian stamps to denote the restoration of the Hungarian National Government at Szeged 1919.

Ne Pas Livrer la Dimanche (French for "do not deliver on Sunday") on the dominical labels or bandalettes attached to Belgian stamps 1893–1914.

Netta di Fuora e di Dentro (Italian for "clean outside and inside") applied to disinfected mail.

Netta Fuori e Sporca Dentro (Italian for "clean inside and dirty outside") applied to disinfected mail.

Nezavisna Drzava Hrvatska (Croat National State) Croatia 1941–44.

N.F. overprint on Nyasaland stamps for use by the Nyasaland Field Force in German East Africa 1916.

Nieuw Guinea Dutch New Guinea.

Nieuwe Republiek New Republic (South Africa).

Nippon (literally "land of the rising sun") Japan.

NIWIN acronym for *National Inspanning Welzijnszorg in Nederlandsch Indie* (Dutch Indies Relief Organisation) overprint on definitive stamps 1947 with a surcharge.

No Hay Estampillas (Spanish for "there are no stamps") inscribed on postmasters' provisional issues of Cauca.

Norddeutscher Postbezirk North German Confederation.

Noreg or **Norge** Norway.

Notopfer Steuermarke (German for "tax stamp for victims of need") on compulsory tax stamps of West Germany to raise funds to defray the costs of beating the Soviet blockade of Berlin.

Noviny overprint on Czech stamps for newspaper use 1926.

N.S.B. Nossi-Be.

N.S.W. New South Wales.

Nueva Granada Colombia.

N.W. Pacific Islands overprint on Australia for use in German colonies occupied in 1914.

N.Z. New Zealand.

O.A.T. wartime handstamps denoting Onward Air Transmission.

O.B. Overprint on Philippine stamps denoting Official Business.

Ob Ost (abbreviation for *Oberbefehlshaber Ost,* German for "Eastern Command") overprint on German stamps for use in occupied Lithuania 1916–17.

Occupation française overprint on Hungarian stamps for use in the Arad region 1919.

Oceanie French Oceania (now French Polynesia).

Oesterreich Austria.

Oeuvres de Solidarité Française (French solidarity works) on charity stamps of the French colonies 1943–44.

Oeuvres de Guerre (war works) overprint on stamps of Cameroun.

Oeuvres Sociales (social works) overprint on St Pierre et Miquelon for war charities.

O F (abbreviation for *Occupation Française*) overprint on French stamps for use at Castellorizo 1920.

Off. or **Offentlig Sak** (Norwegian for "official matter") on stamps intended for official correspondence.

Official Service overprint on Liberia for official use.

Officiel overprint on stamps of Luxembourg and Switzerland for official use.

Offisieel Afrikaans for "official" inscribed on stamps of South Africa and South West Africa for official use.

Oficial inscribed on stamps of Latin America for official use.

O.H.E.M.S. (abbreviation for "On His Egyptian Majesty's Service) on official stamps of Egypt 1922.

O.H.H.S. (abbreviation for "On His Highness's Service") on Egyptian official stamps of 1907–22.

O.H.M.S. (abbreviation for "On His or Her Majesty's Service") overprinted on stamps of Canada and India for official use.

Ohu Post Estonian airmail stamps

Oltre Giuba (Italian for "beyond the Juba River") Jubaland.

O.M.F. (abbreviation for *Occupation Militaire Française,* French Military Occupation) overprint on French stamps for use in Cilicia or Syria 1920.

On CGS (abbreviation for "On Cochin Government Service") on official stamps of Cochin.

O.N.F. (abbreviation for *Occupation Navale Française*) on stamps of Castellorizo 1920.

On H.M.S. (abbreviation for "On His Majesty's Service" overprint on British colonial stamps for official use.

On KSD (abbreviation for "On Kishengarh State Diwan") for official use in Kishengarh, India.

On SS (abbreviation for "On State Service") on official stamps of Travancore.

On S.S.S. (abbreviation for "On Sirmoor State Service") on official stamps of Sirmoor.

On State Service overprint on Iraq, under British mandate.

O.N.U. *(Organisation des Nations Unies)* United Nations.

O.P.S.O. (abbreviation for "On Public Service Only") on New Zealand stamps for postal departmental use 1892–1901.

Oranje Vrij Staat Orange Free State.

Ordinary overprint on Liberian official stamps making them valid for use by the general public.

Organisation Internationale por les Refugies overprint on Swiss stamps for use by the International Refugee Organization 1950.

Oro Pastas Lithuanian airmail stamps.

Orphelins de la Guerre on French stamps raising money for war orphans.

Orts-Post (German for "regional post") on federal issues of Switzerland 1850.

OS (abbreviation for *Offentlig Sak,* official matter) inscribed on Norwegian stamps for official use.

OS (abbreviation for "On Service") overprint on Liberian stamps for official use.

O.S.E. (abbreviation for *Oeuvres Sociales de l'Enfance*) on airmail stamps of Morocco with a surcharge in aid of child welfare.

O.S. G.R.I. (On Service, Georgius Rex Imperator) overprint with new values on stamps of German New Guinea during the Australian occupation 1915.

O.S.G.S. (abbreviation for "On Sudan Government Service") overprint on Sudanese stamps for official use.

Ostland overprint on German stamps for use in "Eastland" – Parts of Russia under Nazi occupation 1941–43.

O.T. (abbreviation for *Obchodni Tiskopis,* Czech for "printed matter") overprint on Czechoslovak and Bohemian stamps for newspapers and periodicals.

Otvorenie Slovenskeho Snemu overprint on Czech stamp 1939 to mark the independence of Slovakia.

Oubangui-Chari Ubangi-Shari.

Oubangui-Chari-Tchad Ubangi-Shari-Chad.

O.W. Official overprint on British stamps for use by the Office of Works 1896–1904.

P (with a crescent and star in an oval) overprint on Straits Settlements for use in Perak 1878.

Pacchi Postale (Italian for "postal parcels") on parcel stamps of Italy and San Marino.

Packenmarke (German for "parcel stamp") on stamps of Wenden 1863.

Padroes da Grande Guerra (Portuguese for "comrades of the Great War") on compulsory tax stamps raising funds for war veterans 1925.

Pago el Agente Postal Manuel E. Jiminez ("paid to the postal agent...") Cauca 1903.

Paketmarke (German for "parcel stamp").

Palacio de Comunicaciones (Spanish for "palace of communications") on compulsory tax stamps of Colombia for the building of a new general post office in Bogota.

Para os Pobres (Portuguese for "for the poor") on compulsory tax stamps of Portugal and the Azores 1915.

Par Avion (French for "by aeroplane") inscribed on airmail labels of most countries in accordance with UPU regulations.

Particular overprint on Nicaraguan official stamps 1921 to convert them for ordinary postal use.

P.D. (abbreviation for *Paye a Destination,* Paid to Destination) on handstruck markings before the advent of the UPU flat rates in 1875.

Pechino Italian post office in Peking (Beijing).

Pelita overprint on Indonesian charity stamps to raise funds for war victims 1948.

Pen. abbreviation for penni, pennia, unit of currency in Finland and thus distinguishing stamps of the Grand Duchy of Finland from similar stamps used in Tsarist Russia.

Perçue (French for "paid") on post paid labels, handstamps and printed impressions used by many countries in accordance with UPU international regulations.

Per Luchtpost (Dutch) by airmail.

Per Lugpos (Afrikaans) by airmail.

Per Nachnahme (German) on cash on delivery labels.

Per Pacchi (Italian for "by parcel post" on parcel stamps of the Vatican.

Persane(s) Persia.

Pilipinas Philippines.

P.I.-U.S. abbreviation for Philipinne Islands to United States, overprinted on Philippine air stamps of 1935 for the China Clipper trans-Pacific service.

Pjonustumerki (Icelandic for "official stamp") overprinted on stamps of 1930 for official mail.

P.M. (abbreviation for *Posta Militare*), overprinted on Italian stamps 1943 for use by military personnel on active service.

Poblact na hEireann (Irish Gaelic for "Republic of Ireland") on stamps of 1949–50.

Poche de l"Atlantique (French for "Atlantic Pocket") St Nazaire under German occupation, February 1945.

Poczta Polska Polish Post.

Pohjois Inkeri North Ingermanland.

Polska Poczta overprint on Austrian stamps 1918 for use in Galicia.

Por Aviacao on airmail labels of Portugal and colonies, and Brazil.

Por Avion on airmail labels of Venezuela.

Por Correo Aereo on airmail labels of Colombia.

Porteado Receber (Portuguese for "postage due") on postage due labels of Portugal and colonies.

Porte de Conduccion on parcel stamps of Peru 1897.

Porte de Mar (Spanish for "seaport") on stamps of 1875 for mail going overseas and denoting the fee payable to ships' captains for taking it.

Porte Franco (Portuguese for "postage franked") on franking stamps used by several charitable or national institutions between 1889 and 1938.

Porte Franco (Spanish for "postage paid") on stamps of Peru 1852–72.

Port Gdansk overprint on polish stamps for use in the Polish post offices in Danzig 1925–37.

Porto on postage due labels of Austria, Croatia, Denmark, Liechtenstein, Poland, Slovenia and Yugoslavia.

Porto Betalt (Norwegian for "postage paid") on Norwegian handstamps denoting bulk postings prepaid in cash.

Porto Gazetei on newspaper stamps of Moldavia 1858.

Portomaerke on postage due labels of the Danish West Indies.

Porto-Marke on postage due labels of Baden 1862.

Portomarke on postage due labels of Austria, Norway and Bosnia.

Porto Pflichtige Dienst Sache (German for "postage obligatory official matter") on official stamps of Wurttemberg 1875–1921.

Porto Scrisorei on postage stamps of Moldavia 1852.

Port Paye (French for "postage paid") on postage paid impressions and postmarks denoting bulk postings prepaid in cash.

Portzegel overprint on Dutch commemoratives of 1907 converting them into postage due labels.

Posesiones Espanolas del Sahara Spanish Sahara.

Posseel (Afrikaans for "postage stamp") on stamps of South Africa and South West Africa.

Posta Aeriana Roumanian airmail stamps.

Posta Aerore or **Ajrore** Albanian airmail stamps.

Posta Ceskoslovensko Czechoslovakia.

Posta Ceskoslovensko Armady Sibirske Czechoslovak field post in Siberia 1919–20.

Postage Tax on postage due labels of Sudan.

Postalari Turkey.

Postalar Takse Pulu on postage due labels of Turkey.

Postal Charges overprint on postage due labels of Papua New Guinea 1960.

Post & Receipt on stamps of Hyderabad.

Posta Pneumatica (Italian for "pneumatic post") on stamps provided for this urban express service 1913.

Posta Romana Constantinopol overprints on Roumanian stamps for use at the Roumanian post office in Constantinople 1919.

Postas le h'Ioc postage due labels of Ireland

Postat e Qeverries se Perkoheshme Albania 1913.

Poste Aerienne (French for "air posts") on airmail stamps of many countries.

Poste Coloniali Italiane Italian colonies general issues.

Poste Estensi Modena.

Poste Italiane Italy.

Poste Locale Switzerland 1850.

Postes (French for "posts") on stamps of many French-speaking countries, as well as those using various non-European scripts with a brief French text in line with UPU regulations (e.g. Afghanistan, Egypt, Korea, Saudi Arabia).

Postes de Coree Korea.

Postes Ethiopiennes Ethiopia.

Postes Imperiales de Coree Korea 1903.

Postes Ottomanes Turkey.

Postes Persanes Persia.

Postes Serbes overprint on French stamps for use of the Serb government in exile at Corfu 1916–18.

Poste Vaticane Vatican.

Postgebiet Ob. Ost German occupation of Lithuania 1916–17.

Postluchtdienst (Flemish for "airmail service") on air stamps of the Belgian Congo 1920.

Postmarke (German for "postage stamp") on stamps of Brunswick.

Postpaketmarke (German for "parcel post stamp").

Postpakket verrekenzegels (Dutch for "parcel postage due stamps").

Posttaxe Bayer. Bavarian postage due labels.

Postzegel (Dutch for "postage stamp") on many stamps of the Netherlands and colonies.

Pour Nos Chomeurs Intellectuels ("for our unemployed intellectuals") on several French charity issues of the 1930s.

P.P. (abbreviation for *Port Paye*, postage paid) overprinted on French postage due labels for use as stamps in French Morocco 1903.

Prensa (Spanish for "press") on newspaper stamps of Uruguay 1922–26.

Preussen Prussia

Primer Vuelo Postal (Spanish for "first postal flight") overprint on air stamps of Guatemala.

Primo Valores Declarados Servicio Interior (Spanish for "fee on insured packets of the domestic postal service") overprint on stamps of the Dominican Republic 1933 and 1940–68.

Primo Volo (Italian for "first flight") overprint on air stamps of Cyrenaica and Italy.

Principaute de Monaco Monaco.

Pro Aero (Latin for "for air") overprint or inscription on Swiss airmail stamps.

Pro Cartero (Spanish for "for the postman") on Argentine charity stamps raising funds for postal employees.

Pro Combattenti (Italian "for combatants") on charity stamps of San Marino.

Pro Desocupados (Spanish "for the unemployed") on charity stamps of Peru.

Pro Educacion Fisica (Spanish "for physical education") on compulsory tax stamps of Panama.

Pro Fondazione Studio (Italian "for study foundation") on charity stamps of Fiume.

Pro Infancia (Spanish "for infant welfare") on compulsory tax stamps of Mexico.

Pro Juventute (Latin for "for youth") inscription on Swiss child welfar stamps since 1913.

Pro Patria (Latin "for the fatherland") on Swiss charity stamps.

Pro Plebiscito Tacna y Arica on compulsory tax stamps of Peru raising funds to pay for the plebiscite in Tacna and Arica.

Pro Union Iberoamericana (Spanish for "on behalf of the Spanish-American Union") on airmail stamps of 1930.

Proteccion a la Infancia (Spanish for "protection of infancy") on compulsory tax stamps of Mexico.

Proteccion al Anciano (Spanish for "protection of the aged") on charity stamps of Uruguay.

Proteja a la Infancia (Spanish for "protect infancy") on compulsory tax stamps of Mexico.

Pro Tuberculosos Pobres (Spanish for "on behalf of the tubercular poor") on compulsory tax stamps of Spain.

Provinz Laibach Slovenia under German occupation 1943–44.

Provisorio (Spanish for "provisional") overprint on stamps converted to other uses or brought back into service.

Pro Vivienda Obrera (Spanish for "on behalf of the working way of life") on obligatory tax stamps of Bolivia for the workers' home building fund.

Przesylka Urzedowa official stamps of Poland 1933–35.

P.S. in an elaborate monogram—Cauca, Colombia.

P.S.N.C. initials of the Pacific Steam Navigation Company which appear in the corners of the first stamps of Peru 1857.

Pto Rico Puerto Rico.

P.T.T. F.F. (abbreviation for "Posts, Telegrtaphs and Telephones" and monogram of King Ferdinand) overprint within a circle on Roumanian stamps to denote the recovery of Transylvania from Hungary 1919.

Puolustusvoimat Finnish military post stamps 1943–44.

Puttialla Patiala.

P.W.P.W. (abbreviation for *Polska Wytwornia Papierow Wartosciowych*, Polish State Printing Office) initials found in the margins of many Polish stamps.

Qarku Koritsa, Albania.

Qeverria e Shqipnis Mesme (Albanian for "Government of Central Albania") on stamps of Central Albania 1915.

R initial of Raghbar Singh, prominently featured on stamps of Jind.

R inscribed on registration labels according to UPU regulation introduced in 1883, and on registered letter stamps of Colombia 1883–1904.

R overprint on stamps of Panama for registered letters 1916–17.

R overprint with new values on French colonies for use in Reunion.

Ratni Doprinos Croatia.

R.B.S. Danish abbreviation for *Rigsbankskilling*, on stamps of 1851.

R. Commissariato Civile Territori Sloveni Occupati Lubiana overprint on Yugoslav stamps for use in Slovenia under Italian civil administration 1941.

R. de C. (abbreviation of the Spanish *Reconstruccion de Comunicaciones,* rebuilding of the general post office) on compulsory tax stamps of Nicaragua.

R. de C. Garzon Tolima, a state of the Republic of Colombia.

Recapito Autorizzato (Italian for "authorised delivery") inscribed on special stamps for use of circular delivery companies authorised by the Italian post office to deliver local mail without going through postal channels.

Recargo (Spanish for "surcharge") inscribed on war tax stamps of Spain.

Receber (Portuguese for "due") on postage due labels of Angola.

Recommande (French for "registered") inscribed on registration labels of many countries.

Recommendada on registration labels of Colombia.

Recommendata on registration labels of Italy and colonies.

Recouvrements (French for "recoveries") inscribed on postage due labels of Algeria, Andorra, France, Monaco and Morocco.

Regatul Romaniei ("Roumanian Government") Transylvania.

Regence de Tunis Tunisia.

Regierungs Dienstsache (German for "government service matter") overprinted on official stamps of Liechtenstein 1932–41.

Regno d"Italia (Italian for "Kingdom of Italy") overprinted on stamps of Fiume when that territory was annexed by Italy in 1924.

Reichspost (German for "state post") inscribed on German stamps 1872–1901.

Rejistro on registered letter stamps of Colombia 1870–77.

Relais on Persian labels permitting passengers to travel on postal vehicles.

Rep di S. Marino San Marino.

Repoblika Malagasy Malagasy Republic (Madagascar).

Repoeblik Indonesia.

Repoeblik Serikat United Republic of Indonesia.

Repubblica Sociale Italiana Italian Social Republic 1944.

Repub. Franc. French Republic.

Republica Espanola Spanish Republic 1931–38.

Republica Oriental Uruguay 1864.

Republica Peruana Peru.

Republica Portuguesa Portugal.

Republika ng Pilipinas Philippines 1944.

Republik Oesterreich Austria.

Republique Centrafricaine Central African Republic.

Republique Française France.

Republique Georgienne Georgia.

Republique Khmere Khmer Republic (formerly Cambodia, now Kampuchea).

Republique Libanaise Lebanon.

Republique Malgache Malagasy Republic (Madagascar).

Republique Rwandaise Rwanda.

Republique Syrienne Syria.

Repulo Posta (Magyar for "airmail") on the first Hungarian air stamps 1918.

Resellada (Spanish for "revalidated") overprinted on obsolete stamps brought back into service during a shortage of the regular series, on stamps of Ecuador and Venezuela.

Resello overprint on demonetised stamps of Nicaragua to restore validity.

Resmi Turkish inscription signifying official mail.

Retardo Spanish denoting a late fee, on stamps of Colombia and Panama.

Retourbrief (German for "returned letter") inscribed on Bavarian franking labels affixed to undeliverable letters and packets.

Revalidado (Portuguese for "revalidated") overprinted on obsolete stamps brought back into use.

R.F. (abbreviation for *Republique Française*) inscribed on many French stamps.

R.H. (abbreviation for *Republique Haitienne*) inscribed on postage due labels of Haiti.

Rheinland-Pfalz Rhineland Palatinate under French administration 1947–49.

Rhein-Ruhr-Hilfe overprint on German stamps with a charity premium in aid of the Rhine-Ruhr flood disaster 1923.

R.H. Official overprint on British stamps for official mail of the Royal Household 1902–04.

Rialtas Sealadac na hEireann (Gaelic for "provisional government of Ireland") overprinted on British stamps used in the 26 counties of southern Ireland 1922.

RIS abbreviation for *Repoeblik Indonesia Serikat*, denoting the Republic of the Indonesian States, overprinted on stamps of the former Dutch East Indies 1950–51.

R.O. (abbreviation for *Roumelie Orientale*), overprinted on stamps of Turkey for use in Eastern Roumelia (South Bulgaria) 1880.

Rodi Rhodes.

Romana, Romina Roumania.

Roode Kruis (Dutch for "Red Cross") on charity stamps of the Netherlands.

Rossija Russia.

Roumelie Orientale Eastern Roumelia (South Bulgaria).

Royaume de l'Arabie Soudite Kingdom of Saudi Arabia.

Royaume du Burundi Kingdom of Burundi.

Royaume du Cambodge Kingdom of Cambodia.

Royaume du Laos Kingdom of Laos.

Royaume du Royaume literally Kingdom of the Kingdom, an error of overprint on stamps of Ruanda-Urundi intended for use in Burundi.

Rpf abbreviation for **Reichspfennig**, overprinted on stamps of Luxembourg under German occupation.

R.R. (abbreviation for *Republik Rheinland* or *Republique Rhenanie*) overprinted with new values on German stamps 1923 for use in the Rhenish Republic, a French-backed breakaway state.

RSA Republic of South Africa.

R.S.M. Republic of San Marino.

R.U.A. (abbreviation for *Republique Unie Arabe,* United Arab Republic) overprinted on stamps of Syria.

Russisch-Polen (German for "Russian Poland") overprint on German stamps for use in occupied Poland 1915.

S overprint on stamps of the Straits Settlements for use in the Malay state of Selangor 1878–82.

Saare overprint on stamps of Bavaria and Germany during the French administration of the Saar 1920.

Saargebiet (German for "Saar district") overprinted or inscribed on stamps of the Saar 1920–35.

Saarland inscription on the stamps used in the Saar under German administration 1957–59.

Sachsen Saxony.

Sahara Espanol Spanish Sahara 1941–46.

Sahara Espanol Occidental Spanish Western Sahara 1924–31

S.A.I.D.E. (abbreviation for *Services Aeriennes Internationaux d'Egypte*) overprinted on stamps required on mail carried on international air services from Egypt to Athens and Rome 1948.

Salonicco overprint on Italian stamps for use at Salonika 1909–11.

Salonique French overprint on Russian stamps used at Salonika 1910.

Samoa I Sisifo Western Samoa.

Sandjak d'Alexandrette Alexandretta 1938.

Saorstat Eireann (Gaelic) overprint on British stamps for use in the Irish Free State 1922.

SAR Syrian Arab Republic.

Sarkari (Hindi for "service") overprinted on stamps of Soruth for use on official mail 1933–49.

Saurashtra Soruth.

Scadta acronym from *Sociedad Colombo-Alemana de Trasportes Aereos*, Colombo-German Air Transport Company, which issued its own stamps.

S.d.N. Bureau International du Travail (French for "League of Nations, International Labour Office") overprint on Swiss stamps 1923–43.

Secours (French for "help") on obligatory tax stamps of Saudi Arabia.

Secours aux Refugies ("aid to refugees") overprint on charity stamps of Syria.

Secours aux Victimes de la Guerre ("aid to victims of the war") on compulsory tax stamps of Haiti.

Segnatasse (Italian for "stamp tax") inscription on postage due labels of Italy, Italian colonies, San Marino and Vatican.

Seguro Postal on insured letter stamps of Mexico.

Seguro Social del Campesino (Spanish for "social security for the peasant") overprint on compulsory tax stamps of Ecuador.

Sello Postal (Spanish for "postage stamp") overprint on demonetised stamps of Nicaragua to revalidate them.

Serbien Bosnian stamps overprinted during the Austrian occupation of Serbia 1916 and Yugoslav stamps thus overprinted during the German occupation 1941.

Service overprint on stamps of India, Indian states and Turkey (1903–15) for official use.

Servicio Aereo Interior overprint on Guatemalan airmail stamps 1930.

Servicio Aereo Sobretasa on airmail stamps of Argentina.

Servicio Centroamericano overprint on Nicaraguan air stamps for mail to other Central American countries.

Servicio Postal Mexicano on official stamps of Mexico 1884–93.

Servizio Commisioni overprint on Italian stamps denoting charges on mail addressed to government departments 1913–38.

Servizio di Stato (Italian for "state service") overprint on air stamps of Italy and colonies for official use.

SF abbreviation for *Soldater Frimaerke* (soldiers' stamp) overprinted on Danish stamps for military use.

SG abbreviation for Sudan Government, overprinted on stamps for official use.

SH Schleswig-Holstein.

Shkoder, Shkodra, Shkodre or **Shkodres** Scutari, Albania 1914–20.

Shqipenia, Shqiperia or **Shqiperise** Albania.

Shqipni or **Shqipnija** Albania

Shqiptar or **Shqyptare** Albania.

S.H.S. abbreviation signifying "Serbs, Croats and Slovenes" overprinted on Bosnian and Hungarian stamps for use in Croatia 1918–19.

Sicilia Sicily.

Sigillum Nov. Camb. Aust. (Latin for "seal of New South Wales") on the first stamps of New South Wales, the so-called Sydney Views, 1850.

Slovenija Slovenia.

Slovensko Slovakia.

Slovensky Stat Slovak State 1939.

Smirne or **Smyrne** Smyrna.

Sobreporto (Spanish for "extra charge") on Colombian stamps of 1866 denoting additional fees on mail addressed to countries with which Colombia had no postal treaty.

Sobre Cuota para Buitos Postales (Spanish for "extra fee for postal parcels") on parcel stamps of Mexico 1950–54.

Sobretasa (Spanish for "surcharge") overprint on Colombian stamps denoting use for compulsory postal tax purposes 1947.

Sobretasa Aerea On Colombian air stamps 1929 denoting additional fees on foreign letters transferred to domestic air routes.

Sociedade Humanitaria Cruz de Oriente (Portuguese for "Cross of the East Humanitarian Society") on compulsory tax stamps of Mozambique.

Societe des Nations League of Nations.

SO (abbreviation for *Silesie Orientale*) overprint on stamps of Czechoslovakia and Poland for use in Eastern Silesia during the plebiscite 1918–20.

Soudan Français French Sudan.

Sowjetische Besatzungs Zone (German for "Soviet Occupation Zone") overprinted on German stamps for use in the Soviet Zone 1948.

S.P. (abbreviation for **Service Publique**) overprint on stamps of Luxembourg for official use 1881–93.

SPM overprint on French colonial general issues for St Pierre et Miquelon 1885–91.

Spoorwegen (Flemish for "railways") on Belgian railway stamps.

Srba Hrvata i Slovenaca Kingdom of the Serbs, Croats and Slovenes (later Yugoslavia).

Srodkowa Litwa Central Lithuania 1920.

S. Thome e Principe St Thomas and Prince Islands.

Stadt Berlin Post Berlin 1948.

Stadt Post Basel Basle 1843.

Stati Parmensi Parma.

STT Vuja Yugoslav zone of Trieste 1945–50.

SU overprint on stamps of the Straits Settlements for use in Sungei Ujong 1878–83.

Suid-Afrika South Africa.

Suidwes-Afrika South West Africa.

S Ujong Sungei Ujong 1891–94.

Sul Bollettino (Italian for "upon bulletin or list") inscribed on the part of the parcel stamp affixed to the way-bill.

Sulla Ricevuta (Italial for "upon the receipt") inscribed on the part of the parcel stamp affixed to the sender's receipt.

Sultanat d'Anjouan Anjouan.

Suomi Finland.

Surcharge Postage inscription on the postage due labels of Trinidad and Tobago and Grenada 1892.

Surgos inscribed on Hungarian special delivery stamps 1916–19.

S.W.A. South West Africa.

Syrie, Syrienne Syria.

SZ (abbreviation for *Sluzba Zamek*, Czech for "official stamp") on postwar official stamps of Czechoslovakia.

T (abbreviation for *Taxe*, French for "charge") found on labels and handstruck marks denoting charges to be raised on international mail, under the regulations of the Univeral Postal Union.

T in the corners of the design, on postage due labels of the Dominican Republic.

T in a circle overprinted on stamps of Peru for use at Huacho in 1884, at the end of the war with Chile.

T in a triangle, overprinted on stamps of Monaco 1917 for use as postage due labels.

Takca on Bulgarian postage due labels.

Takse overprint or nscription on Albanian postage due labels.

Tasa inscription on postage due labels of Uruguay.

Tasa por Cobrar (Spanish for "tax to collect") on postage due labels of Chile.

Tassa Gazzette (Italian for "newspaper charge") on newspaper stamps of Modena.

Taxa on postage due labels of Uruguay.

Taxa de Factagiu overprint or inscription on Roumanian parcel stamps.

Taxa de Guerra inscription on war tax stamps of Portugal and colonies.

Taxa de Plata inscription on postage due labels of Roumania.

Taxa Devida Portuguese inscription on postage due labels of Brazil.

Taxa Recebida Portuguese inscription on postage due labels of Mozambique 1946.

Taxe a Percevoir French for "tax to pay" on the postage due labels of France and colonies.

Taxe de Retard French for "late fee".

Taxe Perçue (French for "charge paid") inscribed on air stamps of Mozambique 1947 and on marks denoting cash prepayment on international mail.

T.C. overprint on stamps of Cochin for use in Travancore-Cochin 1950.

T.C.Postalari Turkey.

T.C.E.K. Turkey compulsory tax stamps 1946.

Tchad Chad.

Te Betaal (Afrikaans for "to pay") on postage due labels of South Africa and South West Africa.

Te Betalen (Flemish for "to pay") on postage due labels of Belgium and colonies.

Telegrafenmarke on German telegraph stamps.

Telegrafos (Spanish for "telegraphs") on stamps of the Philippines, Costa Rica and other Latin American countries.

T.E.O. (French abbreviation for *Territoires Ennemis Occupies*, Occupied Enemey Territories) overprinted on French stamps for use in parts of the former Turkish empire under French administration (Syria and Cilicia).

Terre Adelie overprint on Madagascar stamps for use in Adelie Land 1948.

Terres Australes et Antarctiques Francaises French Southern and Antarctic Territories.

Territoire des Afars et Issas Territory of the Afars and Issas.

Territoire de l'Inini Inini.

Territoire du Niger Niger Territory.

Territoires Australes et Antarctiques Françaises French Southern and Antarctic Territories.

Territorio de Ifni Ifni.

Territorios Espanoles del Golfo de Guinea Spanish territories in the Gulf of Guinea.

Thrace Interalliee Thrace under inter-Allied administration 1919–20.

Thrace Occidentale Western Thrace.

Thuringen Thuringia.

Tidningsfrimarke Swedish newspaper stamps.

Timbre Complementario inscription on Mexican postage due labels.

Timbre de Reconstruccion (Spanish for "reconstruction fund stamp") on compulsory tax stamps of Guatemala.

Timbre du Souvenir on charity stamps of Luxembourg.

Timbre Imperial Journaux inscription on French newspaper stamps 1868.

Timbre Patriotico on compulsory tax stamps of Ecuador.

Timbre Taxe inscription on postage due labels of France and colonies and Vietnam.

Timbrul Aviatei Roumanian compulsory tax stamps for the national aviation fund.

Timbru Binefacere ("charity stamp") on Roumanian welfare fund stamps 1906–07.

Timbru de Ajutor ("assistance stamp") overprint or inscription on postal tax stamps of Roumania 1915–16.

Timbru Official Roumanian stamps for official use.

Tjanste inscription on Swedish stamps for official use.

Tjenestefrimerke inscription on Norwegian stamps for official use.

Toga Tonga.

Toscano Tuscany.

Touva Tuva.

Traite de Versailles (French for "Treaty of Versailles") overprint on stamps used at Allenstein (Olsztyn) during the plebiscite of 1920.

Tripoli di Barberia Italian post office in Tripoli, Barbary Coast 1909.

T.S. de C. (abbreviation for *Tribunal Superior de Cuenta*, Superior Tribunal of Accounts) on ordinary and airmail stamps of Honduras 1931.

Turkiye Cumhuriyeti Republic of Turkey.

Turk or **Turkiye Postalari** Turkish Posts.

UAR abbreviation for "United Arab Republic" overprinted or inscribed on stamps of Egypt and Syria 1958.

U-Boot Post German submarine mail 1916 and Hela (Baltic peninsula) 1945.

U G abbreviation for "Uganda Government" inscribed on the first typewritten stamps of 1895.

U.H. overprint on a stamp of Ecuador 1945 to denote a late fee.

Uhuru (Swahili for "independence") inscribed on stamps of Tanganyika (1961) and overprinted on stamps of Zanzibar (1963).

U.K.T.T. (abbreviation for "United Kingdom Trust Territory") overprinted on Nigerian stamps for use in Cameroons.

Ultramar (Spanish for "overseas") inscribed on stamps of Cuba, Puerto Rico, Portuguese Guinea and Macao.

UNEF (abbreviation for United Nations Emergency Force) overprint on Indian stamps for use of Indian personnel serving in Gaza 1965.

Uniao dos Atiradores Civis (Portuguese for "Union of Civilian Shooters") inscribed on franking stamps used by rifle clubs 1899–1910.

UNTEA abbreviation for United Nations Temporary Executive Authority, overprinted on stamps of Dutch New Guinea for use in that territory pending its transfer to Indonesia under the name of West Irian.

UPAE abbreviation for *Union Postal de America y Espana*, the Postal Union of the Americas and Spain, inscribed on many stamps of Spain and Latin America since 1962.

Urgencia or **Urgente** on special delivery stamps of Spain.

U.S.T.C. abbreviation for United States of Travancore and Cochin, overprinted on stamps of Travancore 1949.

V motif of the compulsory tax stamps of Cuba 1942–44

signifying victory in the Second World War.

V overprinted on stamps of Belgium and Norway during and immediately after the Second World War to denote victory.

V in each corner of triangular stamps of Czechoslovakia, denoting a special personal delivery service 1937.

Vale (Spanish for "worth" or "valid") overprinted on stamps revalidated for postal use or surcharged with a new value.

Vale correo de 1911 overprint on the back of reveue stamps authorised for postal use in Nicaragua.

Valeur Declarée (French for "declared value") on the insured mail labels issued under UPU regulations.

Valevole per le stampe overprint on Italian parcel stamps to indicate validity for printed matter 1890.

Vallees d'Andorre Andorra.

Valor Declarado (Spanish for "declared value") on insured parcel labels of Spain and colonies.

Valore Globale (Italian for "global value") overprinted on stamps of Fiume to denote international validity 1919–20.

Valparaiso Multada inscription on Chilean postage due labels of 1894.

Van Diemen's Land Tasmania.

Venezia Tridentina Italian or Austrian stamps overprinted for use in Trentino under Italian occupation 1918.

Viva Espana ("long live Spain") slogan on many Nationalist stamps of the Civil War 1936–39.

Vojenska Posta ("military post") inscribed on Czechoslovak stamps used by troops in Siberia 1919–20.

Vojna Uprava Jugoslavenske Armije (Yugoslav Military Government) overprint on Yugoslav stamps for use in Venezia Giulia and Istria 1947.

Volksdienst (Dutch for "national service") overprint on stamps of 1944 with a charity premium for social services.

Volksstaat Bayern People's State of Bavaria.

Volksstaat Wurttemberg People's State of Wurttemberg.

Vom Empfanger Einzuziehen (German for "collect from the recipient") inscribed on postage due labels of Danzig 1921–22.

Vom Empfanger Zahlbar (German for "chargeable to the recipient") on postage due labels of Bavaria 1862–76 and Danzig 1929–39.

Voor Het Kind (Dutch "for the child") inscribed on child welfare stamps of the Netherlands and colonies.

Voor Krijgsgevangenen (Dutch "for prisoners of war") overprint on air stamps of Curacao.

Voortrekker (Afrikaans for "pioneer") on many stamps of South Africa.

Vox Hiberniae (Latin for "voice of Ireland") on Irish air stamps 1949.

VPK (abbreviation for *Veld Post Kantoor,* Dutch or Flemish for "field post office") on military postmarks of Belgium and South Africa.

V.R.I. (abbreviation for *Victoria Regina Imperatrix,* Victoria Queen Empress) overprint on Transvaal 1900, following the British occupation.

V-R-I (with **Cancelled** above) overprint on stamps of the South African Republic for use at Wolmaransstad 1900.

V.R. Special Post overprint on 1895–96 Transvaal stamps, converting them for use in Cape Colony.

V.R. Transvaal overprint on stamps of the South African Republic following the first British occupation 1879.

Vuelo Inaugural (Spanish for "inaugural flight") on cachets and postmarks of Latin American airmails.

Vuja or **Vujna STT** Yugoslav military administration of Trieste 1945–50.

V Via Aerea airmail stamps of Paraguay 1929–31.

War overprint on stamps of British Honduras 1916–17 denoting a wartime tax on letters.

War Charity overprint with a date on stamps of the Bahamas 1918–19.

Warschau overprint on German stamps 1917–18 for use in those parts of Poland formerly under Russian rule.

Watersnood (Dutch for "flood relief") overprint on stamps of the Netherlands in aid of flood victims 1953.

Weens Rubli ("one rouble") surcharge on Latvia 1920.

Wendensche Kreis Brief Post Wenden regional letter post 1862.

WHO World Health Organization

W.H.W. (abbreviation for *Winter Hilfs Werk,* German for "winter relief") overprint on stamps of Danzig.

Winterhulp (Dutch for "winter help") on Dutch charity stamps 1944.

Y 1 numeral obliterator on Hong Kong stamps denoting use at the British post office in Yokohama, Japan.

Y 1/4 surcharge on stamps of Cuba and Puerto Rico 1855–57.

Y.A.R. Yemen Arab Republic.

Yca provisional issue made at Yca or Ica, Peru during the Chilean–Peruvian War of 1879–82.

Yca Vapor ("steamship, Ica") overprint on Peruvian stamps

YCTAB Cyrillic overprint on Montenegro to mark the new constitution 1905.

Z. Afr. Republiek South African Republic (Tansvaal).

Z.A.R. overprint with new values on stamps of Cape of Good Hope for use at Vryburg in the South African Republic 1899.

Zegelregt (Dutch for "fiscal stamp") inscribed on stamps of the Transvaal subsequently overprinted for postal use.

Zeitungsmarke (German for "newspaper stamp") on German newspaper stamps.

Zelaya overprint on Nicaraguan stamps for use in this province, owing to the fact that its currency had a different value from the rest of the country.

Zentraler Kurierdienst (German for "central courier service") on official stamps of the German Democratic Republic.

Zimska Pomac (Serbo-Croat for "winter relief") overprint on Italian stamps for use in Slovenia under German occupation 1944.

Zomerzegel (Dutch for "summer stamp") on charity stamps of the Netherlands.

Zona de Occupatie 1919 Romana overprint on Hungarian stamps used in Transylvania occupied by the Roumanian army.

Zona Protectorado Espanol en Marruecos Spanish Protected Zone of Morocco 1916–18.

Zona Occupata Fiumano Kupa overprint on Yugoslav stamps for the Fiume and Kupa Zone occupied by Italy.

Zuid Afrika South Africa

Zuid Afrikaansche Republiek South African Republic (Transvaal)

Zuid-west Afrika South West Africa

Zulassungsmarke (German for "admission stamp") inscribed on parcel stamps used by German military personnel 1942–44.

Zurno ("urgent") overprint on Hungarian express letter stamps for use in Croatia 1918.

BOOKS OF THE YEAR

Below is a brief summary of the catalogues and handbooks published within the past year and reviewed or noticed in the British philatelic press. Where possible the number of pages and type of binding are given. Although these titles are currently available from the authors or publishers whose addresses are given at the end of each entry, readers are advised to try their favourite stamp supplier or Vera Trinder Limited, 38 Bedford Street, London WC2E 9EU, especially in the case of many of the foreign catalogues.

A. CATALOGUES

ACS COLOUR CATALOGUE OF NEW ZEALAND STAMPS

The 17th edition of this semi-specialised catalogue, illustrated in full colour, it includes postage and revenue stamps as well as many Cinderalla items.
Auckland City Stamps Ltd, PO Box 3496, Auckland, New Zealand. NZ$5.00

THE AMATEUR COLLECTOR'S STAMP CATALOGUE OF SWITZERLAND

H.I. Katcher and D. Houtris (eds.)
176 pages. Card covers. This is the 32nd edition of the catalogue devoted to the stamps of Switzerland and the international offices of the League of Nations and UN located in that country. Semi-specialised, it also lists and prices the hotel posts and soldiers stamps.
The Amateur Collector Ltd, PO Box 242, London N2 0YZ. £9.75 post paid

ANFIL CATALOGO OFICIAL SELLOS DE ESPANA

A full-colour simplified catalogue of Spanish stamps and postal stationery.
Anfil Sede Asociacion, Calle Mayor 18-2, Madrid, Spain. 900 pesetas

BALE CATALOGUE OF ISRAEL POSTAGE STAMPS 1994

330 pages. Card covers. A specialised catalogue illustrated in black and white, covering Israel and its forerunners.
Negev Holyland Stamps, PO Box 1, Ilfracombe, Devon EX34 9BR. £21.50

BOLAFFI CATALOGO ITALIANO

Three volumes, dealing with the stamps of Italy, San Marino and the Vatican, and the Italian colonies, post offices abroad and occupation issues respectively. Semi-specialised with colour illustrations in volume 1 and black and white in the others.
Alberto Bolaffi, Via Roma 101, Turin, Italy.

CATALOGO DO SELOS DO BRASIL, VOLUME 1: 1798-1890

An old-established catalogue, widely regarded as the standard work on the subject, the 49th edition has been considerably revised and expanded, notably regarding the Bulls Eyes of 1843.
RHM Ltda, Caixa Postal 3577, Ag Central, CEP 01060-970, Sao Paulo, SP, Brazil.

CATALOGO ENCICLOPEDICO ITALIANO 1994-5

A highly detailed catalogue in two volumes covering the Italian states and colonies.
Della Casa Editore, Via Bardia 6, Modena 41100, Italy.

CATALOGO UNIFICATO AREA ITALIANA 1995

580 pages. Laminated card covers. A semi-specialised catalogue of Italy and colonies, San Marino and Vatican, with illustrations in colour.
Commercianti Italiani, Via Priv Maria Teresa 11, 20123 Milan, Italy.

CATALOGUE OFFICIEL DE TIMBRES-POSTE BELGIQUE 1995

A specialised, full-colour catalogue of the stamps of Belgium and colonies.

Galerie du Centre, Bureau 343, Brussels 1000, Belgium.

CERES CATALOGUE 1995

A specialised, full-colour catalogue of the stamps of France and colonies.

Ceres, 23 rue du Louvre, Paris 75401, CEDEX 01, France.

CHINESE STAMP CATALOGUE— PEOPLE'S POST, 1949–93

170 pages. Card covers. A full-colour listing of the stamps and pre-stamped envelopes of the people's republic. Text in Japanese with an English key.

Japan Philatelic Society, Box 1, Shinjuku, Tokyo 163-91, Japan. 750 yen

COLLECT AIRCRAFT ON STAMPS

Alan Sterckx

252 A4 pages. Laminated card covers. The first stamp depicting an aeroplane appeared in 1912, only nine years after the Wright Brothers made their first flight with a powered machine. Since then there have been more than 12,000 stamps depicting some 1400 aircraft of all kinds, from the first Montgolfier balloon of 1783 to the latest supersonic fighter. The stamps are arranged in country order, and priced mint and used. Appendices chronicle the progress of aviation, classify aircraft and provide a detailed cross reference to the main catalogue.

Stanley Gibbons. £17.95

COLLECT BRITISH POSTMARKS

332 pages. Card covers. The catalogue pioneered by the late Dr Tim Whitney, now expanded and revised under the joint editorship of Colin Peachey and Brian Crooks. The book has increased by a third in page length, while the reduction in the size of illustrations has enabled the new compilers to effectively double the amount of data included. The text itself has been thoroughly overhauled and many errors from earlier editions are now eliminated. Effectively this sixth edition is an entirely new work.

British Postmark Society, 19 Moorland Road, Hemel Hempstead HP11 1NH. £12.50 + £1.50 (UK)

COLLECT BRITISH STAMPS

138 pages, card covers. The forty-seventh edition. Fully illustrated in colour. Lists all official first day covers and presentation packs as well as stamps.

Stanley Gibbons. £5.95

COLLECT CHANNEL ISLANDS AND ISLE OF MAN STAMPS

234 pages. Card covers. The twelfth edition of the volume combining all the stamps of the British offshore islands, it provides a simplified listing, with black and white illustrations and includes booklets, first day covers and presentation packs.

Stanley Gibbons. £7.95

COLLECT GB FIRST DAY COVERS

248 pages. Card covers. A well-illustrated straightforward guide to British FDCs, from letters posted on the first day of the Uniform Fourpenny Post (5 December 1839) to special covers of the present day. All First Day and sponsored handstamps and machine cancellations are listed and priced.

First Day Publishing Company, PO Box 947, Lewes, East Sussex BN8 6ZS. £4.99 + £1.00 (UK)

COLLECT SHELLS ON STAMPS

Tom Walker

202 pages. Card covers. The latest in the popular Gibbons thematic series, dealing with everything from the early stamps of Travancore and the celebrated Uganda Missionaries (denominated in cowrie shells). The first stamps to feature an identifiable shell hailed from the Bahamas in 1859 which showed conch shells in the lower corners. Many of the older stamps listed, in fact, depict shells as ornaments in their borders, but the bulk of the catalogue is devoted to the colourful shell stamps of more recent times. As usual, there are indices giving common and scientific names as well as a classification by species.

Stanley Gibbons. £16.95

COLLECT SHIPS ON STAMPS

Peter Bolton

322 A4 pages. Laminated card covers. A detailed catalogue, country by country, of all stamps depicting boats and ships, with a cross-referenced index according to type of ship.

Stanley Gibbons. £17.95

COLLECTING BRITISH FIRST DAY COVERS

N. C. Porter

A comprehensive price-guide to British FDCs, together with all the special postmarks associated with the first day of issue. Many illustrations in black and white and several in full colour.

A.G. Bradbury, 3 Link Road, Stoneygate, Leicester LE 2 3RA. £4.95 + 1.05 postage (UK)

COLLECTING IRISH STAMPS

A simplified catalogue of the stamps of Ireland, fully illustrated in colour.

Ian Whyte Ltd, 27 Mount Street Upper, Dublin 2, Ireland. £4.95

COLOMBIA 1994–1995 CATALOGO

A simplified catalogue with colour illustrations.
Filatelia Colombia, Apartado 53.404, Bogota, Colombia

COSMOS CATALOGUE DES COSMODROMES DU MONDE 1994

320 pages. Card covers. A lavishly illustrated catalogue of covers and cards with the space theme. Text in five languages.
Editions Lollini, BP 635, F-06011, Nice CEDEX 1, France.

DANMARKS FRIMERKEKATALOG 1994–95

A specialised, all-colour catalogue of Denmark and associated territories, including Christmas seals.
AFA-Forlaget, Bruunsgade 42, DK-8000, Aarhus, Denmark. Dkr175.00

DARNELL STAMPS OF CANADA

300 pages. Card covers. A full-colour, semi-specialised catalogue of Canadian stamps, with a good introductory text.
Darnell Stamp and Coin Dept., Eaton, 677 Ouest, Ste Catherine, Montreal QC, Canada H3B 3Y6. $C15.95

DNK DEUTSCHLAND BRIEFMARKEN-KATALOG 1994

800 pages. Card covers. A full-colour simplified catalogue of German and Europa stamps.
Leuchtturm Albenverlag GmbH, Postfach 1340, Geesthacht 21495, Germany. DM15.90

ESPANA 1994

A semi-specialised catalogue of Spain, illustrated in colour.
Edifil, Calle Mayor 29, 28013 Madrid, Spain. 1300 pesetas.

FACIT SPECIAL 1994–95

752 pages. Soft covers. A semi-specialised catalogue of the Scandinavian group, with emphasis on Sweden (whose postal administration have donated a sheet of map stamps with a face value of 30Skr in each volume). Black and white illustrations throughout.
Facit Forlag AB, Parkgatan 12, S-112 30 Stockholm, Sweden. £24.00

FILABO CATALOGO DE SELLOS DE ESPANA

300 pages. Card covers. The 15th edition of a simplifed catalogue of Spain, colonies, Andorra and Equatorial Guinea. Many illustrations in colour, but others in black and white.
Filabo, 08970 San Juan Despi, Barcelona, Spain. 1250 pesetas

FILIGRANO FIRST DAY COVER 1994

A fully illustrated catalogue of first day covers from Italy since 1948, San Marino, the Vatican, Trieste and the Order of Malta.
GSE Editori Srl, Via Filippo Guarini 8, 47000 Forli, Italy. 15,000 lire

HONG KONG POSTAGE STAMP CATALOGUE 1994–5

64 pages. Card covers. A concise, full-colour catalogue devoted to the stamps and stationery of Hong Kong.
International Stamp & Coin Sdn Bhd, GPO Box 12016, 50764 Kuala Lumpur, Malaysia. £5.00

GREAT BRITAIN CONCISE CATALOGUE

274 pages. Laminated card covers. A semi-specialised catalogue of British stamps, offering collectors a midway approach between Collect British Stamps and the five-volume specialised catalogue.
Stanley Gibbons. £12.95

JAPANESE POSTAGE STAMP CATALOGUE 1995

200 pages. Card covers. Illustrated in full colour, semi-specialised catalogue with text in Japanese.
Japan Dealers Association, 2-16-1-612, Shinbashi, Minato-ku, Tokyo 195, Japan. 600 yen

JB CATALOGUE OF MALTA STAMPS AND POSTAL HISTORY

150 pages. Card covers. A semi-specialised catalogue of Maltese stamps, together with a survey of the postal markings.
Joseph Buttigieg, Sliema Stamp Shop, 93 Manwel Dimech Street, Sliema, Malta.

JSDA JAPANESE STAMP SPECIALISED CATALOGUE 1994

A specialised catalogue of the stamps of Japan and associated territories. Black and white illustrations. Text in Japanese.
Japan Philatelic Publications Inc. Tokyo, Japan. 2300 yen

KOREAN STAMP CATALOGUE

216 pages. Card covers. A guide to the stamps of North Korea from 1946 onwards, all illustrations in full colour.
Korean Stamp Corporation, Pyongyang, People's Democratic Republic of Korea.

LOLLINI COSMOS

A catalogue devoted to covers pertaining to the theme of space travel and exploration.
Lollini, BP 635, 06011 Nice, CEDEX 1, France.

MAGYAR BELYEGEK KATALOGUSA 1994

A full-colour simplified catalogue of Hungary and associated territories. Text in Hungarian.
Philatelia Hungarica, PO Box 600, Budapest H-1373, Hungary

MICHEL ASIEN KATALOG

2400 pages. Soft covers. A two-volume catalogue of the stamps of Asia, arranged by countries (A-J and K-Z respectively) on a simplified basis, with black and white illustrations. DM98.00
Schwaneberger Verlag, Muthmannstrasse 4, Munich 80939, Germany.

MICHEL AUTOMATENMARKEN SPEZIAL KATALOG 1994

176 pages. Soft covers. A comprehensive catalogue of the automatic vending machine stamps by Frama, Dassault and Klussendorf for countries of the world, illustrated in black and white.
Schwaneberger Verlag. DM32.00

MICHEL BRIEFE-KATALOG DEUTSCHLAND 1994/5

712 pages. Soft covers. An incredibly detailed listing of covers, entires, postmarks and all kinds of ancillary markings found on German mail: 10,000 classifications, 8500 illustrations and 28,000 prices quoted.
Schwaneberger Verlag. DM46.00

MICHEL BRIEFMARKEN-KATALOG DEUTSCHLAND

A semi-specialised catalogue, illustrated in full colour, dealing with the stamps of German and associated territories and colonies.
Schwaneberger Verlag. £14.00

MICHEL DEUTSCHLAND SPEZIAL KATALOG 1994

A highly specialised catalogue of Germany, states and colonies, illustrated in black and white with numerous line diagrams.
Schwaneberger Verlag. DM62

MICHEL EUROPA KATALOG OST 1994–5

1700 pages. Soft covers. A simplifed catalogue with black and white illustrations devoted to the countries of eastern Europe (the former Communist bloc).
Schwaneberger Verlag. £26.50

MICHEL EUROPA KATALOG WEST 1995

3000 pages. Soft covers. A two-volume catalogue arranged by countries A-L and M-Z, listing and pricing over 50,000 stamps.
Schwaneberger Verlag. DM64.00

MICHEL GANZSACHEN KATALOG EUROPA OST 1994–95

600 pages. Soft covers. A specialised catalogue of the postal stationery issued by the countries of eastern Europe, from Albania to Western Ukraine.
Schwaneberger Verlag. £50.00

MICHEL JUNIOR KATALOG 1994

A full-colour simplified catalogue of Germany, states, occupations and colonies.
Schwaneberger Verlag.

MICHEL AUSTRALIA, MALAISCHER ARCHIPEL, OZEANIEN 1994

A simplified catalogue of Australasia, the Pacific Islands and South-east Asia, illustrated in black and white.
Schwaneberger Verlag.

NETTO AUSTRIA 1994–5

A specialised catalogue with illustrations in colour, covering Austria, occupations and plebiscites.
Netto, Postfach 55, A 1935 Wien, Austria.

NORGESKATALOGEN 1994

A specialised catalogue, with illustrations in colour, and an introduction in English and German.
Oslo Filatelistklubb, Wennergren Cappelen A/S, Oslo, Norway. 240kr.

PRIFIX 1995

400 pages. Soft covers. A semi-specialised catalogue of Luxembourg and Europa stamps, illustrated in black and white. Bilingual text (French and German).
Prifix, 17 bd Prince Henri, L-1724 Luxembourg. 450fr

QUEEN ELIZABETH II DECIMAL DEFINITIVE ISSUES

674 pages. Laminated card covers. Volume 4 of the Specialised Catalogue, taking due account of recent developments, notably the Enschede printings, the extension of elliptical security perforations, the changes in the Castle high values and the introduction of the £10 stamp.
Stanley Gibbons. £19.95

QUEEN ELIZABETH II PRE-DECIMAL ISSUES

442 pages. Laminated card covers. Volume 3 of the Specialised Catalogue, dealing in great depth with the British stamps from 1952 to 1971.
Stanley Gibbons. £22.50

SAKURA CATALOG OF JAPANESE STAMPS 1995

270 pages. Card covers. A semi-specialised catalogue in full colour. Text in Japanese, with an English section.
Japan Philatelic Publications, PO Box 2, Suginami-Minami, Tokyo 168-81, Japan. £7.00

SCANDINAVIEN FRIMAERKEKATALOG 1994–95

Lars Boes (ed.)

428 pages. Card covers. A semi-specialised catalogue of the Scandinavian countries, together with the UN offices in New York, Geneva and Vienna.
AFA-Forlaget, Bruunsgade 42, DK-8000, Aarhus, Denmark. Dkr155.00

SCHWEIZ-LIECHTENSTEIN 1995

520 pages. Casebound. Full-coloured specialised catalogue of Switzerland and Liechtenstein, with text in French and German throughout.
Zumstein, Zeughausgasse 24, 3000 Bern 7, Switzerland. Sfr22.00

SCOTT 1995 SPECIALIZED CATALOGUE OF UNITED STATES STAMPS

The standard work on US stamps, illustrated in black and white.
Scott Publishing Co., 911 Vandemark Road, Sidney, Ohio, USA 45365. $32.00

SCOTT 1995 STANDARD POSTAGE STAMP CATALOGUE

A fairly basic catalogue of the whole world arranged in five volumes. Volume 1 deals with the stamps of the USA, Canada, the United Nations, the UK and the British Commonwealth, while volume 2 covers the rest of the world from A to C, volume 3 D-I, volume 4 J-Q and volume 5 R-Z, on a simplified basis with black and white illustrations.
Scott Publishing Co., 911 Vandemark Road, Sidney, Ohio, USA 45365.

SELOS POSTAIS 1994

320 pages. Card covers. A full-colour semi-specialised catalogue of Portugal, Azores, Madeira and Macao.
Afinsa, Rua Ricardo Jorge 55-4 Dt, Porto 4000, Portugal

STAMPS OF AUSTRALIA WITH AUSTRALIAN ANTARCTIC TERRITORY

A full-colour semi-specialised catalogue including Framas, OS perfins and Pre-stamped stationery as well as stamps, coils and booklets.
Stamp Factory, Box 1455, Dubbo, New South Wales 2830, Australia. $A7.95.

STAMPS OF THE WORLD

3168 pages. Limp covers. Three volumes covering the whole world on a simplified basis: Volume 1, Foreign countries, A-J; Volume 2, Foreign countries, K-Z; Volume 3, Commonwealth countries. Soft covers, A4 format.
Stanley Gibbons. £72.50 complete + £3.00 (UK) or £6.00 (overseas)

STANLEY GIBBONS STAMP CATALOGUE PART 1: BRITISH COMMONWEALTH

676 and 742 pages. Casebound. Divided into two volumes, the first covering the UK and countries from A to J, and the second covering countries from K to Z. This massive two-volume catalogue is revised and updated annually, and as well as a careful revision of prices the opportunity has been taken to expand the listings of stamp booklets and stamps used on cover.
Stanley Gibbons. £27.50 each volume

STANLEY GIBBONS STAMP CATALOGUE: AUSTRIA AND HUNGARY

292 pages. Soft covers. The fifth edition of the second part of the green catalogue, it has been updated especially in light of the dramatic political changes in Hungary since 1989, which is reflected in the hardening of market values.
Stanley Gibbons. £14.95

STANLEY GIBBONS STAMP CATALOGUE: CZECHOSLOVAKIA AND POLAND

251 pages. Soft covers. The fifth edition of the fifth part of the green catalogue. The title is something of a misnomer in view of the fact that the Czech Republic and Slovakia have parted company. It includes the wartime issues of Bohemia and Moravia, the plebiscite issues for Eastern Silesia, the Czech Legion in Siberia, occupation issues and Polish post offices abroad.
Stanley Gibbons. £15.95

STANLEY GIBBONS STAMP CATALOGUE: FRANCE

644 pages. Soft covers. A thorough revision of the sixth part of the green catalogue devoted to France and colonies, including Andorra and Monaco and now expanded to include many of the former colonial territories omitted in previous editions.
Stanley Gibbons. £18.95

STANLEY GIBBONS STAMP CATALOGUE: SCANDINAVIA

277 pages. Soft covers. A new edition of volume 11, the final part of the green (Europe) sectional catalogue, covering the stamps of Denmark Norway, Sweden and Finland, together with Iceland, Greenland, Faroe Islands and Aland Islands, and the former Danish West Indies.
Stanley Gibbons. £14.95

STANLEY GIBBONS STAMP CATALOGUE: UNITED STATES

318 pages. Soft covers. A much-needed new edition of part 22 of the Gibbons sectional catalogue, covering the stamps of the USA, the Confederate States and associated territories, and providing a useful survey of the modern issues, complicated by the use of different printing contractors and using different sheet formats.
Stanley Gibbons. £12.95

SUOMI FINLAND ALAND AND EESTI 1994

196 pages. Card covers. A full-colour catalogue of the stamps of Finland, the Aland Islands and Estonia.
Lauri Peltonen Ky, Hango 10901, Finland. 30Fmk

VLASTOS CATALOGUE OF GREECE 1994–5

460 pages. Soft covers or casebound. A full-colour specialised catalogue dealing with the stamps of Greece, Crete, Cyprus, Thessaly, Thrace and the Aegean Islands, supplied with a 40-page supplement in English.
Vlastos, 40 Vass Georgiou St, Halandri 152 33, Greece. £9.00 / £16.00

YVERT & TELLIER 1995 VOLUME 1 FRANCE, VOLUME 1B MONACO

360 pages / 232 pages. Soft covers. The standard catalogues for France and Monaco.
Yvert & Tellier, 37 rue des Jacobins, F-80036, Amiens, CEDEX 1, France. 80fr / 50fr

---

B. HANDBOOKS AND MONOGRAPHS

THE AEROGRAMMES OF THE ARABIAN GULF, POST INDEPENDENCE ISSUES

T. F. Jones

A survey of the aerogrammes of the Gulf states, from Abu Dhabi to the United Arab Emirates, together with estimated values.
From the author at 36 Cobham Road, Accrington, Lancashire BB5 2AD. £3.50 + 50p (UK) or £1.50 (overseas)

AIR SERVICES IN NATIONALIST SPAIN DURING THE CIVIL WAR

F. Gomez Guillamon

246 pages A4. Card covers. The fascinating story of the air services during the Spanish Civil War, 1936-39, including the contribution by foreign air lines, especially those operated by Nazi Germany and Italy. The stamps, labels, cachets, postmarks, distinctive stationery and ephemera associated with these services, many of them extremely shortlived, are fully documented.
R.G. Shelley, 9 Chanctonbury Road, Hove. £20 + £2.25 postage

AIRWAY LETTERS OF THE UNITED KINGDOM

Peter Lister

54 pages. Card covers. A record of the services provided in the British Isles by the airlines from 1934 until 1988, together with the stamps, covers, cachets and postal markings associated with them.
From the author, 97 Albany Park Avenue, Enfield Highway, Middlesex EN3 5NX. £8.95 + £1.00 (UK), £2.00 (Europe) or £3.00 (overseas)

AN ANNOTATED BIBLIOGRAPHY OF BURMA PHILATELY

Alan Meech

A comprehensive listing of the literature on the philately of Burma, including postal stationery and postal history, with descriptions and comments.
British Philatelic Trust, 107 Charterhouse Street, London EC1M 6PT. £2.50 (UK) or £3.50 (overseas)

AUSTRALIA—A NUCLEAR WEAPONS TESTING GROUND

Michael Dobbs

142 pages. Plasticised cover. An account of British nuclear testing in the South Pacific between 1952 and 1958, with special reference to the postal facilities for troops and civilian personnel stationed on Christmas Island and at Maralinga in Australia. Full details are given of the pictorial stationery as well as the postal markings and cachets, as well as the bogus stamps of the Monte Bello local post. The book also chronicles the activities of the Woomera Rocket Range up to 1975.
Forces Postal History Society, 4 Kashmir Close, New Haw, Weybridge, Surrey KT15 3JD. £16.00

BEE AND BEE INTEREST POSTAGE STAMPS OF THE WORLD: SUPPLEMENT 1

Dorothy E. Shaw and J. Stuart Ching

20 pages. Card covers. This supplement includes material overlooked when the main thematic listing was published, together with a wealth of new material.

International Bee Reearch Association, 18 North Road, Cardiff CF1 3DY. £4.25

BOLAFFI 1970-90 INTERNATIONAL
BOLAFFI 1994 INTERNATIONAL

These two volumes respectively provide a summary of important prices achieved at auction over a twenty year period, and a more detailed examination of the auction scene in the course of 1993 alone. Previous volumes dealt with 1991 and 1992 and it was their success which encouraged the publishers to provide an overview of the previous two decades. The same format is used in both volumes, each item being illustrated in full colour, together with the name and date of the sale, the starting price and the final sales price.

Alberto Bolaffi, Via Cavour 17, Turin 10123, Italy. Volume 1, £35; volume 2, £40; both volumes £55

BORNEO: JAPANESE POW CAMPS, PART 2

Neville Watterson

342 pages. Laminated card covers. A follow-up to the original volume dealing with the mail of prisoners of war and civilian internees, including a considerable amount of additional material brought to light as a result of reaction from readers. The account given in the first volume has thus been amplified and expanded, while much that is entirely new is now presented for the first time. The postal history of this grim period is fully documented.

From the author at Park View, 449 Abington Park Parade, Wellingborough Road, Northampton NN1 4EZ. £20.00

BRITISH EMPIRE CIVIL CENSORSHIP DEVICES WORLD WAR II, TRINIDAD & TOBAGO

R. G. Wike

80 pages. Card covers. An exhaustive survey and analysis of wartime censorship as practised in Trinidad and Tobago, with full illustration of marks, labels and seals, and identification of the censor numbers assigned to Trinidad, Tobago, Bermuda and Jamaica.

Chavril Press, Bloomfield, Perth Road, Abernethy, Perth PH2 9LW. £15.00

BRITISH MEGATON BOMB TRIALS IN THE PACIFIC

Michael Dobbs

66 pages. Plasticised cover. A companion volume to the author's work on the nuclear tests in Australia, it deals with postal material associated with the hydrogen bomb tests conducted by the UK in the South Pacific in 1957-8 from Task Force Grapple based on Christmas Island.

Forces Postal History Society, 4 Kashmir Close, New Haw, Weybridge, Surrey KT15 3JD. £11.00

BRITISH POSTAGE DUE MAIL, 1914-1971

Michael Furfie

75 A4 pages. Card covers. An account of the handling of unpaid and underpaid mail in the period from the introduction of postage duel labels in April 1914 until the demise of the original design on the introduction of decimalisation in February 1971, with 50 covers, postcards and wrappers illustrating the various methods of processing these items and the infringements of the regulations which provoked the surcharging of mail.

From the author, 37 Town Tree Road, Ashford, Middlesex TW15 2PN. £6.50 (UK), £8 (overseas)

BRITISH STAMP DESIGN 1993: THE WORK OF THE STAMP ADVISORY COMMITTEE

James Negus

36 pages. Card covers. This is *British Philatelic Bulletin* Publication number 2, and follows up the previous volume of 1993 dealing with the work of the Committee and the background to its decisions concerning the stamps of 1992. It provides an invaluable insight into the way in which British stamp subjects are selected and the designs evolved.

British Philatelic Bureau, 20 Brandon Street, Edinburgh EH3 5TT. £4.99

CATALOGUE DE MARQUES DE PASSAGE, 1661–1875

James Van der Linden

336 pages. Casebound. A detailed alphabetical listing of over 3500 postal markings recorded on European mail, applied in transit and at frontier crossings between countries, from their inception until they were discontinued as a result of the formation of the Universal Postal Union.

James Bendon Ltd, PO Box 6484 Limassol, Cyprus. £85.00 (ordinary) or £145.00 (de luxe)

CATALOGUE OF INDIAN CENSORSHIP, 1914-1920

Alan Baker (ed. Charles R. Entwistle)

32 pages A4. Card covers. A detailed survey of censorship applied to Indian mail during and immediately after the First World War, with listings of the labels, handstamps and cachets employed.

Chavril Press, Bloomfield, Perth. £10

CENSORSHIP IN THE ROYAL AIR FORCE 1918 TO 1956

Dr. N. Colley and W. Garrard

76 pages. Card covers. A major contribution to RAF postal history, detailing the censor labels and cachets found on RAF mail from its inception in April 1918 until the Suez crisis of 1956, with full identification of the censor numbers.

Chavril Press, Bloomfield, Perth Road, Abernethy, Perth PH2 9LW. £17.50 (UK), £18.50 (Europe) or £19.50 (overseas)

CHECK LIST OF ROYAL NAVAL VESSELS IN THE LOG BOOK AND ON STAMPS

A.W. Fenton and D.A. Rouse

A listing of the stamps described in volumes 1-20 of Log Book, the periodical of the Ship Stamp Society, arranged in alphabetical order.

Ship Stamp Society, 7 Meadway, Warlingham, Surrey CR6 9RW. £2.80 (UK) or £3.50 (overseas)

CHECKLIST OF JAPANESE SCENIC CANCELLATIONS, 1948–93

Seiko Tomooka

520 pages. Card covers. A comprehensive list of the pictorial handstamps of Japan, fully illustrated with transliterations of the Japanese names into the Roman alphabet.

Japan Philatelic Publications, PO Box 2, Suginami-Minami, Tokyo 168-91, Japan. 3090 yen + 1080 yen postage

CHECKLIST OF SCOUT, GUIDE AND BOYS BRIGADE STAMPS OF THE WORLD

David McKee

Detailed listings of the stamps, carriage labels, Christmas seals, charity labels, postal stationery, even coins and banknotes, which have the principal youth organisations of the world as their subject.

From the author, 3 South Park Drive, Foxrock, Dublin 18, Ireland. £6.50

CHRISTOPHER COLUMBUS, THE DISCOVERER OF THE NEW WORLD

C. J. Stapley

236 pages. Card covers. At the turn of the century Columbus was, next to Queen Victoria, the most widely portrayed person on stamps. The numerous stamps marking the 450th anniversary of the discovery of America (1942) boosted this, but they are as nothing to the prolific issues from all over the world in the past two years marking the 500th anniversary. This book provides background details on all the portraits, ships, maps and scenes depicted, and a check-list of the stamps and postal stationery connected with Columbus.

From the author at Xanadu, Green Lane, Leominster, Herefordshire HR6 8QN. £15.00 + £1.00 postage

COMPARISONS OF HELLENIC STAMPS 1861–1923

Orestes G. Vlastos

Casebound. A sumptuously produced and lavishly illustrated book, particularly useful for indicating the differences between genuine and forged stamps. English text.

Vera Trinder, 38 Bedford Street, London WC2E 9EU. £350 + £3.50 postage and packing

DOMINICA POSTAL HISTORY, STAMPS AND POSTAL STATIONERY TO 1935

E. V. Toeg

A lifetime's research distilled into this excellent monograph.

British West Indies Study Circle, 28 Orchard Close, Hall Weston, St Neots, Cambs PE19 4LF. £42.00 + £4.15 postage and packing

EAST AFRICAN AIRMAILS TO 1939

Bill Colley

A survey of the airmails of Kenya, Uganda, Tanganyika and Zanzibar, with a great deal of useful background information, together with maps and illustrations of all postmarks, cachets and covers recorded.

Pierpoint Publishing, 21 Lynton Close, Hurstpierpoint, Hassocks, West Sussex BN6 9AN. £13.95 + 75p postage (UK)

ENCYCLOPAEDIA OF RARE AND FAMOUS STAMPS. VOL. 1 THE STORIES

L. N. Williams

382 pages. Casebound. Norman Williams, and his late brother Maurice, produced a number of books from 1940 onwards - *Famous Stamps, More Famous Stamps, Stamps of Fame* and *Rare Stamps.* Much of the content of this volume therefore goes over the same ground and brings the story up to date. The projected second and third volumes will contain the provenance and histories of each rarity and a catalogue of values based on market and auction realisations.

David Feldman SA, PO Box 81, Route de Chancy 175, 1213 Onex, Geneva, Switzerland. SF150 + SF15 postage and packing

ENGLISH COMPANION TO THE MICHEL DEUTSCHLAND SPEZIAL KATALOG
Will Payne

An English translation and commentary on the volume of the specialised German catalogue dealing with the stamps of the Third Reich 1933–45.
From the author at Rosemead, Wyddial, Buntingford, Herts SG9 0EX. £10 + 50p (UK)

FALKLAND ISLANDS HISTORY THROUGH PHILATELY
G.D. Moir

56 pages. Card covers. A fascinating account of the turbulent history of the islands as illustrated by its postage stamps, and giving considerable detail on the designs.
Croydon Stamp Centre, St George's Walk, Croydon.

FIRST GUIDE TO STAMP COLLECTING
Neil Granger

92 pages. Casebound. Written for beginners and children from about eight upwards, this is succinct and very nicely illustrated, covering the basics and fundamentals of stamp collecting in an easy manner.
OUP, £9.99

GETTING THE MESSAGE
Christopher Browne

201 pages. Casebound. A rambling, superficial and often factually inaccurate account purporting to be the first complete history of the Post Office, with good illustrations marred by jokey captions.
Alan Sutton. £14.99

GREAT BRITAIN AND IRELAND RAILWAY LETTER STAMPS 1957–1992
Neill Oakley

72 pages. Card covers. Railway letter stamps were in use in the UK from 1891 till the early 1920s but then lapsed. They were revived in 1957 by the Talyllyn Railway and since then have been extensively issued by the light railways and preserved lines of the British Isles.
From the Railway Pilatelic Group, 16 Caves Lane, Bedford MK40 3DR. £7.00 + 50p (UK) or £1.00 (overseas)

GREAT BRITAIN USED ABROAD: CANCELLATIONS AND POSTAL MARKINGS
John Parmenter

370 pages. Casebound. A thorough account of the British post offices and postal agencies established in many foreign countries as well as the colonies in the 19th century, with appendices and an excellently cross-referenced index.
Postal History Society, £35 (£30 to members)

GREEK RURAL POSTMEN AND THEIR CANCELLATION NUMBERS
Derek Willan

76 A4 pages. Card covers. A tabular listing of the numbered handstamps, from 1 to 1195, used by Greek rural postmen to cancel mail on their routes. The different types of handstamp are illustrated and described, with earliest and latest dates recorded.
Hellenic Philatelic Society of Great Britain, 37 Alders View Drive, East Grinstead, West Sussex RH19 2DN. £20.00

GUATEMALAN TELEGRAPH STAMPS & STATIONERY
James C. Andrews

24 pages. Card covers. An exhaustive study of the 17 telegraph stamps from 1897 to the present day, with a great deal of background history and ancillary material, proofs and essays, telegram forms, delivery envelopes, postal announcements and other ephemera.
Michael J. Barrie, PO Box 1445, Detroit MI, USA 48231. $5.00 (USA) or $7.00 (overseas)

A GUIDE TO THE POSTCARD CACHETS OF LAND'S END
John Owen

47 pages. Card covers. A study of the various handstruck marks found on tourist postcards from Land's End from 1901 to the present day.
From the author, 36 Oxford Drive, Kippax, Leeds LS25 7JG. £8.95 + £1.00 (UK)

HANDBOOK OF POSTAL MECHANISATION
Douglas N. Muir (ed.)

A thorough account of the origin, development and current state of postal mechanisation in all its aspects, with special reference to the markings on mail from the first Transorma codes of 1935 to the present day.
Postal Mechanisation Study Circle, 27 Elizabeth Road, Hunters Ride, Henley-on-Thames, Oxon, RG9 1RA. £9.00

HONG KONG POSTAGE STAMPS OF THE QUEEN VICTORIA PERIOD
Air Commodore R.N. Gurevitch

144 pages. Card covers. Sub-titled "a collector's notebook", this is a distillation of a lifetime's research into

the early philately of Hong Kong, somewhat less than the intended definitive monograph perhaps but representing the state of research reached at the present time, in the hope that some of the problems and queries which it has thrown up will be solved by readers. It is, in fact, extremely thorough and well illustrated.

From the author, 54 Hawker Street, Torrens, ACT 2607, Australia. £25.00

HONG KONG SECURITY MARKINGS

Ming W. Tsang

A copiously illustrated account of the perfins, chop-marks and other forms of endorsement applied to stamps to control their use and prevent pilferage by employees in the crown colony of Hong Kong.

Hong Kong Stamp Society, PO Box 206, Glenside, PA, USA 19038. £20.25 (surface mail) or £25.35 (airmail)

HOSPITAL BARGES IN FRANCE: CORRESPONDENCE FROM A NURSING SISTER WITH THE BRITISH EXPEDITIONARY FORCE DURING WORLD WAR I

Peter L. High (ed.)

20 pages. Card covers. An edited transcript of a correspondence recently discovered, covering the period from September 1917 to December 1918. In 1916 alone no fewer than 17,000 battle casualties were transported by canal barge, many of them after the first battle of the Somme, and some 53,000 casualties in all were carried to safety in this manner. Accompanying the extracts from Sister Millicent Peterkin's letters are details of the field post office marks, unit censor markings and stationery.

Chavril Press, Bloomfield, Perth Road, Abernethy, Perth PH2 9LW. £3.50 (UK), £4.50 (Europe) or £5.50 (overseas)

INSECTS ON STAMPS OF THE WORLD

Don Wright

Lists over 2000 identified species of insect depicted on stamps, arranged in sections covering moths and butterflies, then other insects, listed by country of issue and taxonomy. The 123rd publication from the ATA and the first to include colour illustrations.

American Topical Association, PO Box 630, Johnstown, PA, USA 15907. $15.00 post-paid

JUSQU'A AIRMAIL MARKINGS, A STUDY

Ian McQueen

116 pages. Card covers. In the early days of airmail it was necessary to indicate the route of a letter and which section was conveyed by air and which by surface mail. UPU regulations stipulated the use of an endorsement prefixed with the French word Jusqu'a (as far as). Distinctive handstamps and labels associated with this period are fully described and illustrated.

W. A. Page, 138 Chastillian Road, Dartford, Kent DA1 3LG. £10.00 + £1.00 (UK) or £1.50 (overseas)

LINN'S FOCUS ON FORGERIES: A GUIDE TO FORGERIES OF COMMON STAMPS

Varro E. Tyler

168 pages. Card covers. An extremely useful survey of the forged stamps and faked covers which may be encountered and which often trap the unwary, arranged alphabetically from Albania to Wuhu.

Linn's Stamp News, PO Box 29, Sidney, OH 45365, USA. $30 + $4 postage

MADAME JOSEPH FORGED POSTMARKS

Derek Worboys

128 pages. Casebound. A detailed account of the work of the master forger known as Madame Joseph, with illustrations of the 450 implements imitating the postmarks of the Commonwealth and often employed by the dishonest London dealer Gordon Rhodes to transform a heavily mounted mint stamp into a superb lightly used example.

Royal Philatelic Society, 41 Devonshire Place, London W1N 1PE. £25.00

MAILBOATS TO LUNDY

Stanley Newman

40 pages. Card covers. A survey of the postal history of this island with reference to communications by sea from 1830 onwards, long before the post office was established in 1887. Emphasis is laid on the mail since 1929 with reference to special cachets and ships' markings.

Channel Islands and Lundy Auctions, Gemini Business Centre, 136-140 Old Shoreham Road, Hove, East Sussex BN3 7BD. £4.95 + 50p (UK)

MEDICAL HISTORY THROUGH POSTAGE STAMPS

Akira Furukawa

496 pages. Casebound. A superbly produced book detailing the history and development of medicine in all its branches through the centuries, as illustrated on stamps. Separate chapters deal with different medical systems, surgery, nursing, the treatment of leprosy, malaria and other specialised diseases, medical equipment, famous physicians and surgeons, etc.

Gazelle, Falcon House, Queen Square, Lancaster LA1 1RN. £87.99

MISSIONARY LETTERS FROM SAMOA
Brian Purcell

20 pages. Plastic covers. A succinct account of missionary mail from Samoa in the 19th century, with a record of the postal rates, manuscript marks, ship letter marks, New South Wales transit stamps and other postmarks found on missionary letters.

From the author at 1 Ashton Way, Keynsham, Bristol BS18 1JY. £10 + 75p postage (UK), £1,50 (Europe) or £3.50 (overseas)

NATIONAL POSTAL MUSEUM REVIEW OF 1993
This annual survey records the work of the National Postal Museum, material acquired, exhibitions mounted, and work on the arrangement, classification and writing-up of the collections in progress. It highlights the development of historic designs and in a series of contributed articles discusses various aspects of British stamps.

National Postal Museum, King Edward Street, London EC1A 1LP, £5.00

NORDDEUTSCHER LLOYD BREMEN 1857–1970
Edwin Drechsel

An exhaustive chronicle of the shipping company which served the route from North America to Germany. Although it is primarily a history of the company, its ships and their development, it is crammed with detailed information which will be invaluable to the maritime postal historian.

Cordillera Publishing Co., 8415 Granville Street, Box 46, Vancouver, BC, Canada V6P 4Z9.

OLD LETTER BOXES
Martin Robinson

32 pages. Card covers. A new edition of this popular guide, first published in 1987 and providing a concise history of pillar boxes, wall-boxes, lamp-boxes and other forms of posting-box used in the UK since Anthony Trollope's experiment of 1852. All the different types are illustrated and described in detail.

Shire Publications. £2.25

PITCAIRN ISLANDS POSTAL MARKINGS 1883–1991
Cy Kitching

A comprehensive study of the handstamps, cachets, airmail and route markings of Pitcairn, including the 'No Stamps Available' series.

Pitcairn Islands Study Group, 39 Marine Road, Penrhyn Bay, Llandudno, Gwynedd LL30 3NA. £6.00.

THE POLISH PRISONER OF WAR CAMP POSTS
Autolycus

During the Second World War four POW camps for Polish prisoners in Germany—Grossborn, Murnau, Neubrandenburg and Woldenberg—operated their own postal services and issued stamps, many of them printed singly from engraved wood-blocks using any scrap of paper available. The result constitutes one of the most fascinating but least known aspects of wartime philately.

Caldra House Ltd, 23 Coleridge Street, Hove, East Sussex BN3 5AB. £9 + £1 postage

POSTAGE STAMPS OF RUSSIA, 1917–1923, VOLUME 4 TRANSCAUCASIA, PART 8–12, GEORGIA SECTIONS A AND B
Dr R. J. Ceresa

This is the latest contribution to one of the truly great philatelic compilations of this century which will eventually encompass the stamps, stationery and postal markings of the Russian Revolution and the series of civil wars which ensued. Section A provides a historical and political background to Georgia which emerged as an independent state in May 1918, and deals with the Russian stamps used from then until the first distinctive Georgian stamps a year later. Subsequent chapters deal with the other adhesives of the short-lived republic. Section B analyses the surcharges and overprints, postmarks, forgeries and bogus material.

From the author, Fairways Cottage, Quarry Lane, Ross-on-Wye, Herefordshire HR9 7SJ. £25 each section (UK), £26 (Europe)

THE POSTAL HISTORY OF BRITISH AIR MAILS
Edward B. Proud

The rather clumsy title has been deliberately chosen as the emphasis of this book is on the history of those airmail services which operated on a regular basis and carried genuine mail, as opposed to those flights devoted to philatelic mail. It ranges from the balloon and pigeon posts of the Siege of Paris, for which special arrangements were made by the British Post Office, down to airmails of the present time.

Proud Bailey Ltd, PO Box 74 Heathfield, East Sussxe TN21 8PZ. £5.00 + £2 (UK) or £3 (overseas)

POSTBUS COUNTRY: GLIMPSES OF RURAL SCOTLAND
Joan Burnie

112 pages. Casebound. Intended to celebrate the first quarter century of the postbus system in Scotland, it is an ideal introduction to the subject, excellent on the socio-economic aspects especially as they affect tourism, but woefully inadequate and inaccurate as an actual history of

the postbus services and the many special covers, cachets, postmarks and tickets connected with them.
Canongate Press, Edinburgh. £12.99

POSTMARKS OF BRITISH RAILWAY STATIONS
W. T. Pipe and G. J. Blackman
94 pages. Card covers. A detailed survey of the postmarks used at post offices which happened to be located in or alongside railway stations in the British Isles, together with those offices which, though incorporating the word 'station' in their name, were not actually in the railway station although they may originally have been. More often than not, however, a village acquired such a name merely because houses developed round an isolated station, several miles from the village or town which it served. Interestingly, quite a few station villages have changed their names in recent years thanks to the closure of lines under the Beeching Axe.
Railway Philatelic Group, 16 Caves Lane, Bedford MK40 3DR. £7.50 + 75p postage

REFERENCE BOOK OF OVERPRINTS ON HUNGARIAN STAMPS
David Miles
A detailed guide to the occupation issues of 1919, local issues of 1919 and 1944-5, uprising issues of 1956, as well as private and bogus issues.
From the author, 7 Tennyson Avenue, St Ives, Huntingdon, Cambs PE17 4TU. £15.00 + £2.60 (UK) or £7.50 (overseas airmail)

ROYAL HOUSEHOLD MAIL
Glenn H. Morgan
224 A4 pages. Card covers. A history of mail from the royal household, from the messenger service of King John to the present day, with emphasis on the stationery, postmarks and certifying stamps.
British Philatelic Trust, 107 Charterhouse House Street, London EC1M 6PT. £20.00 + £2.50 (UK) or £3.50 (overseas)

ROYAL MAIL SPECIAL STAMPS
The eleventh annual devoted to the commemorative and special stamps of Great Britain, each chapter dealing with a particular issue in great detail with a wealth of fascinating 'behind the scenes' data.
British Philatelic Bureau, 20 Brandon Street, Edinburgh EH5 5TT. £22.50 (ordinary) or £75.00 (de luxe leather-bound)

RUBBER DATESTAMPS OF CUMBRIA
M. J. Mapleton
58 A4 pages. Card covers. A detailed listing of the Climax dater cancellations used in Cumbria between 1885 and the 1930s, in alphabetical order of post office, with earliest and latest dates recorded.
Cumbria Postal History Society, 84 Charnwood Avenue, Thurmaston, Leicester LE4 8EJ. £6.00 + £1.50 (UK).

RUSSIAN RAILWAY POSTMARKS
A. V. Kiryushkin and P. E. Robinson
180 A4 pages. Card covers. Data on more than 2600 railway postmarks of Russia, arranged in tabular form, with many illustrations, maps and a rarity guide.
J. Barefoot, PO Box 8, York YO3 7GL. £20 (UK) or £25 (abroad)

SCOUT STAMPS OF THE BRITISH COMMONWEALTH
Gordon C. Sampson
64 pages. Card covers. The first part of a trilogy which will eventually encompass all the scout and guide stamps of the world, grouped into four sections (UK, Commonwealth, non-postal issues and charity post labels).
From the author, 76 Goathland Avenue, Longbenton, Newcastle upon Tyne NE12 8HF. £5

A SHORT MARITIME POSTAL HISTORY OF NORWAY
Eric N. Jackson
A succinct account of the ship mail to and from Norway over the past 200 years, well illustrated with maps of routes, diagrams of postmarks and cachets and actual seaborne covers.
Scandinavia Philatelic Society, 6 Rydens Court, 43 Adelaide Road, Surbiton, Surrey, KT 6 4TG. £8 + 70p (UK)

SPECIAL EVENT POSTMARKS OF THE UNITED KINGDOM VOLUME III
Alan Finch and Colin Peachey
172 pages. Card covers. This is intended as a supplement to the main work and deals with the period from 1984 till the end of 1993, listing all the special event handstamps used in that period, and accompanied by clear line drawings, with estimated values.
British Postmark Society, 19 Moorland Road, Hemel Hempstead, Herts HP1 1NH. £9.50 + £1 (UK) or £1.50 (abroad)

STAMP COLLECTING: A FIRST GUIDE

Neill Granger

A beginner's book with a fairly basic approach but excellent, full-colour illustrations.

Oxford University Press. £9.99

STAMPS OF LUNDY ISLAND

Stanley Newman

80 pages. Card covers. An account of the stamps issued by Lundy in the Bristol Channel since 1929, together with postal markings and a great deal of background information.

Channel Islands and Lundy Auctions, Gemini Business Centre, 136-140 Old Shoreham Road, Hove, East Sussex BN3 7BD. £9.50 (postage extra)

THE STORY OF GREETINGS STAMPS

Tim Shackleton

48 pages. Card covers. The detailed background to the British Greetings stamp booklets since their inception, with a mass of fascinating information on the design problems and their solutions. The book contains a unique sheet of 45 greetings labels.

British Philatelic Bureau, 20 Brandon Street, Edinburgh EH3 5TT. £9.95

THE TÊTE-BÊCHE VARIETIES OF TRANSVAAL

Dr Alan R. Drysdall and Major Harold M. Criddle

42 pages. Casebound. A sumptuously produced account of the tête-bêche varieties found on the early issues of the Transvaal by the two leading authorities on the philately of the original South African Republic.

BPA Expertising Ltd, PO Box 137, Leatherhead, Surrey KT22 0RG. £35.00

THREE HUNDRED YEARS OF THE STAMP OFFICE AND STAMP DUTIES

Harry Dagnall

122 pages. Casebound. A history of the Stamp Office established in 1694 in the reign of King William III, and continuing to the present time, published in connection with the exhibition held in 1994 to celebrate the tercentenary. The detailed historic text is well illustrated with the various stamps and markings used,

HMSO. £1.95

THE TRAVELLING POST OFFICES OF CEYLON

Derek Walker

Although a railway was surveyed as early as 1842 it was not until 1865 that the first line was laid. TPOs were introduced in 1892 and within a few years almost twenty routes were in operation. This book recounts the history of each line, its TPO routes and their postal markings.

Ceylon Study Circle, 42 Lonsdale Road, Cannington, Bridgwater, Somerset TA5 2JS. £5.00 + 50p (UK), £1.00 (overseas)

WATER IN HUNGARIAN PHILATELY

Mervyn Benford

A thematic approach to Hungarian stamps, dealing with those featuring rivers, lakes, water birds, water sports, fishes and fishing, ships and boats of all kinds.

Hungarian Philatelic Society, Cloudshill Cottage, High Street, Shutford, Banbury, Oxon OX156 6HE. £3.00

WOMEN ON STAMPS

Helen Cockburn

A series of volumes (three so far) listing in alphabetical order the women of the world who have been portrayed on stamps. Each entry has brief biographical data.

American Topical Association, PO Box 630, Johnstown, PA, USA 15907. $17 each

WWF—WORLD WIDE FUND FOR NATURE AND WORLD WILDLIFE FUND LIST OF STAMPS

G. P. Doggett

A check-list of stamps bearing the Giant Panda logo, and issued to publicise or raise funds for the WWF since 1969.

9 Wheelwright Mews, Milton Keynes MK14 6HU. £2.00

65 YEARS IN STAMPS: A PHILATELIC HISTORY OF THE SHOWA PERIOD

Nishioka Tatsuji

136 pages. Casebound. The author celebrated his 90th birthday in July 1994 by re-publishing his memoirs of 65 years in the stamp trade, covering the most turbulent and momentous years in modern Japanese history. This work originally appeared in Japanese in 1989 and has now been translated and edited by Scott Gates and Robert Elliot.

James Bendon Ltd, PO Box 6484, Limassol, Cyprus. £17.50 (US $27.50)

EUROPEAN POSTAL MUSEUMS AND PHILATELIC COUNTERS

This directory lists the philatelic, postal and communications museums of Europe (including the British Isles). Opening times are given where known, together with admission charges current in 1994 where applicable. Most museums also sell stamps, stationery and other philatelic products and have facilities for the cancellation of philatelic souvenir mail.

The main post offices in most countries provide some form of philatelic sales, but the quality of service is variable and the range of products not always comprehensive. Philatelic counters, on the other hand, are usually staffed by personnel who have been specially trained to cater to the needs of collectors. The details of such outlets are appended at the end of each section. It is hoped to extend this list to include other continents in subsequent editions of this yearbook.

ALAND ISLANDS
Maritime Museum, Mariehamn. Opened 1954 and devoted to all aspects of transportation by sea, including exhibits of sea mail. Daily, 12–4pm; Sunday 1pm–4pm.
Philatelic Counter, Head Post Office, Mariehamn. Has a fine display of Aland Islands stamps, stationery and first day covers.

AUSTRIA
Post and Telegraph Museum, Technisches Museum fur Industrie und Gewerbe, 212 Mariahilferstrasse, Vienna XIV. Tuesday–Friday, 9.30am–4pm; weekends, 9am–1pm. 5sch.
Philatelic Counter, Hauptpostamt, Postgasse 8, Vienna 1.

BELGIUM
Postal Museum, 2 Petite Rue des Minimes, Brussels (just off the Place du Grand Sablon). Tuesday-Saturday, 10am–4pm. Free.
Musee des Chemins de Fer Belges (Belgian Railway Museum), Brussels Nord Station. Contains exhibits of railway stamps. Open daily, 10am –5pm. Free.
Philatelic Counter, Regie des Postes, Place de la Monnaie, Brussels; and at the head post offices of Antwerp, Charleroi, Ghent, Liege and Namur.

Temporary facilities are also offered in the tourist season and on the first day of issue, at Courtrai, Ostend and Hasselt.

BULGARIA
Postal Museum, Sofia, Central Post Office, Sofia.
Philatelic Counter, Central Post Office, Graf Ignatiev Street, Sofia.

CYPRUS
Philatelic Counter, Head Post Office, Metaxas Square, Nicosia. Philatelic sales are also provided at the main post offices in Larnaca, Limassol, Paphos and Kyrenia.

CZECH REPUBLIC
Postal Museum, 10 Holeckova Street, Prague V. Open daily. Free.
Technical Museum, 42 Kostelni Street, Prague VI. All modes of transport by land, rail, sea and air, with much of postal and telegraph interest. Open daily. Free.
Prodejna Filatelie, Ortemovo nàm. 16, 225 06, Prague 7.
Philatelic Counter, Central Post Office, Jindrisska ulice 14, Prague and *Postovska ulice 3, Brno.*

DENMARK

Post and Telegraph Museum, 9 Valkendorfsgade, 1151 Copenhagen. Thursday and Sunday, 10am–4pm (May-October); other days throughout the year, 1pm–3pm (except Easter Sunday, Whitsunday and Christmas Day). Free.

Philatelic Counter, Vesterbrogade 67, DK-1620, Copenhagen V. Monday–Friday, 10am–3pm; Saturday 10am–12 noon; Thurs.late opening till 6pm.

FAROE ISLANDS

No postal museum as yet, but a fine display of stamps and philatelic material in the head post office, Torshavn, which also has a good philatelic counter. Open daily.

FINLAND

Post and Telegraph Museum, 21B Tehtankatu, Helsinki. Tuesday and Friday, 12–3pm; Wednesday, 6pm–8pm. 1mk.

Railway Museum, Helsinki Station. Contains exhibits of TPO interest.

Philatelic Counter, Department of Posts, 11 Mannerheimintie, Helsinki.

FRANCE

National Postal Museum, 34 Boulevard de Vaugirard (near Montparnàsse Station), Paris. Daily (except Tuesday), 9.30am–12.30pm and 3pm–7pm (summer); 10am–5pm (winter). 10fr.

Regional Postal and Telecommunications Museum, *Château de Wurtemberg-Montbeliard, Riquewihr, Haut Rhin.* (April–October), daily, 10am–12 noon; 2pm–6pm. 15fr.

Amboise Postal Museum, 6 Rue Joyeuse, 37400 Amboise. A private museum with excellent French postal historical material. Daily except Tuesday, 9.30am–12.30pm; 3pm–7pm (summer); 10am–5pm (winter). 25fr.

National Railway Museum, Rue du Paturage, Mulhouse. Open daily.

French Naval Museum, Palais de Chaillot, Paris XVI. Daily, 10am–5pm; Wednesday 10am–11pm. 10fr.

Philatelic Counters are located at main post offices near the Louvre and next to the Postal Museum, Paris; also at the head post offices in Bordeaux, Lyon, Marseille and Strasbourg.

GERMANY

Postal Museum, 69–75 Mauerstrasse, Berlin 1066. The former Reichspost Museum and later postal museum of the GDR, it is currently undergoing extensive refurbishment in time for its centenary in 1997. Open daily. DM1.00.

Bundespostmuseum, 53 Schaumainkai, Frankfurt-am-Main. Monday–Friday, 9am–4pm.

Postal Museum, 1–5 Stephanplatz, Hamburg. Tuesday–Friday, 8am–2pm; Thursday, 8am–6pm.

Mittelrheinisches Postmuseum, 14–20 Friedrich-Ebert-Ring, Koblenz D-54. Monday–Friday, 8am–1pm; 1.30pm–4pm.

Transport Museum, 6 Lessingstrasse, Nuremberg,

Denmark's Philatelic Counter in Vesterbrogade, Copenhagen.

Bavaria. Monday–Friday, 8am–12; 2pm–4pm. Includes all kinds of postal and telegraph equipment, mailvans, etc.

Philatelic Library, City Library, 5 Sparkassenstrasse, Munich. Monday and Wednesday, 8am–4.30pm; Tuesday, 11am–7pm; Thursday and Friday, 8am–3.30pm. Contains 40,000 volumes of philatelic and postal history interest.

Philatelic Counters at all main post offices.

GIBRALTAR

The Gibraltar Museum contains a philatelic and numismatic section, and stages regular exhibitions in John Mackintosh Hall. Daily, 11am–1pm; 4pm–7pm; Sunday, 10.30am–1pm. Free.

Philatelic Sales, GPO, 104 Main Street.

GREAT BRITAIN

National Postal Museum, King Edward Building, King Edward Street, London EC1. Monday–Friday, 10am–4.30pm; Saturday, 10am–4pm. Closed Sundays and public holidays. Free.

Bruce Castle Museum, Lordship Lane, Tottenham, London N17 8NU. Postal history of the UK from 1450 to the present day. Daily, 10am–12.30pm; 1.30pm–5pm. Closed Sundays and Wednesdays. Free.

British Library, Great Russell Street, London WC1 (but due to move to a new location at King's Cross in 1996). The Tapling Collection is displayed in the King's Library. Daily, 10am–5pm; Sunday, 2.30pm–6pm. Closed Christmas Day and Good Friday. Free.

Imperial War Museum, Lambeth Road, London SE1 6HZ. Daily, 10am–6pm. £3.70 (OAPs, £2.70, children £1.85). Contains war stamps and military postal history material.

National Maritime Museum, Romney Road, Greenwich, London SE10 9NF. Contains the Frank Staff collection of trans-Atlantic mail, and other material of maritime postal history. Daily, 10am–6pm; Sunday, 2.30pm–6pm. £7.45.

Bath Postal Museum, Pulteney Bridge, Bath, Avon, BA2 4AY. Open daily.

City Museum and Art Gallery, Chamberlain Square, Birmingham, B3 3DH. Contains a good general collection, with emphasis on British stamps, together with a study of Birmingham postal history. Open daily. Free.

Museum of Transport, Bunhouse Road, Glasgow G3. Contains many exhibits of postal interest, including mail-coaches and mailvans. Daily, 10am–5pm; Sunday, 2.30pm–6pm. Free.

Transport Museum, Witham Street, Belfast, Northern Ireland. Much of postal interest, with plans to expand the philatelic and postal history aspects. Daily, 10am–5pm; Sunday, 2.30pm–6pm. Free.

Plans are in hand to open postal museums at the post office at Castle Street, Llangollen, North Wales (opening spring 1995), and in the world's oldest operational post office, Main Street, Sanquhar, Dumfriesshire (opening 1996).

Philatelic Counters: London Chief Office, (recently transferred to Lombard Street, EC1). Until recently there were 66 philatelic counters attached to the main regional post offices but these have been drastically reduced and currently operate at the head offices in Canterbury, Exeter, Leeds, Leicester, Oxford and Truro.

Postshops Plus: Bath, Belfast, Birmingham, Brighton, Bristol, Cambridge, Colchester, Coventry, Croydon, Durham, Edinburgh, Glasgow, Guildford, Newcastle, Nottingham, Portsmouth, Romford, Southampton, Southend and Stratford-upon-Avon.

Collections: Cardiff, Chester, Gloucester, Liverpool, London (Trafalgar Square), Manchester, Windsor and York.

The distinctions between Philatelic Counters, Postshops Plus and Collections (often incomprehensible to the philatelic public) appear to lie mainly in the quality of service offered, the level of competence of the counter staff and the range of products available.

GREECE

Philatelic Counter, Head Post Office, Kotzias Square, 1 Kratinou Street, Athens, and sales outlet at the *Philatelic Bureau, Haftia, 100 Aiolou Street, Athens.* Open weekdays.

GUERNSEY

Postal Museum, Head Post Office, Smith Street, St Peter Port. Daily, 9am–12.30pm; 2pm–5pm; Thursday, 9am - 1pm. Free.

Castle Cornet, St Peter Port, Guernsey has a fine display of postal history as well as the full range of stamps issued since 1969.

Philatelic Counter, Head Post Office, Smith Street. Opening times as above.

HUNGARY

Museum of Stamps (Belyegmuzeum), Dob utca 75–81, Budapest VII. Open daily.

Postal Museum (Postamuzeum), Krisztina kurut 6–8, Budapest XII. Concentrates on postal history

material and artefacts, uniforms and equipment. Open daily.
State Philatelic Shops, November 7 ter 3, Budapest VI and *Szabadsajto utca 6, Budapest V.*

ICELAND
National Museum of Iceland, Sudurgata, Reykjavik, Iceland. Contains a complete collection of Icelandic stamps, coins, banknotes and postal history material. Tuesday, Thursday, Saturday and Sunday, 1.30pm–4pm (1 September–31 May); daily, same hours (1 June–31 August). Free.
Philatelic Counter, Head Post Office, Reykjavik.

IRELAND
There is no postal museum, although from time to time plans have been considered. Exhibits of postal interest are to be found in the National Museum.
Philatelic Counter, General Post Office, O'Connell Street, Dublin 1.

ISLE OF MAN
The Manx Museum, Douglas contains stamps, coins, paper money and postal history material. Open daily. Free.
Philatelic Counter, Head Post Office, Regent Road, Douglas.

ITALY
Museum of Posts and Telecommuncations, Via Andreoli, Rome. Open daily except Mondays, 9am – 1pm.
Naval Museum, Piazza Bonavino, Genoa-Pegli. Contains much of maritime postal interest. Tuesday–Saturday, 10am–12; 2pm–5pm; Sunday, 10am–noon. Free.
Philatelic Counter, Head Post Office, Piazza San Silvestro, Rome. Philatelic windows also located in the main post offices of the leading provincial cities.

JERSEY
Postal Museum and Philatelic Counter, Head Post Office, St Helier, Jersey. Daily, 9am–5pm; Saturday, 9am–1pm. Free.

LIECHTENSTEIN
Postal Museum, Englanderbau Building, Vaduz, Liechtenstein. Daily, 10am–12.15pm; 2pm–6pm. Free.
Philatelic Counter, Center-Haus (next to the Vaduzer Hof Hotel), Vaduz. Daily, 8am –12; 2pm–5pm.

LUXEMBOURG
Postal Museum, Postal Centre, Rue du Commerce, Luxembourg-Ville. Open daily.
Philatelic Counter, Postal Centre. Open daily. Free.

MALTA
Postal Museum and Philatelic Counter, General Post Office, Merchants Street, Valletta. Open daily. Free.

MONACO
Postal Museum, La Terrasse de Fontvielle, Monaco Ville, Monaco MC 98050. Opened late 1994 and containing the collection and postal archives from the Prince's Palace. Open daily. 10fr.
Philatelic Counters at the Philatelic Bureau, 23 Avenue de Prince Hereditaire Albert I, Fontvielle, and at the main post offices in Monaco Ville and Place Beaumarchais, Monte Carlo.

NETHERLANDS
Postal Museum, 82 Zeestraat, The Hague. Monday–Saturday, 10am–5pm; Sunday, 1pm–5pm. 5.00g.
Philatelic Counters, Prinses Beatrix Laan 11, The Hague and *Head Post Office, Dam Square, Amsterdam.* Monday–Friday, 2pm–4pm.

NORWAY
Post Office Museum, General Post Office, Dronningensgate 15, Oslo. Tuesday, Thursday and Friday, 10am–3pm; Sunday, noon–3pm. Free.
Philatelic Counter, Schweigaardesgate 33B, Oslo. Monday–Friday, 8am–3.45pm.

POLAND
Museum of Posts and Telecommunications (Muzeum Poczty i Telekomunikacji), Ul. Krasinskiego 1, Wroclaw (formerly Breslau). The remnants of the prewar museum were transferred thither from Warsaw in 1956. Daily (except Tuesday), 10am–1pm; Sunday, 11am–12 noon.
Philatelic outlets: over 100 shops operated by Ruch, the principal ones in Warsaw being at 14 Swietokrzyska, Rynek Starego Miasta and Wiejska.

PORTUGAL
Postal Museum (Museo do CTT), Rua de Dona Estefania 175, Lisbon 1. Daily, 3pm–6pm; Sunday, 10am–1pm.
Maritime Museum (Museo de Marinha), Praca do Imperie, Lisbon, contains much of maritime postal historical interest. Daily, 10am–5.30pm (except

Mondays). 50e.

Philatelic Counters (Portuguese stamps), *Rua de Sao Jose 20, Lisbon 2.* (Portuguese overseas territories) *Agencia Geral do Ultramar, Praca do Comercio, Lisbon 2.*

ROUMANIA

Philatelic Counter, Central Post Office, 29 Calea Victorei, Bucharest.

RUSSIA

A. S. Popov Museum of Communications, 7 Soyuz Street, St Petersburg. Open daily. Free.

Philatelic Counter, Central Post Office, ulitsa Kirova 26a, Moscow. Open daily, 9am–5pm.

SAN MARINO

Postal Museum (Museo Postale e Filatelico), Palazzo di Borgo Maggiore, Piazza Belzoppi, San Marino. Open daily, 10am–5pm.

Philatelic Counter, Piazza Garibaldi. Open daily, 8.30am–12; 3pm–5pm.

SLOVAKIA

No Postal Museum as yet, although stamps and postal history material are exhibited in the National Museum, Bratislava. Open daily.

Philatelic Counter, Central Post Office, Namesti Slovenskeho narodniho povstani 39, Bratislava.

SPAIN

Postal Museum, Central Post Office, Madrid. Open daily.

Fabrica Nacional de Moneda y Timbre, Calle de Jorge Juan 106, Madrid. A permanent display of stamps, coins and banknotes at the state mint and printing works. Open daily. Free.

Maritime Museum (Museo Maritimo), Puerto de la Paz 1, Barcelona. Includes exhibits of maritime postal history. Daily (except Monday), 10am–1.30pm; 4pm–6pm. 100p.

Naval Museum (Museo Naval), Montalban 2, Madrid. Contains archives and postal history material. Daily (except Monday), 10am–1.30pm. 90p.

Philatelic Counter, Palacio de Comunicaciones, Plaza de la Cibeles, Madrid 1. Daily, 9am–2pm; 5pm–9pm.

SWEDEN

Postal Museum (Kungliga Poststyrelsen Postmuseum), Lilla Nygatan 6, Stockholm 1. Housed in the original post office which functioned as such from 1718 till 1905. Daily, 11am–4pm. 20kr.

Swedish Railway Museum, Gavle, has stamps and covers pertaining to the TPOs and railway parcel services. Open daily.

Philatelic Counter, Postens Filateliavdelning, Birger Jarlsgatan 18, Stockholm and also at the chief post offices in Stockholm (*Vasagatan 28-34*), Goteborg (*Drottningtorget 6-7*) and Malmo (*Skeppsbron 1*).

SWITZERLAND

Swiss Postal Museum, Helvetiaplatz 4, Berne. Daily, 9am–12; 2pm–5pm; Sunday, 10am–12; 2pm–5pm. Free.

Swiss Institute of Transport and Communications, Lidostrasse 5, Lucerne. Many exhibits of postal and telegraph interest in what is arguably the world's finest museum of its kind. Open daily.

Philatelic Museum, United Nations, Palais des Nations. Open daily.

Philatelic Museum, International Bureau of the Universal Postal Union, Weltpoststrasse 4, Berne. Open daily.

Philatelic counters: Parkterrasse 10, Bollwerk Passerelle, Berne; Elisabethenanlage 7, Basle; Fraumunsterstrasse 16, Zurich; Avenue d'Ouchy 4, Geneva; Rue de Mont Blanc 18, Geneva; Astoriahaus, Kauffmanweg 4, Lucerne; Via Pretorio 5, Lugano; and *head post office, St Gallen.*

The UN philatelic outlet is in the post office at the Palais des Nations, Geneva.

VATICAN

Museo della Citta Vaticane contains collections of stamps and postal history. Monday–Saturday, 9am–2pm.

Philatelic Counter, Post Office, St Peter's Square, Vatican. Daily, 9am–12.15pm; 3.30pm–5.45pm.

YUGOSLAVIA (SERBIA AND MONTENEGRO)

National Postal Museum, Majke Jevrosime Street 13, Belgrade. Monday–Friday, 9.30am–5pm.

Philatelic Counter, Biro za Postanske Marke, Palmoticeva 2, Belgrade. Philatelic outlets at the main post office, *2 Takovska Street, Belgrade.*

PHILATELIC BUREAUX OF THE WORLD

The following list gives the countries which maintain their own philatelic bureau, or are represented by an agency which handles their stamps exclusively. Countries which are handled by one or other of the large international agencies are listed separately. In some cases, however, there is an overlap; in such cases the local bureau will handle orders from individuals, whereas the international agencies tend to cater for the philatelic trade.

ABKHAZIA Philatelic Export Division, Ministry of Posts, Soukhoumi, Abkhazia

AFGHANISTAN Philatelic Service, Ministry of Communications, Kabul, Afghanistan

AITUTAKI Head Postmaster, Aitutaki, Cook Islands

ALAND ISLANDS Filateliservicen, PO Box 100, FIN-22101, Mariehamn, Aland Islands

ALBANIA Philatelic Department, Artimex, Tirana, Albania

ALGERIA Service Philatelique, Ministere des Postes et Telecommunications, Alger, Algeria

ANDORRA (French P.O.) see under FRANCE

ANDORRA (Spanish P.O.) see under SPAIN

ANGOLA Secretaria Filatelia, Servicos dos Correios, Sao Paulo de Luanda, Angola

ANGUILLA Philatelic Section, General Post Office, The Valley, Anguilla, West Indies

ANTIGUA Philatelic Bureau, General Post Office, St John's, Antigua

ARGENTINA Servicio Filatelico (Encotel), Central Post Office, Buenos Aires, BA, Argentina

ARMENIA State Philatelic Enterprise, Ministry of Posts, Erivan, Armenia

ARUBA Philatelic Bureau, J. Irausquinplein 9, Oranjestad, Aruba, West Indies

AUSTRALIA Australia Post Philatelic Group, PO Box, Melbourne, VIC, 2000, Australia

AUSTRIA Briefmarkenversandstelle, Postgasse 8, Wien A-1011, Austria

AZERBAIJAN Philatelic Export Department, Ministry of Posts, General Post Office, Baku, Azerbaijan

AZORES Loja de Coleccionismo do Ponta Delgada, Av. Antero de Quental, 9500 Ponta Delgado, Acores

Between them the Aland Islands team speak English, German and French as well as all Scandinavian languages.

BAHAMAS Philatelic Bureau, Nassau, Bahamas

BAHRAIN Philatelic Bureau, General Post Office, Bahrain

BANGLADESH Philatelic Bureau, General Post Office, Dhaka-1000, Bangladesh

BARBADOS Philatelic Bureau, General Post Office, Bridgetown, Barbados

BARBUDA Philatelic Bureau, Codrington, Barbuda, West Indies

BELARUS Philatelic Export Department, Ministry of Posts, Minsk, Belarus

BELGIUM Regie des Postes, Direction de la Philatelie, Centre Monnaie, B-1000, Bruxelles, Belgium

BERMUDA Philatelic Bureau, General Post Office, Hamilton, Bermuda

BOLIVIA Direccion Nacional de Correos, Departamento Filatelico, La Paz, Bolivia

BRAZIL Departamento de Filatelia, SCS Quadra 4, Bloco A No 230, Edificio Apolo, 7o Andar, 70300-500, Brasilia DF, Brazil

BRITISH VIRGIN ISLANDS Philatelic Bureau, General Post Office, Tortola, British Virgin Islands, West Indies

BULGARIA Bulgarska Filatelia, Boul. Totleben 8, Sofia 1606, Bulgaria

BURUNDI Agence Philatelique, PO Box 45, Bujumbura, Burundi

CAMEROUN Agence Philatelique, Ministere des Postes et Telecommunications, Duala, Cameroun

CANADA National Philatelic Centre, Antigonish, NS, Canada B2G 2R8

CHILE Empreso de Correos, Servicio Filatelico, Moneda 1155, 3er Piso, Santiago, Chile

CHINA (People's Republic) China National Stamp Corporation, Hepingmen, Beijing, China

CHINA (Taiwan) Directorate General of Posts, Philatelic Department, 55 Chin Shan South Road, Sec. 2, Taipei 1063, Taiwan, Republic of China

COLOMBIA Oficina de Filatelia, Administracion Postal Nacional, Edificio Murillo Toro, Oficina 209, Bogota, Colombia

CONGO Centre Philatelique, CCP 103-20, Brazzaville, R.P. Congo

COOK ISLANDS Philatelic Bureau, Ministry of Posts, Avarua, Rarotonga, Cook Islands

COSTA RICA Oficina Filatelica, Apartado Postal 8000-1000, San Jose, Costa Rica

CROATIA HPT Philatelic Service, Zagreb, Croatia

CUBA Director General of Posts, Ministry of Communications, Philatelic Division, ECOFIL, Apartado 1000, Havana, Cuba

CYPRUS Philatelic Section, Department of Postal Services, Nicosia, Cyprus

CZECH REPUBLIC PTT Philatelic Service, Postfila Export Department, 225 06 Praha 7, Ortenovo nam. 16, Czech Republic

DENMARK Postens Frimaerkecenter, Vesterbrogade 67, DK-1620, Kobenhavn V, Denmark

DOMINICAN REPUBLIC Servicio Filatelico, Ministerio de Correos, Santo Domingo, Republica Dominicana

ECUADOR Departamento Filatelico, Direccion General de Correos, Museo Postal del Estado, Quito, Ecuador

EGYPT Philatelic Services, Postal Organisation, Cairo, Egypt

EL SALVADOR Departamento de Filatelia, Direccion General de Correos, San Salvador, El Salvador, CA

EQUATORIAL GUINEA Servicio Filatelico, Departamento de Correos, Bata, Rio Muni, Guinea Ecuatorial

ESTONIA Eesti Postmark, PO Box 2933, EE 0031 Tallinn, Estonia

ETHIOPIA Philatelic Services, Ministry of Posts, Addis Ababa, Ethiopia

FAROE ISLANDS Postverk Foroya Philatelic Office, FR-159, Torshavn, Faroe Islands

FINLAND Philatelic Section, Postimerkkikeskus, Box 654, Laippatie 4B, 00880 Helsinki, Finland

FRANCE Service Philatelique, 18 rue Hippolyte Bonvin, 75758 Paris, CEDEX 15, France

FRENCH POLYNESIA Centre Philatelique, Papeete, Tahiti, Polynesie Francaise

GABON Service Philatelique, Ministere des Postes et Telecommunications, Libreville

GERMANY Versandstelle fur Postwertzeichen, Postfach 2000 W-8480, Weiden, Germany

GIBRALTAR Philatelic Bureau, PO Box 5662, Gibraltar

GREAT BRITAIN British Philatelic Bureau, 20 Brandon Street, Edinburgh EH3 5TT

GREECE Philatelic Bureau, 100 Aeolou Street, Athens, Greece

GREENLAND Kalaallit Allakkeriviat, Filatelia, DK-3913 Taslilaq, Greenland

GUATEMALA Departamento Filatelico, Ministerio de Correos, Ciudad Guatemala, Republicade Guatemala

GUERNSEY Philatelic Bureau, Postal Headquarters, Guelles Road, PO Box 432, St Peter Port, Guernsey, GY1 3ZE

The German Philatelic Bureau has a mobile post office for use at stamp shows.

GUINEA Agence Philatelique, Boite Postale 814, Conakry, Guinea

GUINEA-BISSAU Reparticao de Filatelia, Aministracao dos Correios, Guinea-Bissau

HAITI Office du Timbre, PO Box 3, Port-au-Prince, Haiti

HONDURAS Departamento Filatelico, Ministerio de Correos, Tegucigalpa, Honduras, CA

HUNGARY Philatelia Hungarica, PO Box 600, H-1375, Budapest 5, Hungary
Magyar Posta, Budapest 12, Krisztina Krt 6-8, H-1540, Hungary

ICELAND Frimerkjasalan, Postholf 8445, 128 Reykjavik, Iceland

INDIA Philatelic Bureau, Room 106, Department of Posts, Dak Bhavan, Parliament Street, New Delhi 110001, India

INDONESIA Philatelic Sub Division, 34 Jalan Jakarta, Bandung 40272, Indonesia

IRAN Philatelic Section, General Directorate for Postal Services, Tehran, Iran

IRAQ Stamp Section, the State Enterprise for Telecommunications and Posts, Ministry of Transport and Communications, Baghdad, Iraq

IRELAND Philatelic Bureau An Post, General Post Office, Dublin 1, Ireland

ISLE OF MAN Philatelic Bureau, PO Box 10M, Circular Road, Douglas, Isle of Man

ISRAEL Philatelic Service, Israel Postal Authority, 12 Sderot Yerushalayim, Tel Aviv-Yafo, Israel 68021

ITALY Ufficio Filatelico Centrale, Amministrazioe delle Poste e Telecommunicazioni, Divisione V,
Sez. 1, Direzione Centrale Servizi Postali, 00100 Roma, Italy

JAMAICA Philatelic Bureau, General Post Office, Kingston, Jamaica

JAPAN Philatelic Section, Central Post Office, Box 888, Tokyo 100-91, Japan

JERSEY Philatelic Bureau, PO Box 304, St Helier, Jersey, JE1 1AB, Channel Islands

JORDAN Philatelic Service, Ministry of Posts, Amman, Jordan

KAMPUCHEA Agence Philatelique, Ministere des Postes, Phnom Penh, R.P. Kampuchea

KAZAKHSTAN Eberhardt Colle, PO Box 700118, 70571 Stuttgart, Germany

KIRIBATI Philatelic Bureau, General Post Office, Butaritari, Kiribati, Central Pacific

KOREA (South) Korean Philatelic Centre, 170-12 Guro 3-dong, Guro-gu, Seoul 152-053, Korea
Versandgrosshandel Jurgen Wolff, Steinweg 23, 51107 Koln, Germany (European agent)

KOREA DEMOCRATIC PEOPLE'S REPUBLIC Korea Stamp Corporation, Pyongyang,DPR Korea

LAOS Bureau de Philatelie, Departement des Services Postaux, Vientiane, Laos

LATVIA Latvijas Pasts, 21 Brivibas Boulevard, Riga PDP, LV-1000, Latvia

LEBANON Agence des Timbres-poste, Ministere des Postes, Beirut, Lebanon

LIBYA Ministry of Communications, Department of PTT, Stamps and Philatelic Section, Tripoli, Libya

LIECHTENSTEIN Official Philatelic Service, FL-9490, Vaduz, Liechtenstein

LITHUANIA Pasto Zenklas, Giedraiciu STR 60e, 2042 Vilnius, Lithuania

LUXEMBOURG Administration des Postes, 8A avenue Monterey, L-2020, Luxembourg

MACAO Correios de Macau, Divisao de Filatelia, Largo Senado, Macao

MADAGASCAR Centre d'Approvisionnement en Timbres-poste, Service Philatelique, Tananarive, Republique Malgache

MADEIRA Loja de Coleccionismo do Funchal, Av. Zarco, 9000 Funchal, Madeira

MALTA Philatelic Bureau, Posta Malta, Auberge d'Italie, Merchants Street, Valletta, CMR 02, Malta

MARSHALL ISLANDS Unicover World Corporation, 1 Unicover Center, Cheyenne, WY, USA 82008-0001

MEXICO Gerencia de Filatelia, Departamento de Promocion Filatelica, Netzahualcoyotl 109 CCL, Centro C.P. 06080, Mexico, D.F.

MICRONESIA Unicover World Corporation, 1 Unicover Center, Cheyenne, WY, USA 82008-0001

MOLDOVA Philatelic Export Department, Ministry of Posts, Chisinau, Moldova

MONACO Bureau Philatelique, La Terrasse de Fontvielle, Monaco Ville, Principaute de Monaco

MONTSERRAT Philatelic Bureau, GPO Plymouth, Montserrat, West Indies

MOROCCO Service de la Philatelie, Direction Centrale des Postes, Rabat, Morocco

MYANMAR Philatelic Bureaau, General Post Office, Rangoon, Myanmar

NAMIBIA Intersapa, 152 Proes Street, Pretoria 0002, South Africa

NEPAL Philatelic Bureau, Sundhara, Kathmandu, Nepal

NETHERLANDS PTT Post Filatelie Versamelservice, PO Box 30051, 9700 RN Groningen, The Netherlands

NETHERLANDS ANTILLES Philatelic Service, Waaigatplein 1, Curacao, Netherlands Antilles

NEW CALEDONIA Bureau Philatelique, Ministere des Postes, Noumea, New Caledonia

NEW ZEALAND Philatelic Bureau, Private Bag, Wanganui, New Zealand

NICARAGUA Oficina de Control de Especies Postales y Filatelia, Apartado Postal 325, Managua, Distrito Nacional, Nicaragua

NIUAFO'OU CPA Consultants Ltd, PO Box 40C, Esher, Surrey, KT109LE

NIUE Philatelic Bureau, General Post Office, Alofi, Niue, South Pacific

NORFOLK ISLAND Philatelic Bureau, Post Office, Norfolk Island

NORTHERN CYPRUS Philatelic Bureau, Department of Posts, Lefkosa, Mersin 10, Turkey

NORWAY Norway Post Stamp Bureau, PO Box 9350, N-0135, Oslo, Norway

PAKISTAN Philatelic Bureau, Malir Halt, Karachi 27, Pakistan 75100

PALESTINE Georg Roll Briefmarken Agenturen, Germany

PANAMA Filatelia y Museo Postal, Direccion General de Correos, Apartado 3421, Panama 4, Republica de Panama

PARAGUAY Servicio Filatelico, Ministerio de Correos, Asuncion, Paraguay

PERU Division de Filatelia, Direccion General de Correos, Jr. Conde de Superunda 170, Lima 1, Peru

PHILIPPINES Bureau of Posts, Stamps and Philatelic Division, Manila D-406, Philippine Islands

POLAND Foreign Trade Enterprise Ars Polona, Krakowskie Przedmiescie 7, PO Box 1001, 00-068 Warsaw, Poland

PORTUGAL Direccao dos Servicos de Filatelia, Avenida Casal Ribeiro 28-6o, 1096 Lisboa CODEX, Portugal

QATAR Philatelic Bureau, Department of Posts, Doha, Qatar

ROUMANIA Rompresfilatelia, Cal. Grivitei 64-66, Bucuresti c.p. 201-12, Roumania

RUSSIA Philatelic Department, Mezhdunarodnaya Kniga, Ul. Dimitrova 39, Moscow G-200, Russia

RWANDA Agence Philatelique, Ministere des Postes, Kigali, Rwanda

ST HELENA Philatelic Bureau, General Post Office, Jamestown, St Helena

ST KITTS Philatelic Bureau, General Post Office, Basseterre, St Kitts, W.I.

ST PIERRE ET MIQUELON Bureau Philatelique, Place General de Gaulle, St Pierre, St Pierre et Miquelon

SAN MARINO Azienda Autnoma di Stato Filatelica e Numismatica, Casella Postale 1, San Marino 47031

SAUDI ARABIA Philatelic Bureau, General Post Office, Riyadh, Saudi Arabia

SINGAPORE Philatelic Bureau, Postal Services, 1 Killiney Road, Singapore 0923, Republic of Singapore

SLOVAKIA Postova Filatelisticka Sluzba, Nam.

Slobody c.6, 817 61 Bratislava, Slovakia

SLOVENIA Philatelic Service, Ministry of Transport and Communications, SLO 61000 Ljubljana, Presernova 23, Slovenia

SOMALIA Ministry of Posts, Philatelic Service, Mogadishu, Somalia

SOUTH AFRICA Philatelic Services and Intersapa, 152 Proes Street, Pretoria 0002, South Africa

SPAIN Direccion General de Correos y Telecomunicaciones, Palacio de Comunicaciones, Madrid 28070, Spain

SUDAN Philatelic Office, Posts & Telegraphs Public Corporation, Khartoum, Sudan

SWEDEN Sweden Post Stamps, S-164 88 Kista, Sweden

SWITZERLAND General Directorate of PTT, Philatelic Office, Parkterrasse 10, CH 3000 Berne, Switzerland

SYRIA Directorate of Posts, Philatelic Office, Damascus, Syria

THAILAND Philatelic Division, Communications Authority, 99 Chaeng Watthana Road, Donmuang, Bangkok 10002, Thailand

TONGA Philatelic Bureau, General Post Office, Nuku-alofa, Tonga
CPA Consultants Ltd, PO Box 40C, Esher, Surrey KT10 9LE

TRINIDAD & TOBAGO Philatelic Bureau, General Post Office, Port of Spain, Trinidad, West Indies

TURKEY PTT General Direction, Presidence of Department of Posts, Filateli Servisi PK 900, TR-06045, Ankara, Turkey

TURKMENISTAN Philatelic Bureau, PO Box 560, Rego Park, NY 11374, USA

TUVALU Philatelic Service, General Post Office, Funafuti, Tuvalu, Central Pacific

UKRAINE Philatelic Export Service, Ministry of Posts and Telecommunications, Central Post Office, Kiev 1, Ukraine

UNITED NATIONS Philatelic Service, UN Postal Administration, Palais de Nations, CH-1211, Geneva 10, Switzerland
Postverwaltung der Vereinten Nationen, Postfach 900, A-1400, Wien (Vienna office)

UNITED STATES OF AMERICA US Postal Service Philatelic Fulfillment Center, Box 449997, Kansas City, MO 64144-9997, USA

URUGUAY Direccion Nacional de Correos, Servicio Filatelico, Montevideo, Republica Oriental del Uruguay

UZBEKISTAN State Philatelic Enterprise, Ministry of Posts and Telecommunications, Samarkand, Uzbekistan

VATICAN Ufficio Filatelico, Amministrazione delle Poste, Citta di Vaticano

VENEZUELA Oficina Filatelica Nacional, Ministerio de Comunicaciones, Caracas, Venezuela

VIETNAM Xunhasaba Philatelic Department, 32 Hai Ba Trung Street, Hanoi, Vietnam

YEMEN Philatelic Service, General Post Office, Sana'a, Yemen

YUGOSLAVIA (SERBIA AND MONTENEGRO) RO Jugomarka, Palmoticeva 2/V, Beograd, Serbia

ZAIRE Bureau Philatelique Exterieur, PB 1981, Kinshasa 1, Zaire

ZAMBIA Philatelic Bureau, General Post Office, Ndola, Zambia

ZIMBABWE Philatelic Bureau, Private Bag 199H, General Post Office, Harare, Zimbabwe

Jersey's friendly team are a regular feature of UK stamp shows.

BUREAUX OR AGENCIES HANDLING THE STAMPS OF SEVERAL COUNTRIES

AUSTRALIAN STAMP BUREAU, Melbourne, VIC, Australia and Old Inn House, 2 Carshalton Road, Sutton, Surrey, SM1 4RN (for customers in the UK):
Australia, Australian Antarctic, Christmas Island, Cocos (Keeling) Islands, Norfolk Island

CPA CONSULTANTS LIMITED, PO Box 40, Esher, Surrey, KT10 9LE:
Niuafo'ou, Tonga

CROWN AGENTS STAMP BUREAU, Old Inn House, 2 Carshalton Road, Sutton, Surrey, SM1 4RN:
Ascension, Bahamas, Barbados, Belize, Bermuda, Botswana, British Antarctic Territory, British Indian Ocean Territory, Brunei, Cayman Islands, Falkland Islands, Fiji, Gibraltar, Hong Kong, Isle of Man, Jamaica, Jersey, Kenya, Kiribati, Liberia, Malawi, Malaysia, Mauritius, Nauru, Nigeria, Norfolk Island, Oman, Pitcairn Islands, St Helena, St Kitts, Samoa, Seychelles, Solomon Islands, South Georgia and South Sandwich Islands, Sri Lanka, Swaziland, Tokelau Islands, Trinidad and Tobago, Tristan da Cunha, Vanuatu, Zambia, Zil Elwannyen Sesel

HARRY ALLEN LIMITED, PO Box 5, Watford, Herts WD2 5SW:
Aitutaki, Angola, Austria, Azores, Canada, Cape Verde Islands, China (People's Republic), Cook Islands, Hungary, Ireland, Israel, Macao, Madeira, Monaco, Mozambique, New Zealand, Penrhyn Island, Portugal, Ross Dependency, Singapore, Sweden, USA

INTER-GOVERNMENTAL PHILATELIC CORPORATION, 460 West 34th Street, New York, NY 10001, USA:
Antigua and Barbuda, Azerbaijan, Dominica, Gambia, Ghana, Grenada, Grenadines of Grenada, Guyana, Lesotho, Maldive Islands, Mongolia, Nevis, Nicaragua, Palau, St Vincent and Grenadines, Tanzania, Togo, Turks and Caicos Islands, Uganda

UNICOVER WORLD CORPORATION, Unicover Center, Cheyenne, WY, USA:
Marshall Islands, Micronesia

PROFESSIONAL DIRECTORY

Throughout the world there are literally thousands of dealers who trade professionally in stamps, covers, postal history and items of every conceivable philatelic interest, as well as related books and accessories. Many are large companies with shops, others deal only by post; some have dozens of employees, others are simply one-man operations. All of these dealers are comprehensively listed, together with their specialities, in other publications such as the *Philatelic Exporter Stamp Directory* and the *Membership Directory* of the Philatelic Traders' Society. Here for simple convenience we list the major dealers and philatelic auctioneers in the United Kingdom.

A J H Stamps
243 Manchester Road, Accrington, Lancashire BB5 2PF.

A W Stamps
182 Basing Way, Finchley, London N3 3BN.

Abbey Philatelic Company Ltd
83 London Fruit Exchange, Brushfield Street, London, E1 6EP.

Abdullah's Stamp Agency (ASA)
1 Wilson Street, Bristol, BS2 9HH.

Acorn Philatelic Auctions
Unit 6 Astra Business Centre, Guinness Road, Trafford Park, Manchester, M20 6UZ.

Acorn Stamps
26 Overlea Road, London E5 9BG.

Admiral Stamps
Cordreys Collectors Centre, East Grinstead Road, Lingfield, Surrey RH7 6EP.

B. Alan Ltd
2 Pinewood Avenue, Sevenoaks, Kent TN14 5AF.

Richard Allan
The Stamp Centre, 77 The Strand, London WC2R 0DE.

Harry Allen,
P. O. Box 5, Watford, Hertfordshire, WD2 5SW.

R. M. Andrews
The Barn, Brockhampton, Cheltenham, Gloucestershire, GL54 5XL.

Antiques Collectors Centre
35 St Nicholas Cliff, Scarborough, North Yorkshire YO11 2ES.

Antiques & Collectors Market, David Wells
37 Catherine Street, Salisbury, Wiltshire, SP1 2DH.

D. L. Archer
2 Litchfield Way, Broxbourne, Hertfordshire, EN10 6PT.

Argyll Etkin Limited
48 Conduit Street, New Bond Street, London W1R 9FB.

Ark Stamps
P. O. Box 6, Ravenshead, Nottingham, NG15 9EY.

J & M Arlington
45 Lakenheath, Southgate, London N14 4RL.

John Auld, Alliance Auctions
1 Hillview Villas, Hastingwood, Nr Harlow, Essex, CM17 9JK.

Avalon Stamp & Postcard Shop
1 City Walls, Rufus Court, Northgate Street, Chester, CH1 2JG.

Avion Stamps
P. O. Box 99, Nottingham, NG16 5QN.

Avon Stamps/Omniphil
P. O. Box 23, Rugby, Warwickshire, CV22 6SQ.

J. M. Bailey
22 Woodend Lane, Stalybridge, Cheshire, SK15 2SR.

Malcolm Bailey
Unit 16, Royal Exchange Antique Gallery, Exchange Street, Manchester, M2 7DB.

Clive Baker
48 Yarrow Close, Broadstairs, Kent, CT10 1PW.

Frank Baker

Postman's Piece, The Wold, Claverley, Wolverhampton, WV5 7BD.

Rowan S. Baker The Covent Garden Stamp Shop

28 Bedfordbury, Covent Garden, London. WC2N 4RB.

A. Ballard

P. O. Box 780, London, SE13 5QA.

Baptist Missionary Society Stamp Bureaux

3 Barnfield Crescent, Wellington, Telford, Shropshire, TF1 2ES.

J. Barefoot Ltd

P. O. Box 8, York, Yorkshire YO3 7GL.

Bay Stamps

Freepost, Colwyn Bay, Clwyd, North Wales, LL29 9YZ.

Bayview Stamps

P. O. Box 9, Paignton, Devon, TQ4 7YJ.

The Benham Group

Benham House, Tontine Street, Folkestone, Kent CT20 1SD.

A La Bonbernard

Ballacree, Churchtown, Ramsey, Isle of Man, IM7 2AN.

A. G. Bond

6 Rollestone Crescent, Exeter, Devon, EX4 5EB.

Book & Collectors Centre

16 Market Street, Hebden Bridge, HX7 6AA

Border Stamp Centre

23 Abbotsford Road, Galashiels, Selkirkshire, TD1 3DR.

Boscombe Collectors Shop

726a Christchurch Road, Boscombe, Bournemouth, BH7 6BZ.

Bournemouth Philatelic Auctions

42 Woodside Road, Ferndown, Dorset, BH22 9LD.

Bournemouth Philatelic Supply Co Ltd

4 Criterion Arcade, Bournemouth, BH1 1BU.

Graham M. Bowden

P. O. Box 3851, Sutton Coldfield, West Midlands, B72 1DY.

Bradford Stamp Centre

390 Dudley Hill Road, Undercliffe, Bradford, West Yorkshire, BD2 3AA.

Tony Bray

71 Bradford Road, Shipley, West Yorkshire, BD18 3DT.

Bredon Covers

Bredon View, Chapel Lane, Wyre Piddle, Worcs, WR10 2JA.

Bridgnorth Stamp Co Ltd

24A Ludlow Road, Bridgnorth, Shropshire, WV16 5AR.

Bridgwater Collectors Shop, W. Loudon,

Unit 6, Marycourt Shopping Mall, St Marys Street, Bridgwater, Somerset, TA6 3EQ.

Bristol Stamp Co, Norfolk Stamp Co, James Auctioneers Ltd, Suffolk Stamp Co

269 Gloucester Road, Bristol, BS7 8NY.

Peter F. Broadbelt

10 Dragon Road, Harrogate, North Yorkshire, HG1 5DF.

I. Brownlee Stamps Ltd

P. O. Box 116, Macclesfield, Cheshire, SK10 4XZ.

Pat Bullivant

35 Rectory Lane, Little Bowden, Market Harborough, Leicestershire, LE16 8AS.

Bygones, The Collectors Shop

123 South Street, Lancing, West Sussex, BN15 8AS.

Byron Stamps

19 Byron Way, Wistaston, Crew, Cheshire, CW2 8DA.

Caerel Stamps

4 Old Post Office Court, Carlisle, CA3 8LE.

Richard Campbell

P. O. Box 734, Arundel, West Sussex, BN18 0Q5.

Candlish McCleery Ltd

P. O. Box 11, Worcester, WR8 9BQ.

Carmichael & Todd

P. O. Box 494, Wimbledon, London, SW19 8DN.

T. J. Carr

76 Wivenhoe Road, Alresford, Colchester, Essex, CO7 8AG.

Cavendish Philatelic Auctions Ltd

153–157 London Road, Derby, DE1 2SY.

Christie's

8 King Street, St James's, London SW1Y 6QT.

Charminster Auctions, L. Saunders

The Emporium, Mansfield Road, Parkstone, Poole, BH14 0DD.

Chesterfield Stamp Corner

2 Corporation Street, Chesterfield, S41 7TP.

D. J. Church

102 New Century Road, Laindon, Basildon, Essex, SS15 6AQ.

G. Cleveland

12 High Street, Rickmansworth, Hertfordshire, WD3 1ER.

Collectables

3 Rhos Point, Rhos-on-Sea, Clwyd, LL28.

Collectables by Courtenay of Spalding Ltd

36 New Road, Spalding, Lincolnshire, PE11 1DN

Collectors Corner

227 Kingshill, Swindon, Wiltshire, SN1 4NG.

Collectors Corner

13 Welhouse Road, Barnoldswick, Lancashire, BB8 6DB.

Collectors Gallery

6/7 Castle Gates, Shrewsbury, SY1 2AE.

J. C. Collings

P. O. Box 9, Sevenoaks, Kent, TN15 6QT.

Adam Cooke,
132 Riverside, Garnet Street, London, E1 9SY.

C & B Coomber
Ashleigh, 49 Twemlow Parade, Morecame & Heysham, Lancs, LA3 2AJ.

Corbitt Stamps Ltd
5 Mosley Street, Newcastle upon Tyne, NE1 1YE.

Cordesa Cards
10 London Road, Grays, Essex, RM17 5XY.

J. M. Cornish (Machins)
40 Clipton Street, Greenbank, Plymouth, Devon, PL4 8JB.

Cornucopia Collectors
15 King Street, Dundee, Scotland, DD1 2JD.

M. Cottrill
33 Castleton Road, Hope, Sheffield, S30 2RD.

Croft Stamps
4 St Georges Way, Imprington, Cambridge, CB4 4AF.

J. W. Crouch
36 Broadfields Close, Bishops Frome, Worcester, WR6 5DA.

Crown Agents Stamp Bureau
Old Inn House, 2 Carshalton Road, Sutton, Surrey, SM1 4RN.

Kathleen Anne Cudworth
8 Park Avenue, Clayton West, Huddersfield, West Yorkshire, HD8 9PT.

Cumbria Philatelic Auctions
4 Old Post Office Court, Carlisle, Scotland, CA3 8LE.

John Curtin Ltd
P. O. Box 31, Sunbury on Thames, Middlesex, TW16 6HS.

Curtis Rawson Ltd, The Stamp Centre
Theatre Square, 3 Wollaton Street, Nottingham, NG1 5FW.

D & E Stamps
17 Wayfield Drive, Stafford, ST16 1TR.

Dalkeith Auctions
Dalkeith Hall, Dalkeith Steps, 81 Old Christchurch Road, Bournemouth, Dorset, BH1 1YL.

Pete Daniels
70 Moor Park Close, Rainham, Gillingham, Kent, ME8 8QT.

Robert Danzig
P. O. Box 7, Newport, Isle of Wight, PO 2 PY.

Dauwalders
92/94 Fisherton Street, Salisbury, Wiltshire, SP2 7QY.

B. M. Dayman
Three Elms Cottage, 142 Kippington Road, Sevenoaks, Kent, TN13 2LW.

R. A. De Lacy-Spencer
Mount Horeb, Quidenham, Norwich NR16 2PH

Wolfango De Souza
4 Waldegrave Road, North Ealing, London, W5 3HT.

Direct Thematic Supplies
P. O. Box 11, Rayleigh, Essex, SS6 7NF.

Dix & Webb
1 Old Bond Street, London W1X 3TD.

P. G. Dixon
Hemingford Abbots, Huntingdon, PE18 9AX.

B. A. Downham
70 Metcalfe Road, Cambridge, CB4 2DD.

Downsway Stamp Co (V & P Roebuck)
12 Downs Way, Epsom, Surrey, KT18 5LU.

Drake's Stamps
6 Truro Road, St Austell, Cornwall, PL25 5JB.

Steve Drewett
Thornton Lodge, Stanshalls Lane, Felton, Bristol, Avon, BS18 7UQ.

Peter J. Duck
256 St Margaret's Road, Twickenham, Middlesex, TW1 1PR.

G. K. Eldridge (Covers-Cards)
177 Mousehole Lane, Bitterne, Southampton, Hampshire, SO18 4TD.

Elm Hill Stamps & Coins
27 Elm Hill, Norwich, Norfolk, NR3 1HN.

Empire Stamp Auctions
Thornton Lodge, Stanshalls Lane, Felton, Bristol, Avon, BS18 7UQ.

Exmouth Stamps
First Floor, Hayne House, 2 The Parade, Exmouth, Devon, EX8 1RJ.

Far Orient Philatelics
P. O. Box 72B, East Mosley, Surrey, KT8 2RX.

Graham Farnfield
15 Sky Peals Road, Woodford Green, Essex, IG8 9NE.

Fenwick Philatelics
52 Fenwick Street, Liverpool, L2 7ND.

A. Tony Field
8 Wildcroft Gardens, Edgware, Middlesex, HA8 6TJ.

A. Fisher
Flat 2, 22 Victoria Grove, Bridport, Dorset, DT6 3AA.

R. Fleming
1A Parr Street, Warrington, Cheshire, WA1 2JP.

John & Molly Fosbery
63 Sandringham Road, Buckland, Newton Abbot, Devon, TQ12 4HB.

Alan Foster
1 Abbotsbury, Bracknell, Berkshire, RG12 8QU.

Fourpenny Post
30 Dinsdale Avenue, Wallsend, Tyneside, NE28 9JD.

John Fowler
63 Marlborough Road, Broomhill, Sheffield, South Yorkshire, S10 1DA.

Framed Philatelics
P.O. Box 95, Hedge End, Hampshire, SO32 2UE.

B. Frank & Son
3 South Avenue, Ryton, Tyne & Wear, NE40 3LD.

J. A. L. Franks Ltd
7 New Oxford Street, London WC1A 1BA.

G. B. Philatelics & Postcards
Tristan House, Smallack Drive, Crownhill, Plymouth, Devon, PL6 5EB.

G. M. Stamps
25 St Anns, St Anthonys Hospital, North Cheam, Surrey, SM3 9DW.

A. L. Garfield
39 Malford Grove, South Woodford, London, E18 2DY.

Gazebo
Top Floor Fleamarket, Pierrpoint Row, Camden Passage, Angel Islington, London, N1.

Stanley Gibbons Publications
5 Parkside, Christchurch Road, Ringwood, Hampshire, BH24 3SH.

Stanley Gibbons Limited
399 Strand, London, WC2R OLX.

M. Gilbert
30 Park Avenue, Shelley, Huddersfield, HD8 8JG.

Glance Back Books
17/17a Upper Church Street, Chepstow, Gwent, Wales, NP6 5EX.

Glass Slipper, Andrew Hall
c/o The Post Office, Bishop Wilton, York, YO4 1SR.

L. Gleicher
24 Grafton Road, London, NW5 3EJ.

L. Gleicher
7 Allington Street, London, SW1E 5BE.

Frank Godden Ltd
The Barn, Heaton Royds, Shay Lane, Bradford, West Yorkshire, BD9 6SH.

Michael Goodman
111 Green Lane, Edgware, Middlesex, HA8 8EL.

David J. Goulty & Associates
12 Coltsfoot Close, Ixworth, Bury St Edmunds, Suffolk, IP31 2NJ.

Dr Conrad Graham
23 Rotherwick Road, London, NW11 7DG.

Anthony Grainger
42 Lee Lane East, Horsforth, Leeds, LS18 5RE.

Grampian Stamp Shop
38 Union Terrace, Aberdeen, Scotland, AB1 1NP.

Granta Stamp & Postcards
28 Magdalena Street, Cambridge, CB3 0AF.

Gravesend Stamp Centre
7 Queen Street, Gravesend, Kent, DA12 2EQ.

D. L. Green
2A Leanne Business Centre, Sanders Lane, Wareham, Dorset, BH20 4DY.

J. M. A. Gregson Ltd
P. O. Box 11, Patchway, Bristol, BS12 4BH.

Ron Griffiths
47 Long Arrotts, Hemel Hempstead, Hertfordshire, HP1 3EX.

Guardian Stamps
P. O. Box 99, Rochdale, OL11 5JJ.

Guernsey Stamp Co Ltd
P. O. Box 107, St Peter Port, Guernsey, GY1 4DE.

H. H. Sales Ltd
The Barn, Heaton Royds, Shay Lane, Bradford, West Yorkshire, BD9 6SH.

H. M. S. Stamp Fairs
P. O. Box 636, Harrow, Middlesex HA1 1DY.

D. R. Hails
Dalcairn, Pen Y Maes, Ruthin, Clwyd, Wales, LL15 1DD.

Sylvia Hanvey
19 Glenariff Drive, Glen Road, Comber, BT23 5HA.

Hardman Green Philatelics
39 Grange Road, Darlington, Co. Durham, DL1 5NB

Harmers of London Stamp Auctioneers
91 New Bond Street, London, W1A 4EH.

R. Harris
77 Holcombe Road, London, N17 9AR.

Stewart Harris
"Abbotsmead", Mill End Green, Great Easton, Essex, CM6 2DW.

Graeme K. Harrison
Stokes Cottage, Marston Magna, Yeovil, Somerset, BA22 8DQ.

Harrow Stamp Company
Unit 1, 15 Springfield Road, Harrow, Middlesex, HA1 1QF.

Mark R. Harvey
P. O. Box 50, Chiddingfold, Surrey, GU8 4XQ.

Hertstamps
P. O. Box 137, Hatfield, Hertfordshire, AL10 9DB.

George H. Hicks
3 Spring Garden Close, Ormesby, Middlesbrough, Cleveland, TS7 9HT.

Matthew P. Hinton
14 Crofton Avenue, Timperley, Altrincham, Cheshire, WA15 6DA.

William H. Hirst
49 Priory Road, West Bridgford, Nottingham, NG2 5HX.

Mike Holt
P. O. Box 177, Stourbridge, West Midlands, DY8 3DE.

K. Holten
Iver Heath, Iver, Buckinghamshire, SL0 0HR.

Horsham Stamp Auctions, The Stamp Shop
23 Trafalgar Road, Horsham, West Sussex, RH12 2QD.

Hull Stamp Shop
31 Princes Avenue, Hull, HU5 3RX.

R. E. Hunt
Pendennis, Eastcombe, Stroud, Glos. GL6 7EA.

Immediate Stamp Company
81 Walm Lane, London, NW2 4QL.

Interstamps
4 Woods View Road, Bournemouth BH9 2LN.

Geoff Irons
37 Tiverton Road, Potters Bar, Hertfordshire, EN6 5HX.

J. B. Stamps
Stall L2/L3 The Balcony, The Market Hall, Tenant Street, Derby, DE1 2DZ.

J. C. Stamps
The House That Jack Built, Southside Street, The Barbican, Plymouth, Devon, PL1 2LA.

J & K Edge (Stamps)
3 Newborough Avenue, Llanishen, Cardiff, South Glamorgan, CF4 5BY.

A. F. Jackson Hodgson
15 Clarence Street, Southend-on-Sea, Essex, SS1 1BH

Michael Jackson (Philatelists) Ltd
P. O. Box 77, Huntingdon, Cambridgeshire, PE18 6TZ.

W. A. Jacques
Ashville, Cliffe, Selby, North Yorkshire, YO8 7NU.

Janes Philatelic
Cratchit House, 1 Cliff Road, North Petherton, Bridgwater, Somerset, TA6 6NU.

Kelvin Jenkins
19 Maengwyn Street, Machynlleth, Powys, SY 20 8EB.

G. Jenner
31 Queen Street, Leighton Buzzard, Bedfordshire, LU7 7BZ.

Graham Johnson
The White Cottage, 238 Portsmouth Road, Cobham, Surrey, KT11 1HU.

A. C. Jones
47 Marylands Avenue, Hockley, Essex, SS5 5AH.

Ray Jones
Martingale Cottage, Church Lane, Hallow, Worcester, WR2 6PF

S. Jones
20 Pennine Way, Brierfield, Nelson, Lancashire, BB9 5DT.

Katamaras
Collectors Centre, 6 Church Walk (off Head Street), Colchester, CO1 1NS.

Michael Kay
P. O. Box 1243, London, W4 1JP.

Philip Kaye
9 Avondale Road, Hove, East Sussex, BN3 6ER.

Kirby & Fleming
4 Woodside Crescent, Stockport, SK4 2DW.

Kirkfield Press
56 Henley Avenue, Dewsbury, West Yorkshire, WF12 0LN.

B. Kleinberg
40 Waxwell Lane, Pinner, Middlesex, HA5 3EN

Kollectables
51 Parnie Street, Trongate, Glasgow, Scotland, G1 5LU.

Andrew G. Lajer
P. O. Box 42, Henley on Thames, Oxon, RG9 1FF.

Ken Lake
1a Stephen Court, Ecclesbourne Road, Thornton Heath, CR7 7 BP.

Jean Lancaster Auction Agency
20 Milner Road, Kingston upon Thames, KT1 2AU.4

Tony Lester
29 Momus Boulevard, Binley Road, Stoke, Coventry, CV2 5NA.

S. V. Leverton & Co
P. O. Box 54, Stanmore, Middlesex, HA7 4ED.

Peter Lincoln
75 Nags Head Hill, St George, Bristol, BS5 8LP.

John Lister Ltd
Manor Farm House, Common Road, Dorney, Windsor, Berkshire, SL4 6PX.

Stephen Loss BA
6 Andrews Avenue, Flixton, Manchester, M41 8SU.

Graham Loton
Thrums, The Hill, Happisburgh, Norfolk, NR12 0PW.

Robson Lowe
Premier House, Hinton Road, Bournemouth, BH1 2EF.

M & C Stamps
Unit 30, Gloucester Antique Centre, Severn Road, Gloucester, Gloucestershire, GL1 2LE.

M. P. Stamps
P. O. Box 111, Ramsgate, Kent, CT11 9DR.

MacDonnell Whyte Ltd
102 Leinster Road, Dublin 6, Ireland.

Magan Stamps
P. O. Box 413, Holywell, Clwyd, CH8 7DJ.

Maidstone Stamp Emporium
34 Melville Road, Maidstone Kent, ME15 7UY.

A. T. Makey
Newport, Brough, North Humberside, HU15 2QSA

Grahame W. Mann
14 Lakeside Court, Brierley Hill, West Midlands, DY5 3RQ.

Marino-Montero London Stamp Company Ltd
P. O. Box 251, Hedge End, Hampshire, SO32 2ZH.

Stephen Mayer International Ltd
1 Axis Hawkfield Way, Hawkfield Business Park, Whitchurch, Bristol, BS14 OBY.

Peter J. McBride
33 Donegall Street, Belfast, Northern Ireland, BT1 2FG.

A. A. McCarthy
28 Penrice Close, Milton Grange, Weston-super-Mare, Avon BS22 9AH.

Meridian Stamp Co
6 Broadview Road, Chesham, Bucks, HP5 2LY.

T. S. Mills
151 Glendale Gardens, Leigh-on-Sea, Essex, SS9 2BE.

Philip J. Milton
Sterling House, 17 Joy Street, Barnstaple, North Devon, EX31 1BS.

Modern Coins & Stamps, B. M. King
24 Market Hall, Arndale Centre, Luton, Bedfordshire, LU1 2TA.

Peter Mollett, Philatelist
P. O. Box 1934, Ringwood, Hampshire, BH24 2YZ.

Trevor W. Mountford
P. O. Box 1762, Bournemouth, BH7 6BZ.

Robert Murray, Stamp Shop
5 & 6 Inverleith Gardens, Ferry Road, Edinburgh, Scotland, EH3 5PU.

Muscotts
6 Meadrow, Godalming, Surrey, GU 7 3HL.

W. Musgrove (Pandora)
137 Elburton Road, Plymstock, Plymouth, Devon, PL9 8JD.

Nationwide Collectors Fairs
8 Park Avenue, Clayton West, Huddersfield, West Yorkshire, HD8 9PT

New Raynes Stamp Company
2a Corporation Street, Chesterfield, S41 7TP.

Newton Philatelics
Stargate, Ryton, Tyne & Wear, NE40 3EE.

Norbury Stamp Shop
77 Great Underbank, Stockport, Cheshire, SK1 1PE.

North West London Stamp Co
51 Mayflower Lodge, Regents Park Road, Finchley, London, N3 3HX.

Northampton Stamp & Coin Shop
52 Bridge Street, Northampton, NN1 1PA

Eclan O'Kelly
P. O. Box 1346, Dublin 6, Ireland.

Omniphil
P. O. Box 23, Rugby, Warwickshire, CV22 6SQ.

D. R. Owen
12 Wolverley Avenue, Wollaston, Stourbridge, West Midlands, DY8 3PJ.

Palmerston Philatelic Auctions
Loreburn Chambers, 11 Great King Street, Dumfries, Scotland, DG1 1 BA.

Parkstone Philatelics
P. O. Box No 72, Redcar, Cleveland, TS11 8YY.

Murray Payne Ltd
P. O. Box 1135, Axbridge, Somerset, BS26 2EW.

Will Payne
"Rosemead", Wyddial, Buntingford, Hertfordshire, SG9 OEX.

Pennifil
9 Kelsons Avenue, Thornton-Cleveleys, Lancashire, FY5 4DW.

Pennymead Auctions
1 Brewerton Street, Knaresborough, North Yorkshire, HG5 8AZ.

Penrith Coin & Stamp Centre
37 King Street, Penrith, Cumbria, CA11 7AY.

Perry Stamps
"Willow Cottage", 109 Mountnessing Road, Billericay, Essex, CM12 9HA.

Peter's Stamps & Postcards
79 Bracken Road, Brighouse, West Yorkshire, HD6 2HR.

Philangles
Beech House, Wilderspool Causeway, Warrington, Cheshire, WA4 6QP.

Philatelic Traders Society Ltd
107 Charterhouse Street, London, EC1M 6PT.

Philcard International
P. O. Box 1000, London, N3 3TD.

Philcovers, Christopher Phillips
19 Alexander Park, Scarborough, North Yorkshire, YO12 5JN.

Phillips Son & Neale
101 New Bond Street, London, W1Y OAS.

Phoenix International
Monument Lane, Codnor Park, Notts, NG16 5PJ.

Piece Hall Stamp & Collector's Centre
Unit 42, The Piece Hall, Halifax, West Yorkshire HX1 1RE.

Plumridge & Co
P. O. Box 359, Chislehurst, Kent, BR7 6UA.

Portsmouth Stamp Shop
184 Chichester Road, North End, Portsmouth, Hampshire, PO2 0AX.

Prinz Publications (UK) Ltd
13 Fore Street, Copperhouse, Hayle, Cornwall, TR27 4DX.

A. Raikes

37 Julian Road, Ludlow, Shropshire, SY8 1HA.

Ramstamps

Central House, 19 Old Steine, Brighton, Sussex, BN1 1GD.

Brian Reeve Stamp Auctions

Suite 155, Southbank House Business Centre, Black Prince Road, London, SE1 7SJ.

David M Regan

25 Hoghton Street, Southport, PR9 0NS.

Peter C. Rickenback

14 Rosslyn Hill, London NW3 1PF.

G. Robbe Ltd

York Chambers, York Street, St Helier, Jersey, JE2 3RQ.

Wayne Robbins

P. O. Box 719, Ringwood, Hampshire, BH24 1YQ.

UTY M. ROHRS

72 Roebuck House, Stag Place, London, SW1E 5BD

G. Rosen & Son

50 Byron Road, Walthamstow, London, E17 4SW.

Rowland Hill Stamps

Hill House, Cookley, Kidderminster, Worcestershire, DY10 3UW.

Rushstamps

PO Box 1, Lyndhurst, Hants. SO43 7PP.

Arthur Ryan & Co.

2 The Square, The Quadrant, Richmond, Surrey TW9 1DY.

A. P. Ryle Stamps

1 Shoreland Road, Barnstaple, North Devon, EX31 3AA.

Safe Albums (UK) Ltd

16 Falcon Business Park, Ivanhoe Road, Hogwood Lane, Finchampstead, Berkshire, RG11 4QW.

J. Sanders (Philatelist) Ltd

5 Commercial Road, Southampton, SO15 1DB.

Robert Seaman

Copt Hall, Stock, Ingatestone, Essex, CM4 9BA.

David Sedgwick

Station House, Wylam, Northumberland, NE41 8HR.

Chris Shaw Collectables

4 Newlyn Drive, Bilton Hall, Jarrow, Tyne & Wear, NE32 3TW.

David Shaw

63 Mill Hey, Haworth, Keighley, West Yorkshire, BD22 8NA.

Ronald G. Shelley

9 Chanctonbury Road, Hove, East Sussex, BN3 6EL.

Norman Shorrock

2 Arnot Way, Higher Bebington, Wirral, Merseyside, L63 8LP.

Mike Shorten

59 Greengate, Swanton Morley, Dereham, Norfolk, NR20 4 LX.

Simkiss Philatelic

The Hibben, 8 Taubman Street, Ramsey, Isle of Man, IM8 1DH.

J. Smith

47 The Shambles, York, YO1 2LX.

R. G. Smith

6 Tavistock Street, Bletchley, Milton Keynes, MK2 2PF.

Sotheby's

34–35 New Bond Street, London, W1A 2AA.

Stamp Aid "The Club"

32 Bury Street, Radcliffe, Manchester, M26 2QB.

The Stamp Box, G. Bentley

5 Cannon Court, High Street, Lymington, Hampshire, SO41 9AQ.

Stamp Insurance Services

29 Bowhay Lane, Exeter, Devon, EX4 1PF.

The Stamp King

3 Market Street, Mansfield, Notts, NG18 1JQ.

Stamp Magazine

Link House, Dingwall Avenue, Croydon, CR9 2TA.

Stamp Scene (G. B. & K. P. Williams)

1 Elm Grove, Malpas Park, Newport, Gwent, NP9 6JF.

Stamp Searchers

P. O. Box 947, Lewes, East Sussex, BN8 6ZS.

Stamp Shop Avoch

28 High Street, Avoch, Ross-shire, IV9 8PT.

The Stamp Shop

Unit 10, Granby Parade, Water Street, Bakewell, Derbyshire, DE45 1EG.

The Stamp Shop

87 Dean Road, Scarborough, North Yorkshire, YO12 6QS.

Stampede

119 Marsland Road, Sale, Cheshire, M33 3NW.

Stantonbury Stamps

64 Ashfield, Stantonbury, Milton Keynes, MK14 6AU.

Star Philatelic

302 Ferndown Road, Ferndown, Dorset, BH22 9AS.

Studley's Stamp Shop

9 Merrion Centre Superstore, Leeds, West Yorkshire, LS2 8DB.

Sun Philatelic Centre London Ltd

Norbury Avenue, Norbury, London, SW16 3RL.

Swindon Stamps & Postcards

3 Theatre Square, Swindon, Wiltshire, SW1 1QN.

Telford Philatelic Supplies

1980 Holyhead Road, Wellington, Telford, Shropshire, TF1 2DW.

Thames Stamp Auctions

35 Wheathill Road, Anerley, London, SE20 7XD.

The Collectors Centre

Saumarez Street, ST Peter Port, Guernsey, Channel Islands, GY.

W. D. S. Thorn

Shop 2, Georgian Villiage, 100 Wood Street, Walthamstow, London, E17 3HX.

Martin Townsend

P. O. Box 10, Hitchin, Hertfordshire, SG4 9PE.

R. W. Truman

New Close Cottage, Ston Easton, Bath, Somerset, BA3 4DH.

R. G. Tye

331 Wimbledon Park Road, London SW19 6NS.

Urch Harris & Co

1 Denmark Avenue, Bristol, BS1 5HD.

J. Uttley (Stamps)

21 Birch Drive, Whitehouse Common, Sutton Coldfield, West Midlands, B75 6HY.

Valelink Ltd

26 Queens Road, Brighton, Sussex, BN1 3XA.

R. Warren

Oaklands, Crowhurst, Lingfield, Surrey, RH7 6LS.

Warwick & Warwick

Pegeant House, Jury Street, Warwick, CV34 4EW.

G. A. West

12 Dean Way, Storrington, West Sussex, RH20 4Qn.

West Midlands Collectors Centre

9 Heantun House, Salop Street, Wolverhampton, West Midlands, WV3 0SG.

Westerham Stamps

18 Rysted Lane, Westerham, Kent, TN16 1EP.

Western Auctions Ltd

Bank House, 225 City Road, Cardiff, Wales, CF2 3JD.

Wharfedale Stamp Company

P. O. Box 41, Wetherby, West Yorkshire, LS22 5XQ.

Andrew A. Whitworth

1 Prizet House, Helsington, Kendal, Cumbria, LA8 8AB.

Ian Whyte (Ireland) Ltd

30 Marlborough Street, Dublin 1, Ireland.

Eric Wilding

Post Office, High Street, Pevensey, East Sussex, BN24 5JP.

Frank J. Wilson

57A Bourne Road, Spalding, Lincs, PE11 1 JR.

Richard Wilson International

3 Lyndale Terrace, Alstone Lane, Cheltenham, GL51 8JJ.

Windsor Stamps

52 Mount Durand, St Peter Port, Guernsey, GY.

W. D. Winkworth

P. O. Box 386, Steyning, West Sussex, BN44 3HN.

Winstone Stamp & Coin Co

Great Western Antique Centre, Bartlett Street, Bath Avon, BA1 2QZ.

Wyon Classics, Corridor Stamp Shop

7a The Corridor, Bath, BA1 5AP.

YOU ARE WANTED!

Please take time to check the Professional Directory to ensure that your company has been included. As this is the first edition of the **STAMP YEARBOOK** every effort has been made to include as many UK and Irish dealers as possible. If, however your name does not appear in this section, simply complete the form below and return it to us as soon as possible. If your details are included but incorrect, please also use the form below to amend your directory entry.

NAME: ....

ADDRESS: ....

....

....

....

.... *POSTCODE:* ....

TELEPHONE NO: ....

NEW ENTRY/AMENDED ENTRY: ....

....

....

SIMPLY POST OR FAX TO:

TOKEN PUBLISHING LTD,
PO Box 14, Honiton, Devon EX14 9YP

TEL: 01404 831 878   FAX: 01404 831895

WORLD TRADE ASSOCIATIONS

ARGENTINA
Sociedad de Comerciantes Filatelicos De la Republica Argentina (SoCoFiRA), Casilla de Correo Central 3296, 1000 Buenos Aires, Argentina

AUSTRALIA
Australasian Stamp Dealers' Association (ASDA), GPO Box 5378, Melbourne, Victoria 3001, Australia.
Stamp & Coin Dealers' Association of Australia (SCDAA), PO Box 977, St Mary's, NSW 2760, Australia

AUSTRIA
Osterreichischer Briefmarken-Handler Verband (OBHV), Postfach 31, Mariahilferstrasse 105, A–Vienna, Austria

BELGIUM
Chambre Professionnelle Belge des Negociants en Timbres-Poste (CPBNTP), Calelie du Centre, Bureau 343, Rue des Fripiers 17, B–1000, Bruxelles, Belgium

BRAZIL
Associancao Brasileira dos Comerciantes Filatelicos (ABCF), Caixa Postal 3577, 01051 Sao Paulo, Brazil

CANADA
Canadian Stamp Dealers' Association (CSDA), c/o PO Box 123, Adelaide Street Post Office, Toronto, Ontario, Canada M5C 2K5

DENMARK
Danmarks Frimaerkehandlerforening (DFHF), PO Box 12, DK–3000, Helsingor, Denmark

FINLAND
Suomen Postimerkkikauppiaden Liitto RY (SPKL), PO Box 39, FIN–10901, Hanko, Finland

FRANCE
Chambre Syndicale Francaise des Negociants et Experts en Philatelie (CNEP), 4 Rue Drouot, F–75009, Paris, France

GERMANY
Bundesverbandes des Deutschen Briefmarkenhandels (APHV), Geibelstrasse 4, D–50931, Koln, Germany

GREECE
Greek Stamp Dealers' Association, 23 Veranzerou Street, GR–10432, Athens, Greece

INDIA
Indian Stamp Dealers' Association (ISDA), 19 Chandni Chowk Street, Calcutta 700072, India

INDONESIA
Asosiasi Pedagang Prangko Indonesia (APPI), Surabaya Philatelic Centre, Jalan Baliwerti 115–1, Surabaya 60174, Indonesia

IRELAND
Irish Philatelic Trader's Association (IPTA), 30 Marlborough Street, Dublin 1, Ireland

ISRAEL
Israel Stamp Dealer's Association (ISDA), 32 Allenby Road, PO Box 4944, Tel-Aviv 61040, Israel

ITALY
Federazione Nazionale Commercianti Filatelici Italiani (FNCFI), Via Guido Banti 32, 1–00191, Rome, Italy

JAPAN
Japan Stamp Dealers' Association (JSDA), Central PO Box 1003, Tokyo, Japan

NETHERLANDS
Nederlandsche Vereeniging van Postzegelhandelaren (NVPH), Weteringkade 45, NL–2515 Al Den Haag, Netherlands

NEW ZEALAND
New Zealand Stamp Dealers' Association ((NZSDA)
PO Box 5236, Auckland, New Zealand

NORWAY
Norsk Frimerkehandler Forening (NFHF), Postboks 5606, Briskeby, N–0209, Oslo, Norway

PORTUGAL

Portuguese Stamp Dealers' Association (ACOFIL), Rue Ricardo Jorge 551 Dto, P-4050, Porto, Portugal

RUSSIA

Russian Stamp Dealers' Association (ATM), PO Box 271, RU–197198, St Petersburg, Russia

SOUTH AFRICA

South Africa Philatelic Dealers' Association (SAPDA), PO Box 47285, Parklands 2121, South Africa

SPAIN

Asociacion Nacional de Empresarios de Filatelia de Espana (ANFIL), Calle Mayor 18, 2 Dcha, E-28013, Madrid, Spain

SWEDEN

Sveriges Frimarkshandlarforbund (SFHF), PO Box 459, S-10129, Stockholm, Sweden

SWITZERLAND

Schweizerischer Briefmarkenhandler-Verband (ASNP/VSBH), PO Box 1538, CH-8640, Rapperswil, Switzerland

TURKEY

Pul Tuccarlari Dernegi (PTD), Galipded 53, PK 129, Beyoglu, Istanbul 80050, Turkey

UNITED KINGDOM

The Philatelic Traders' Association (PTS), 107 Charterhouse Street, London EC1M 6PT

The ADPS Stamp Dealers' Association (MDPTA), Malcolm Bailey, Unit 16, Royal Exchange Antiques Gallery, Manchester M2 7DB

Scottish Philatelic Trade Association, c/o Cornucopia Collectors, 15 King Street, Dundee DD1 2JD

Universal Dealers' Protection Association (UDPA), 71 Cottage Street, Kingswinford, West Midlands DY6 7QE

USA

American Stamp Dealers' Association (ASDA), 3 School Street, Glen Cove, NY 11542, USA

American Philatelic Society (APS), PO Box 8000, State College, PA 16803, USA

National Stamp Dealers' Association (NSDA), PO Box 7176, Redwood City, CA 94063, USA

From the Publishers of Medal News . . .

MEDAL NEWS YEARBOOK 1996

- Descriptions of all British & Commonwealth Orders, Medals and Decorations *with accurate valuations* (fully illustrated)
- Directory of Dealers
- Directory of Regimental and other Museums
- Guide to Researching Medals
- Bibliography of recent works
- Glossary of Abbreviations on Medals
- Topical Review of the Year
- British Orders *in full colour*
- Storage of Medals
- Medal Ribbons in full colour

And much more . . . nearly 300 pages, FOR ONLY £12.95

STAMPS AND THE LAW

THE Stamp Duties Management Act of 1891, although passed primarily to regulate the use of stamps impressed, struck or affixed to dutiable materials (notably contracts, cheques and legal documents), included Section 17 (2) which made provision for prosecution in cases of adhesive postage stamps and postal stationery obtained fraudulently. This Section was used in the successful prosecution of a number of individuals up to 1904 for trafficking in the British stamps overprinted for the use of government departments. After the case known as R. v. Williams, January 1896, there was a considerable tightening of the procedures for the handling and accounting of official stamps used in local tax offices. As a result of a celebrated case in 1903, involving a prominent philatelist and a senior official of the Board of Inland Revenue, it was decided to abolish official stamps altogether. Section 13 (4) of the Act may be used to prosecute individuals aiding and abetting the fraudulent handling of stamps.

Most prosecutions involving stamps, however, are dealt with under the Larceny Act of 1916, either as simple theft in the case of stealing by customers from a dealer's stock, or stealing as a servant, when stamps are taken dishonestly from a dealer's stock by those in his or her employment.

Fraud may be defined as dishonestly obtaining goods or money from someone, and occurs when someone achieves a practical result by false pretences. For a person to be guilty of fraud, the false pretence must have been made deliberately with the intention of producing that result.

The commonest example of this occurs when someone pays for stamps with a cheque which he knows will not be honoured by his bank. It also applies when a dealer sells as genuine, stamps or postal history material which he knows to be forgeries, fakes or imitations. In such cases the deception may be compounded by the forging of the marks or signatures found on rare items to attest their genuineness, or the forgery of ancillary documents, such as certificates issued by the Expert Committee of the Royal Philatelic Society and other bodies.

For legal purposes a forgery is a total fabrication, something created specifically in imitation of a stamp, postal marking or entire letter. A fake is any alteration to, or tampering with, an article which itself is quite genuine, the object of the alteration being to convert a cheap item into something of value. In this category come such deliberate acts of fraud as the alteration of perforation from a common to a rare gauge, or the changing of a colour or shade to simulate a scarce variety of an otherwise common stamp. Similarly the forging of overprints or cancellations to convert a cheap stamp into one of great value is a criminal offence.

The repair of a damaged stamp or postal history item, however, is still something of a grey area so far as the law is concerned. There are skilled craftsmen who can add generous margins to a closely trimmed or cut-into stamp and who can add a new back to a stamp which has been badly thinned. Since the fashion for unmounted mint has become so widespread, and even many standard catalogues as well as dealers' lists make a substantial difference in the value of unmounted and mounted mint stamps, this has encouraged a veritable industry in regumming stamps which have either lost their gum altogether or which have been heavily hinged. Regumming is often difficult to detect, especially if one does not have a genuine mint stamp for comparison. Fortunately the micrometer and the ultra-violet lamp are a considerable aid in detecting repairs and other alterations.

False pretences may also be a question of degree. In general the law tends to ignore some false pretences, such as "trade puffs". Dealers who puff up or boast about the merits of their wares are not committing fraud so long as it does not amount to deliberate misrepresentation of the facts.

Misrepresentation is a false statement which causes someone to enter into a contract. A fraudulent misrepresentation is created if the person making the statement knows or believes it to be false, or does not believe that it is true, and makes it in order to induce someone to contract with him.

For instance, a dealer might tell a potential customer that an apparently rare cover is genuine, when he knows (or at least suspects) that stamps or postal markings have been added to it to enhance its value.

Negligent misrepresentation may work in reverse, if, for example, an auctioneer fails to describe a stamp or stamps in an auction lot adequately, despite detailed instructions from the vendor, to the latter's loss. On the other hand a misrepresentation is innocent if the person making it is not aware that his statement is false and has taken all due care in making it. This occurs frequently in the saleroom, and it therefore behoves the purchaser, if in doubt about a lot on which he has bid successfully to ask for an extension.

This is the period of time following the sale in which the purchaser has the right to have questionable items expertised. If the experts reject the item as a forgery or a fake, the purchaser can return it to the auctioneer who is then duty bound to return it to the vendor stating clearly the reasons for the cancelled sale. Should the vendor subsequently offer the item for sale, through another auctioneer, knowing the item to be false, then he is committing a fraud and would be liable to prosecution if the offence comes to light.

In an attempt to give customers better protection, the Trade Descriptions Act was passed in 1968. Anyone in the business of selling goods or providing services is under a legal obligation to avoid giving false or misleading information about these to prospective customers.

Any kind of misleading information or indication —spoken, written or pictorial—constitutes a false description under the Act. The maximum penalty for applying a false description to goods or services is a £2000 fine or two years' imprisonment and an unlimited fine if there were a trial by jury.

Anyone who thinks he has been misled by a false trade description should complain to the trading standards or consumer protection department of his regional or county council. It is the department's job to enforce the Act and to report the circumstances to the police (or the procurator fiscal in Scotland) for possible prosecution.

If stamps or postal history material were falsely described by the trader himself, it is not necessary to prove that he knew the description was misleading. The falsity in itself renders him liable, if it is material. However, no matter whether the falsehood relates to goods or services, it is a defence to show that it arose by accident or mistake, or by relying on information supplied by someone else; and that all reasonable precautions were taken to avoid the offence. In addition, a person charged with making a false description of stamps can plead that he did not know (and could not reasonably be expected to know) that they did not fit the description. In practice, this is a defence which no self-respecting dealers or auctioneers would shelter behind, and in the vast majority of cases they would be only too ready to re-imburse the customer.

The law applies only to information disseminated in the course of a trade or business, and does not apply to private transactions. If collector A purchases a stamp from collector B through a club exchange packet, for example, and subsequently discovers that it is not the rare stamp described and priced accordingly, but the cheap version worth a fraction of the price paid, A cannot take action against B under the Trade Descriptions Act, but if the sum involved was large, and if B, on being confronted with the facts, failed to make restitution, then A would have a right at law to sue for fraud in a civil action.

In practice, however, most collectors would let the matter go. If it were not amicably resolved—and most vendors acting in good faith would be only too ready to make a repayment—commonsense would dictate that the aggrieved party would inform the Packet Secretary who would warn the offender in the first instance and probably refuse to handle further material if the offence were repeated. In cases where a customer suffers from such sharp practice on the part of a dealer or auctioneer, then he has recourse to the Philatelic Traders' Society, assuming that the dealer or auctioneer is an affiliated member, and in that case pressure can be brought to bear on the offender to make restitution, or be expelled from the PTS. Membership of the Society is no cast-iron guarantee of reputable dealing but the PTS does have a reputation for integrity and is very prompt to take the appropriate action against those who break the rules. It behoves the collector to purchase material only from members of the PTS or comparable overseas trade bodies.

VALUE ADDED TAX

This is a matter which primarily concerns dealers, but it also applies to those who dabble in stamps and postal history on a part-time basis, and has implications for collectors at all levels. Briefly anyone conducting a business, or in self-employment, who has a turnover in excess of £43,000 per annum, must register with HM Customs and Excise for the collection and payment of Value Added Tax. Anyone whose turnover is less than £43,000 is exempt from the obligation to register, but is at liberty to register if he or she feels that this would be advantageous. It is nice to think that there is an element of choice in this, although one would be hard-pressed to think why anyone would voluntarily register for VAT unless they absolutely had to! Incidentally, the government raised the VAT registration level by 40 per cent to £35,000 in 1991 with the avowed intention of relieving a large number of small businesses from this burden, at a time when the VAT rate was 15 per cent.

Assuming that you are a dealer with a turnover above the magic limit, then you are committing a serious offence if you fail to register. Registration then lays you open to the full machinery of the system. You have to charge VAT on all goods and services, issuing VAT invoices and receipts and keeping detailed accounts which are liable to snap inspection at any time. You must make quarterly returns to Customs and Excise of the amount of tax you have collected. From this you are allowed to deduct the VAT which you yourself have paid out in the course of your business, and you then have to remit the difference to the VAT collector. Of course, should the amount you have paid exceed the tax which you have collected, you receive a repayment in due course. This arises in businesses which handle zero-rated goods and services, but stamps and postal history do not come into that category.

New regulations came into force on 1 January 1995. The special margin scheme of accounting for VAT, currently applicable to certain second-hand goods such as cars, has now been extended to almost all second-hand goods, including stamps which are either postally used or are no longer current. The scheme allows businesses buying and selling eligible goods to account for VAT only on the difference between the buying and selling prices of these items.

Consideration is being given to introducing a special system of accounting which will enable dealers to account for VAT without the need to keep a detailed record of every transaction. At present, certain works of art, antiques and collector's items, including stamps and postal history, defined in Notice 712 Second-hand goods, previously exempt from VAT at import, are now subject to VAT on import at an effective rate of 2.5 per cent. At the time of writing, however, HM Customs and Excise have not produced the practical guide for second-hand dealers on how to implement the Global Accounting Scheme. Apparently the scheme is proving far more complicated than had originally been envisaged, hence the delay in working out the practical details. Both the scheme and the 2.5 per cent import rate have been postponed for the time being, although it was hoped to implement them by May 1995. In the meantime, dealers have been advised to prepare a stock valuation and assessed profit margin as of 1 January 1995, and have it agreed in writing by their local VAT office.

IMPORTING STAMPS BY MAIL

Elsewhere in this volume will be found the names and addresses of philatelic agencies and bureaux around the world from whom it may be possible to obtain stamps and other philatelic products direct. It is a wise precaution to write to these bodies in the first instance for precise details of their sales and distribution. In some cases they appoint a dealer in Britain as an agent and this is a method of purchase that removes a great deal of the hassle and red tape. Nowadays, however, many postal administrations are quite happy to use the credit card system to make it easy to part you from your money. The problem arises when the stamps are despatched. As a rule, bureaux stipulate quite clearly that they will not accept orders prepaid in cash, and it is an offence to send coins or banknotes out of the country as payment. Cheques drawn on British banks should not be used. Indeed, this may be actively discouraged by the imposition of heavy clearance and handling charges at the other end.

Other than credit cards, the Girobank system is probably the best method of remitting currency from one country to another; full details may be obtained from any bank or post office. Details on the preferred method of sending remittances, or transferring cash to another country, will be found in the Royal Mail International Service Guide.

The receipt of postal packets containing stamps and other philatelic products from abroad makes you liable for Value Added Tax on their importation, with the exception of materials from other EC countries since the inception of the Single Market on 1 January 1994. In the latter case VAT at the appropriate rate is charged by the despatching country, so you pay willy-nilly. In the case of imports from other countries, not taxed prior to despatch, you are liable to the tax on delivery, usually denoted by to pay labels. It is the responsibility of the despatching bureau to declare the value of the material being sent to you, so that HM Customs and Excise can raise the appropriate amount of VAT. The same remarks apply to the importation of material purchased at auction abroad. In any event you should consult your local VAT office regarding the position of auction lots which would come under the heading of second-hand goods.

BUYING AND SELLING

When goods are sold, the seller and the buyer enter into a contract which confers rights and imposes obligations on both parties. There is no law governing the quality of goods sold by a private individual. If you purchase a stamp from a fellow-collector as a result of an informal meeting at the local stamp club it is incumbent on you to ensure that what you are buying is what you think you are buying. If you purchase something from a dealer or auctioneer, on the other hand, you are entitled under the Sale of Goods Act to goods of "merchantable quality" which means that they must be reasonably fit for their purpose. Items sold under a specific description, on the other hand, must correspond exactly with that description. If they do not, the seller, even a private individual, can be sued under the Sale of Goods Act. This is an important distinction because there is an erroneous notion that the Act doe not apply to transactions between private individuals. If A sells a stamp to B, purporting it to be a rare variety, and B subsequently discovers that the factor making the stamp rare has been deliberately altered by A, then B can sue A. Even if A claims that he made the sale in good faith, believing the stamp to be genuine in every respect, he will still be liable for restitution (giving B his money back) and may also face a claim for damages. The Sale of Goods Act thus overturns the traditional adage caveat emptor which, in its full formula, translates as "let the buyer beware for he ought not to be ignorant of the nature of the property which he is buying from another party". Traditionally this was the maxim applicable at auctions, and it was in order to overcome this vexation matter that the system of extensions (see above) was devised.

AUCTIONS

There are various legal aspects pertaining to the disposal or acquisition of material by auction. These are not always readily apparent, and it is also important to note that there are subtle differences in law and practice between England and Scotland. These tend to arise in cases where stamps come up for sale at provincial general mixed auctions, rather than in the sales conducted by philatelic auctioneers. Goods up for auction may be subject to an upset price which is made public as the price at which the bidding will start. A reserve price, on the other hand, is known only to the auctioneer, and if it is not reached, the goods will not be sold. Upset prices are common in Scotland, reserve prices in England. If no upset price is specified and the goods are not subject to a reserve price then the highest bid secures them, even though it may not be as high as the vendor hoped for. If a seller notifies other bidders that he is bidding for his own goods, or that he has employed an agent to bid for him, the bidding is legal. If he does not give notice and bids himself, or gets someone else to bid for him, thus forcing up the price, the sale is fraudulent and the buyer can purchase the goods for the amount of the last bid he made before fraudulent bidding started.

One frequently hears dark, but usually apocryphal, tales of "the ring" in action to depress the bidding and secure items below the price commensurate with their actual value. This is a fraudulent practice and in law is regarded as a criminal conspiracy. In practice, however, it would be very difficult for a group of dealers or other individuals to keep the bidding down merely by sitting on their hands. This practice could only operate successfully in sales which were largely, if not entirely, frequented by dealers bidding in the room. But stamp sales, like other specialist collector-oriented auctions, are characterised by a high proportion of private bidders in attendance. Any conspiracy by a ring would merely allow some private bidder to step in and secure the lot at a bargain price. Rings are illegal, but in practice prosecutions are very rare as it is extremely difficult to obtain proof of their operations. What is more likely to happen is that dealers have been known to act in concert to force up the bidding to frighten off some unwelcome interloper. Here again, such tales are legion, but astonishingly lacking in specific details. The golden rule in attending auctions is to know what you are going after, and to have a pretty precise idea of how much you are prepared to pay. Do not be stampeded in the heat of the moment into going way beyond your limit.

TAXATION OF PROFITS ON DISPOSAL

The Inland Revenue define an asset as "any form of property (other than sterling) wherever situated". A disposal includes a sale, exchange or gift of an asset, or the receipt of a capital sum in respect of them. In layman's terms you dispose of an asset when you sell it, give it away, exchange it or lose it. A transfer of assets between husband and wife doesn't count (unless they are legally separated); nor does the transfer of an asset you leave when you die. If a disposal results in a profit you could be liable to tax. Any profit made on the sale of certain assets, including stamps and postal history, constitutes a capital gain and is subject to Capital Gains Tax (CGT) which is currently charged at the same 25 per cent and 40 per cent rates as income tax. However, the government allows you to make a total capital gain in the current tax year of £5500 before tax becomes chargeable. If this is the case, and the total proceeds from disposal do not exceed £10,000, then a simple declaration to this effect is all you need to make in the relevant section of your annual tax return.

Computing the actual capital gain is a complicated matter. Suppose you purchased a stamp in 1960 for £5000 and sold it in 1994 for £15,000. On the face of it, you've made a capital gain of £10,000 and you might think that you were liable to CGT because the gain was well over £5500. However, the length of time you've held the asset also has to be taken into consideration. From 6 April 1988 the law was altered so that only gains made after 31 March 1982 are now taxable. In effect, you are taxed as if you acquired the stamp on 31 March 1982. The initial value of the stamp is deemed to be its market value at that date. If the gain from March 1982 to the time of disposal is greater than the overall gain from acquisition in 1960

to disposal in 1994, you take the lesser of the two figures. If this produces a gain, whereas the old method of working it out would have produced a loss, you will be regarded, for tax purposes, as having made neither a gain nor a loss on disposal. You have a choice of opting for computing from the time of actual acquisition or from March 1982, whichever seems the more advantageous, but once you've made your choice you cannot subsequently change your mind.

How do you establish what the stamp was worth in March 1982? The Inland Revenue tend to regard Stanley Gibbons as their yardstick. The difference between the nominal or catalogue value in 1982 and what you eventually got for the stamp, assuming that the latter was greater, might be regarded as the capital gain, but even then the position is complicated by inflation in the intervening years eroding the real value of the stamp.

At this stage things get really complicated, as you have to work out the indexation allowance. This is determined by the Retail Prices Index (RPI), and you need to know the RPI for (a) the month of disposal, and (b) the month in which you acquired the asset, or March 1982 if later. The RPI is announced each month by the Department of Employment and is published in its Employment Gazette, which ought to be available in your local public library. Take the RPI for the month of disposal and subtract the RPI for the month when indexation commenced. Then divide the result by the RPI for the month when indexation began, and work out this figure to the third decimal place. This is known as the indexation factor, which you then multiply by the initial cost of your stamp. Simple isn't it? In most cases, however, I suspect that you will have made a capital loss in real terms, so these sums, though necessary to satisfy the Inland Revenue, are largely academic.

INSURANCE AND PROTECTION AGAINST THEFT

A stamp collection may be an important asset; indeed, I have known cases where a person's collection far exceeded the value of his house and all other assets combined. It is not unknown for collectors to become so obsessive that they will stop at nothing, or spare no expense, in the vain pursuit of that great rarity which will make the collection complete, or at least worthy of a gold medal in international exhibitions. Because of the specialised nature of stamp collections at this level, however, many insurance companies baulk at offering effective cover against loss through fire or flooding, far less burglary or theft. Stamp collections are only included in normal household insurance cover if they are of a modest value and are not out of proportion to the other assets.

Where a collection is assessed in thousands rather than hundreds of pounds, insurance becomes much more of a problem. Companies will insure such a collection, but will insist on an independent assessment of its value and will then demand a great deal of security for its retention. The collection must be housed in a built-in, fire-proof safe and the house or flat must be fitted with burglar alarms and security-locked doors and windows, subject to regular maintenance and inspection. Failing these requirements, the stamps must be held in a strong-box in a bank vault, which is not always as secure as it might be these days! Such arrangements are often regarded as tiresome and inconvenient, especially by the collector who likes to be able to examine his treasures whenever he likes.

Regrettably this dilemma is all too often resolved by ignoring the question of insurance altogether. In that case, the collector often hopes for the best—which, in these times, is not good enough. If you are unable or unwilling to insure your collection at home, then the only advice is to take steps to protect it as best you can. Fortunately there is now a wide range of anti-burglary devices, from conventional burglar alarms to pressure pads and electronic eyes, locks and safes. The more appliances you employ the better. Get your local police to advise you on overall domestic security; they will check doors and windows and advise on other aspects regarding making your home as safe as possible. Remember that most household thefts are opportunistic, carried out in broad daylight by young thieves mainly intent on seizing cash, or jewellery, television sets, camcorders and the like which can readily be converted into money. In practice, albums stacked in a bookcase along with other books are less likely to attract attention. Even if the burglar is tempted, and steals your collection, stamps are much more difficult to sell, and many's the crook who landed in trouble when he tried to unload his booty at the nearest stamp dealer. As the penalties for receiving stolen property (known in Scots law as reset) are very severe, dealers are constantly on their toes regarding material to which the would-be vendor does not appear to have good title.

In the event of your stamps being stolen, however, it is advisable to have as accurate a record of them as possible to assist the police and the philatelic trade in their recovery. Fortunately photocopying is both cheap and efficient these days; good black and white photocopies of album pages and postal history items should suffice, but for very rare material the additional expense of colour photocopying is worthwhile.

It is also helpful to maintain an inventory, with details of date of purchase, the price paid and descriptions (usually with catalogue numbers for easy reference). This used to be a time-consuming and tedious business, but there are several computer programmes now available which make the task much simpler.

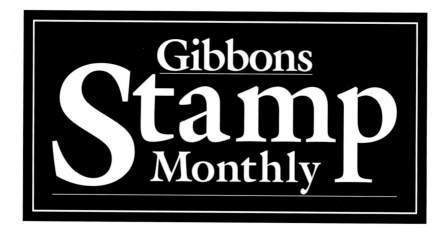

INDEX TO ADVERTISERS

Published by Token Publishing Ltd, PO Box 14, Honiton, Devon EX14 9YP and Printed in England at the
Friary Press, Bridport Road, Dorchester, Dorset DT1 1JL